Prostitution and Feminism

Towards a Politics of Feeling

Maggie O'Neill

Polity

Copyright © Maggie O'Neill 2001

The right of Maggie O'Neill to be identified as author of this work has been asserted in accordance with the Copyright, Designs and Patents Act 1988.

First published in 2001 by Polity Press in association with Blackwell Publishers Ltd

Editorial office:
Polity Press
65 Bridge Street
Cambridge CB2 1UR, UK

Marketing and production:
Blackwell Publishers Ltd
108 Cowley Road
Oxford OX4 1JF, UK

Published in the USA by
Blackwell Publishers Inc.
Commerce Place
350 Main Street
Malden, MA 02148, USA

All rights reserved. Except for the quotation of short passages for the purposes of criticism and review, no part of this publication may be reproduced, stored in a retrieval system, or transmitted, in any form or by any means, electronic, mechanical, photocopying, recording or otherwise, without the prior permission of the publisher.

Except in the United States of America, this book is sold subject to the condition that it shall not, by way of trade or otherwise, be lent, re-sold, hired out, or otherwise circulated without the publisher's prior consent in any form of binding or cover other than that in which it is published and without a similar condition including this condition being imposed on the subsequent purchaser.

ISBN 0–7456–1204–0
ISBN 0–7456–1921–5 (pbk)

A catalogue record for this book is available from the British Library.
Library of Congress Cataloging-in–Publication Data

O'Neill, Maggie.
   Prostitution and feminism : towards a politics of feeling/Maggie O'Neill.
    p.cm.
   Includes bibliographical references and index.
    ISBN 0-7456-1204-0 (alk. paper)—ISBN 0-7456-1921-5 (pbk. : alk. paper)
     1. Prostitution. 2. Prostitutes. 3. Feminism. I. Title.

 HQ117 .O54 2001
 306.74—dc21   00-034704

Typeset in 10.5 on 12pt GaramondThree
by Kolam Information Services Pvt. Ltd, Pondicherry, India
Printed in Great Britain by T. J. International, Padstow, Cornwall

This book is printed on acid-free paper.

Contents

Acknowledgements

Many people have helped directly or indirectly in the progress of this book. I would like to thank the following people. Steve O'Connor and Patrick and James O'Neill. Chris Rojek has given invaluable advice and reassurance. Lynn Dunlop remained calm and reassuring when I wondered if I would ever make it to print. I would also like to thank Sarah Dancy, Frances Maher and Leander Shrimpton at Polity Press. Brian Burtch and Helmut Kuzmics gave advice and critical comments on drafts of the masculinity chapter. Thanks to Nick Tilley and Tony Holden for commissioning the initial pilot study and for their help during the progress of the initial work back in 1990. Thanks to Karen Hughes, Mo McDonald, Sue Johnson, Mandy Hyland, Terry Webster, Jo Ions, Nicola Goode, Michelle Welick, Helen McGregor, Elaine N'Jie, Chris Wilkinson, Hilary Kinnel, Ruth Morgan-Thomas, 'Rights of Women' in London, the British Sociological Association's Violence Against Women study group, the English Collective of Prostitutes (especially Nikki and Nina), Rosemary Barberet, Sue Mulroy, Judith Green, Rosie Campbell, Liz Stokes, Ruth Holliday, Jan Bourne, David Gatley, Nicola Mullenger, Sara Giddens, Dee Lunn, Lee-Jane Nixon, Con Lodziak, John Tomlinson, Roger Matthews, Mike Presdee, Viv Chadder, Joost van Loon, Ian Connelly, Caroline Schwaller, Jalner Hanmer, Vikki Bell, Rolland Munro, Jenny Ryan, Bob Witkin and Richard Harvey Brown. Last, but not least, my thanks go to all the women and young people who took part in the various research projects and to Jackie Clewlow at Staffordshire University for efficient administrative support. Final thanks must go to the reviewers at Polity Press; their constructive criticism was invaluable.

Introduction: Socio-Cultural Contexts – Renewed Methodologies for Research

How do we get to grips with the complexities involved in understanding feminist responses to prostitution at the turn of the century? This book seeks to answer this question by focusing upon the interrelationships between feminist research, feminist theory and feminist practice in late modern/postmodern times. The text provides:

- a feminist socio-cultural analysis of prostitution in changing times;
- a comprehensive introduction to the major feminist debates on prostitution as a cultural practice, as well as an examination of the figure/image/representation of the prostitute through examples of art and literature;
- ethnographic data with women and young people working as 'prostitutes', which serve to demystify and demythologize stereotypical images and representations of 'prostitutes' and prostitution;
- a renewed methodology for social research, defined as ethno-mimesis. Ethno-mimesis combines ethnographic research and the re-presentation of ethnographic data in visual/artistic form. Re-presenting social research in visual/artistic form can provide a rich understanding of the many issues surrounding the lived experiences of women working in prostitution; challenge stereotypes; and also bring the work to a wider audience. Life-history accounts re-presented in visual/artistic form can develop public understanding and feed into social policy (for example, see chapter 3).

This work stresses the importance of critical feminist theory wrapped up in the material and personal experiences of women working as prostitutes. Focusing upon the personal/experiential aspects of women's lives helps to develop an interpretive understanding of prostitution in contemporary society. This enables us to better understand gendered relations, masculinities, male violence against women and the social organization of desire, represented most acutely in the dynamics of destruction and the desire operating between pimp, client and prostitute.

The ethnographic material documented here was gathered over a period of nine years. One of the major obstacles and difficulties in conducting ethnographic fieldwork is the time and emotional energy involved (Murdock 1997). Within the context of the pressure upon researchers in universities to publish, and the depleting resources for research in some universities, involvement in ethnographic research and especially participatory research is, for many, too high a price to pay. However, the benefits and impact upon teaching and learning are considerable. Participatory action research (PAR)[1] provides a renewed focus upon the role and purpose of academic involvement in the public sphere, especially in relation to facilitating processes of social inclusion and regeneration *with* and for the communities involved in the research. The impact of this research upon social policy (via the inclusion of the stereotypical 'subjects' of research, usually seen as 'outsiders' or 'outlaws') may appear to be small scale but has much wider repercussions in terms of the impact upon the groups and communities involved. For example, PAR promotes: the self-esteem of individuals and groups; the development of skills and empowerment; and the ownership of a stake in creating change, in creating praxis.

The research that led to the production of this text takes an ethnographic approach to working with women and young people rooted in the principles of PAR. As a feminist and a researcher, I am committed to challenging and changing sexual and social inequalities with individuals/groups/communities. This commitment forms the driving force for my work.[2] Moreover I am committed to exploring intertextuality and collaboration across genres to explore social worlds and lived cultures. This includes working with the stereotypical subjects of research through PAR as well as working with artists, photographers and performance artists in the re-presentation and analyses of social research (see chapters 2 and 5).

Ethno-mimesis: towards a politics of feeling

A new theoretical concept – ethno-mimesis – is introduced here to capture the process and outcome of doing participatory action research with marginalized groups as well as the re-presentation of the research in artistic form. This concept privileges the interrelationship between the psychic and social processes involved in the process of PAR. It illuminates the researcher's self-reflexive involvement in the research, including being immersed in a physical and emotional/psychic sense in the lived cultures of the individuals and groups who are the co-creators of the research. For the researcher, immersion in 'lived cultures' is necessarily followed by interpretation, commentary and criticism. The concept describes a dialectical, self-reflexive, interpretive relationship based upon mutual recognition. It privileges the exploration of lived experience within the lived cultures of the group that the researcher is working with and the re-presentation of the research in visual, poetic, artistic forms.[3] The process of conducting ethno-mimesis is captured for me by the term a *politics of feeling*.

A politics of feeling is a related concept to ethno-mimesis, and both concepts emerged in the process of conducting ethnographic research with and for women working as prostitutes. A politics of feeling describes the exploration of the politics of everyday life through women's narratives, through their inclusion in the research. It also describes a critical feminist standpoint(s) approach. Immersion in the life-worlds of women and young people working in prostitution, combined with analysis of the interrelationship between the micrology (following Walter Benjamin) of women's lives and broader social processes, underpins the critical feminist standpoint(s) approach outlined here.

One of the central themes of this book is the development of renewed methodologies for socio-cultural research as ways of working and writing in societies that are post-traditional but are also marked by the traditional; in societies that are dis-enchanted but are in the process of being re-enchanted; and, if we agree with Stjepan Meštrović (1997), in societies that are postemotional but also contain possibilities of and for authenticity.

For Meštrović, contemporary Western societies are entering a new phase of development where 'synthetic, quasi-emotions become the basis for widespread manipulation by self, others, and the culture industry as a whole' (1997: xi). What he calls 'postemotional types' are able to 'feel' a vast array of emotions without necessarily being motivated to action. In the postemotional society emotions have not disappeared but rather a 'new hybrid of intellectualized, mechanical, mass produced emotions has appeared on the world scene' (1997: 26). Moreover, in the West we are suffering in part from compassion fatigue (1997: 33). Postemotionalism, for Meštrović, is a 'new theoretical construct to capture the Balkanization, ethnic violence and other highly *emotional* phenomena of the late 1990s that are being treated mechanically – and not just in the Balkans but throughout the industrialized West' (1997: 40). Meštrović draws upon Adorno's thesis regarding the growth and power of the culture industry in helping to create and sustain an almost totally administered society, where spaces to think and feel critically are constantly diminishing.[4]

The work presented and discussed in this text takes a participatory action approach to working with and for women and young people working as prostitutes. This work is influenced by and draws upon Adorno's dialectic of mimesis and constructive rationality. Adorno's use of mimesis was heavily influenced by Walter Benjamin (Adorno 1984; Benjamin 1978; Nicholsen 1997). I have argued elsewhere (O'Neill 1999) that the work of Adorno is very useful for contemporary feminists. He emphasizes negativity and the need for non-identical thinking, for critical analytical thinking; he focuses upon micrology (drawing upon Walter Benjamin) – upon the small scale – upon the minutiae of lived experience and upon living a damaged life, through the ambiguity and ambivalence of modern and hyper-modern times. He develops a relentless attack upon essentializing the feminine at the same time as proclaiming the utter loss of hope in the enlightenment as progress, as the *promesse de bonheur*. He focuses upon the paralysis, the pessimism, contained in the hopelessness of challenging and changing administered society, but at the same time he never gives up hope for transformative possibilities; for him this was contained in the liberating potential of art and aesthetics.

Ethno-mimesis is illustrated in chapter 2 through a combination of ethnographic participatory work and the re-presentation of this work in visual/artistic form. In re-presenting ethnographic work in visual/artistic form we can reach a wider audience, beyond academic communities, thus facilitating understanding, interpretation and maybe even action/praxis in relation to prostitution as a social issue. Certainly, in re-presenting ethnographic data in artistic form we can access a richer understanding of the complexities of lived experience and this can throw light on broader social structures and processes. The complexities of lived experience include the material and the 'immaterial' (Van Loon 1999), the 'Phenomenal' (Battersby 1998) and what Adorno alludes to as the 'unsayable', those aspects of lived experience that are hard to put into words.

Immersion in the life-worlds of women working in prostitution through ethnographic research enables the foregrounding of feelings, meanings and experiences from the multiple standpoints of women, and may facilitate the development of 'thick' descriptions of lived cultures. This may help us to better understand their lived experiences (Geertz 1973). Indeed, such self-reflexive works also help us to understand our own lives and lived cultures. Working with women in participatory ways to develop changes in attitude, policy and practice promotes feminist praxis as purposeful knowledge – from the standpoints of the women concerned. The process of conducting ethnographic participatory research through 'feeling' involvement can give rise to a politics of feeling. Resistance, action, transformation can ensue and be progressed in participatory ways with the co-researchers.

A politics of feeling is developed through participatory research, through a critical feminist standpoint(s) approach and through *ethno-mimesis*. This approach neither romanticizes nor idealizes marginalized peoples (West 1994) and it resists 'postemotionalism' (Meštrović 1997), the domination of our social worlds by synthetic emotions and compassion fatigue.

Postemotionalism mirrors Postman's concern (1987) about what he calls culture-death and is influenced by Meštrović's reading of David Reisman's *The Lonely Crowd* (1950). Our cultural life is being turned into a perpetual round of entertainment; we absorb media images in a state of relative inattention. Postemotionalism is indicative of contemporary 'me-dominated' and media-saturated society (see Tester 1994), where spaces to think and feel critically are diminishing. There is a degree of pessimism and paralysis in our responses to the crisis and plight of others. This paralysis is a marker of postemotionalism. We turn the page, switch off – unmoved. In this book it is accepted, to a degree, that our lived relations are in the throes of what Meštrović terms 'postemotionalism', a loss of 'feeling'. However, this is not so widespread as Meštrović claims, for we are able to – and do – resist this tendency in the politics of everyday life.

Conducting participatory action research (PAR) with individuals and groups promotes purposeful knowledge that may be transformative and certainly counters paralysis and pessimism. The relationship between thinking, feeling and doing (Arendt 1970; Tester 1995), commitment and collective responsibility, is central to PAR, and is illustrated in chapter 2 and Part II through the participatory action research with women and young people working as prostitutes.

A *politics of feeling* privileges emotions, feelings and meanings in accessing 'lived experiences' or 'lived cultures' and explores experiences, meanings, practices through the tension or mediation between feeling and reason involved in critical interpretive ethnography. *Ethno-mimesis* is both a process (methodological tool) and a constellational form (an outcome) of interpretive research. Ethno-mimesis combines ethnographic research and art forms in the development of hybrid texts as one possible outcome of PAR. In chapter 2 I use the example of performance art and video (from collaborative work with Sara Giddens) to re-present life-history narratives of women working in the sex industry. The intertextuality between ethnographic data and artistic re-presentation illuminates the complexity of women's lives through what Taussig (1993) alludes to as 'sensuous knowing'.

Key aims

The key aims of this book are twofold. First, I aim to problematize feminist theorizing and feminist research – specifically the epistemological and methodological issues involved in knowledge production – in late modern/postmodern times. I recommend that we develop more participatory, constellational and hybrid ways of doing and re-presenting research with women and young people working as prostitutes. This may include working with performance artists and/or photographers.[5] Second, I aim to problematize the categories of prostitute and prostitution by drawing upon self-reflexive ethnographic accounts of women's lived experiences, the available literature and fictive or cultural texts, in order to explore neglected gender issues, especially around subjectivities and difference.

The outcomes are also twofold. First, I stress the desperate need for feminists to build bridges across the divides between feminists who are working in the sex industry and feminists who are not (including intra-group differences), as discussed in chapter 1, and I include recommendations for this bridge-building that are founded upon mutual or inter-subjective recognition (J. Benjamin, 1993), collaboration, participation and collective action. Second, I suggest a methodological approach to 'doing sociology', or 'doing cultural studies', combining ethnographic approaches and artistic re-presentations of ethnographic data, which I call *ethno-mimesis*, as a renewed (revitalized by processes of participatory action research and collaboration across genres such as performance art) methodology for doing social research in postmodern times of de-traditionalization and postemotionalism.

This work is influenced by the methodological work of Atkinson and Coffey, Maria Mies, Norman Denzin, William F. Whyte, Orlando Fals Borda, Augusto Boal, Trinh T. Minh-Ha and the critical theory of Jessica Benjamin, Theodor Adorno, Walter Benjamin, Stjepan Meštrović and Michael Taussig. It is, of course, ultimately embedded within a critical hermeneutic project, but one that looks to social research as praxis. This feminist, sociological project involves developing hybrid responses to inter-pretive, qualitative research. Hybrid responses include developing alternative forms of re-presenting the lived experiences and lived cultures of marginalized groups, with their help, in order to counter postemotionalism and foster committed responses to the sexual, social inequalities we live in and through.

Prostitution and Feminism is about creating the intellectual and practical spaces for women's voices to be heard and listened to in order to better understand the lived experiences of women working as prostitutes; to counter 'othering'; to better understand gendered relations, including a focus upon subjectivities, difference and identities; and to work towards collectively resisting, challenging and changing sexual and social inequalities in post-modern times through feminist praxis. It is also about exploring renewed methodologies for social research in order to acquire a better understanding of the complexity of our social worlds through intertextual feeling forms.

The chapters

This book is organized into three parts and each of the parts can be read as a discrete whole or taken together, integrated as part of a larger (unfinished) story.

Part I comprises chapter 1 and chapter 2. Chapter 1 outlines and discusses the feminist debates on prostitution, stressing the importance of collective action, of feminist action research. Feminist action research can develop a more thorough understanding of the complex experiences, meanings and practices involved in understanding the phenomenon of prostitution and the experiences of women. This chapter also calls for feminists working as prostitutes and feminists not working in the sex industry to work together.

Chapter 2 outlines and illustrates *ethno-mimesis* as a renewed methodology for social research in current times. An interpretive feminist account of women's life-histories, rooted in immersion in the feeling worlds of participants is re-presented through fragments of women's narratives, live art and photography. This ethno-mimetic approach is developed from a commitment to:

- the interrelation between feminist thought and practice involving processes of immersion, interpretation, commentary, criticism and praxis;
- critical feminist theory, the usefulness of the work of Adorno, Walter Benjamin and Jessica Benjamin – specifically the role of critical theory as interpretive philosophy, the concept of 'mediation' and the central dialectic of mimesis and constructive rationality;[6]
- interpretive ethnography as a way of understanding women's lived experiences, especially the development of critical standpoint epistemologies (influenced by the work of Maria Mies, Orlando Fals Borda, Augusto Boal, Trinh T. Minh-Ha and Norman Denzin).

Part II (chapters 3 and 4) seeks to tell the stories of certain women, young people and children who sell sex.

Chapter 3 explores women's experiences of routes into prostitution, 'making out' in prostitution, routes into prostitution from local authority care, and possibilities for exiting. The interrelationship between psychic processes and social processes is a key theme, specifically the ways that the micrology of women's lives can shed light on broader socio-economic structures and processes.

Chapter 4 examines child/juvenile prostitution by exploring: the interrelationship between prostitution, homelessness, leaving care and runaways; and the central importance of developing social knowledge as social critique, as feminist praxis. The chapter concludes with a call for changes to attitudes, policy and practice towards the involvement of children and young people in prostitution. We desperately need to stop treating these children and young people as 'social junk', as 'criminals', and to deliver child-centred responses across the spectrum of agencies and services with which young people have contact. Ultimately, the way we respond as a society to this issue is a mark of our 'postemotionalism' or 'compassion fatigue'.

Part III examines neglected gender issues in the debates around modernity and postmodernity by focusing upon fictive texts and lived experience in the area of sexuality and prostitution. Exploring (triangulating) ethnographic texts and fictive texts is, I argue, a useful way of understanding the complexities involved in debates around prostitution, desire, identities and the differences involved in gendered relations in postmodern times.

Through postmodern ethnographies we can better understand the socio-cultural-political (macro) relations and interrelations, and the multiple (micro) 'realities' we might want to transform. Accessing and documenting lived experiences in a self-reflexive, critically aware way can lead us to better understand psychic processes (feelings/meanings/identities) and socio-cultural structures and processes. This knowledge in turn may help us to develop transformative possibilities. This process – *a politics of feeling* – draws upon 'feeling forms' (Witkin 1974), such as art, life-story narratives, film and dance to re-tell, re-present, the multiple stories generated through interpretive ethnographic research. Critical interpretation and reception of multiple stories may lead to new awareness and to changes in attitude and practice towards marginalized social groups like 'prostitutes'.

Chapter 5 explores the interrelationship between prostitution, sexuality and the social organization of desire. The image and representation of the 'prostitute' and the aestheticization of the whore in contemporary culture are examined. In the conclusion it is argued that through a combination of interpretive ethnography focusing upon life-history narratives and fictive texts, such as art, literature and film, feminist research/analysis can move towards changing 'the instruments of culture', our sign worlds of sexuality, by saying the 'unsayable', by telling our stories outside of the dominant discourses that constitute the 'between men' culture (Irigaray 1993). Feminist thought and praxis rooted in interpretive ehnography is potentially transformative, especially when it is linked to PAR.

Chapter 6 explores masculinities and male violence against women by focusing upon pimps and punters. In order to develop a clearer understanding and analysis of the gendered organization of prostitution we must turn our attention to the men involved in prostitution and the organization of the wider sex industry. The narratives of men are explored through interview material with men (and with women on men) who are clients of 'prostitutes' alongside James Boswell's biographical account of his sexual 'wanderings'. Triangulating historical analysis with interview material (narratives from men as clients and from women on male clients) and fictive texts can give us a better understanding of the men involved in prostitution, the social organization of desire through time and the wider sex industry. Historical and fictive sources (critical recovery of history) are useful for uncovering greater knowledge and understanding of social issues. The interrelation between history, philosophy, literature and social theory is vital to a better understanding of our social worlds (Winch 1990).

The Conclusion brings together the main themes in summary and discusses the importance of feminist analyses of prostitution in conditions of reflexive modernity/postmodernity that engage with lived experience and develop feminist praxis through interpretive ethnography. Within this text, *ethno-mimesis* as a politics of feeling provides a theoretical construct which describes a research methodology. As a theoretical concept, ethno-mimesis describes the combination of interpretive ethnography or participatory action research *and* visual artistic re-presentations of the research data.

Ethno-mimesis as a 'politics of feeling' privileges the personal, the 'micrology' of actions and interactions, and in the tension between mimesis and rationality, through critical reflection/interpretation, 'gets at' a thorough understanding of prostitution in current times. By triangulating life-story interviews (narratives of self) and fictive texts (literature, film, photography, art works) this work challenges stereotypes and illuminates ideology and ideological effects surrounding 'prostitutes' and prostitution. Moreover, it accesses the micrology of lived experience, the unsayable, the phenomenal, the immaterial or the non-conceptual, thus serving educative and potentially transformative roles.

Coming to understand the reflexive relationship (mediation) between the lived experience of women working as prostitutes and the wider social and cultural structures, processes and practices through feminist participatory action research is constitutive of what I call a 'politics of feeling'.

The fragments of stories (life narratives, fictive texts, video stills) documented here are fragments of the politics of everyday life. They speak and show the embeddedness of feeling, meaning, being and becoming, in the lived, embodied experiences of the women, men and young people working as prostitutes. There are resonances for all women in the stories that unfold throughout this text. Through these examples of 'lived cultures', there are important implications here for 'doing' sociology and women's, cultural and media studies in postmodern times.

Part I

Feminist Knowledge and Social Research: Understanding Prostitution

One aim of this book is to show that academic involvement in the public sphere, in the articulation of the lived experience of women's lives, can be 'powerful' and have potentially transformative consequences.[1] Furthermore, in the process of conducting participatory action research, I have found that the social construction of academic knowledge is enriched and a 'democratization' effect develops with the groups one is working with, given the reflexive relationship between critical feminist theory, women's lived experience and policy-oriented practice. Women's voices and participation through ethnographic work are central to this process. Feminism is a practice and a politics as well as 'a strong intellectual movement' (A. Gray 1997: 90).

This text is concerned with the development of 'knowledge for', as critical feminist praxis (Stanley 1990), embedded within a cultural politics of difference. The work documented and discussed here is located at the intersection of contemporary feminist theory and socio-cultural research. It is situated at the crossroads of feminist theory, interdisciplinarity, intertextuality and renewed methodologies for social research in late modern/postmodern times.

Renewed methodologies involve ways of researching and writing in societies that are post-traditional but also marked by the traditional. Societies that are 'postemotional' (Meštrović 1997) are marked by mechanical, mass-produced emotions and compassion fatigue; but they also contain possibilities of and for authenticity. Renewed methodologies are a response to the fragmentation, plurality and utter complexity of living in postmodern times.

The crisis in representing ethnographic data, which occurred during the 1980s, encouraged reflexivity around issues of class, race and gender and at the same time critiqued the moral and scientific authority of the ethnographer (Atkinson 1992). Texts produced and re-presented as the outcomes of ethnographic fieldwork are no longer accepted unproblematically (Atkinson and Coffey 1995; Denzin 1997). Ethnographers can no longer presume to produce uncontested 'realist' accounts of the experiences of individuals/groups/ 'others'. Rather the self-reflexivity inherent in the ethnographic process, coupled with the deconstruction of conventional discourses, serve to question the status of ethnographic texts within sociology, cultural studies, women's studies; and the ways in which ethnographers claim to re-present socio-cultural phenomena.

To illustrate: ethnography is a gendered project (Trinh 1989, 1991; Clough 1994; Denzin 1997). Feminist thought, queer theory and post-colonial thought have challenged and deconstructed the 'oedipal logic of the heterosexual, narrative ethnographic text that reflexively positions the ethnographer's gender neutral (or masculine) self within a realist story about the "other"' (Denzin 1997: xiv). As a response, there have been demands for experimentation in the re-presentation of ethnographic data to enable specific gendered and racialized boundaries to be transgressed (Trinh 1991; Denzin 1997).

In this work, what I call renewed methodologies for social research that incorporate the voices of citizens through scholarly/civic research as participatory research can serve not only to enlighten and raise our awareness of certain issues; they can also produce critical reflexive texts which may help to motivate social change (O'Neill et al. 1999). The tension between a modernist ethos of resistance and transformation through participation as praxis (working *with* women through participatory action research) and a postmodern ethos of hybridity, complexity, interdisciplinarity and intertextuality (anti-identitarian thinking, re-presenting women's lived experience through art forms; illuminating the interrelationship between the fictive and the real in our lived cultures) is uneasy but represents the dynamics of the work presented here. Renewed methodologies can uncover important messages about the complexity of everyday life.

In this work, renewed methodologies for social research seek to speak in empathic ways with women, in order to counter postemotionalism, valorizing discourses and the reduction of the Other to a cipher of the oppressed/marginalized/exploited. Renewed methodologies facilitate a politics of feeling. This is illustrated in chapter 2 through live art/performance as a response to the life-story narratives of women working as prostitutes.

The central thread that runs through this work is the relationship between theory, lived experience and practice, articulated in the relationship between psychic processes and social processes; between critical feminist theory and feminist praxis; between theory, lived experience and community activism. An important aspect is the attempt to collect and show in a purposeful way what usually remains hidden in the literature and research on women working as prostitutes and on prostitution. This will be revealed through the combination of women's stories and cultural or fictive texts. The transformative possibilities of doing feminist participatory action research are identified, developed and analysed in the course of this section, which provides a review of the literature and an outline of *ethno-mimesis* – a theoretical concept that describes a research methodology indicative of a politics of feeling.

> All purposeful manifestations of life, including their very purposiveness, in the final analysis have their end not in life, but in the expression of its nature, in the representation of its significance. (W. Benjamin 1972: 73)

1
Feminism(s) and Prostitution

Feminist approaches to prostitution

Feminist approaches to prostitution have shifted over the last ten or so years – linked to later modernity/reflexive modernity/postmodernity, however you decide to label the shifts and transformations that have been taking place since the 1960s but are, of course, rooted in much earlier social and cultural changes. In any consideration of feminist responses it is important to explore the intersection with discourses on health, the law and prostitutes' rights. This chapter is therefore organized into four sections: feminist approaches to prostitution; health perspectives; prostitution and the law; and prostitutes' rights and participatory research.

Although there is no specific work to date on the relationship between critical feminist theory, feminist praxis and prostitution, feminist theorists have addressed the issue of prostitution in their work on women and crime (Smart 1978, 1989, 1992; Edwards 1987, 1988a, 1988b, 1998; Phoenix 1999) or on women, sexuality, social organization and control (Smart 1978; McIntosh 1978, 1992; McLeod 1982; Jarvinen 1993; Brewis and Linstead 1998; O'Connell-Davidson 1998; West 2000). Historical analyses focus upon the relationship amongst women working as prostitutes, the state, working-class communities and the regulation of the body (Walkowitz 1980; Roberts 1992; Finnegan 1979; Bullough and Bullough 1987; Meil Hobson 1990; Corbin 1987, 1990). More recently, texts examining sex tourism in Latin America and Southeast Asia have been published (Truong 1990; O'Connell-Davidson 1994, 1998; Brace and O'Connell-Davidson 1996; Bishop and Robinson 1997; Lim 1998).

In the initial stages of feminist analysis of prostitution in contemporary society, prostitution has been treated in a reductionist way as a deviant activity and as sexual slavery (see Barry 1988; Dworkin 1981; Hoigard and Finstad 1992; Jarvinen 1993). More recently, it has been treated as an understandable (and reasonable) response to socio-economic need within the context of a consumer culture, and within a social framework that privileges male sexuality (Pheterson 1986; O'Neill 1991, 1992, 1995; Green, Mulroy and O'Neill 1997; O'Connell-Davidson 1994, 1998; McLeod 1982; McLintock 1992; Hoigard and Finstad 1992; McIntosh 1978, 1992; Campbell 1996; Phoenix 1999; J. West 2000). Feminist work in this latter area has mostly focused upon violence against women, sexuality and/or the pornography debate (see Hanmer and Maynard 1987; Hanmer and Saunders 1984; Hanmer, Radford and Stanko 1989; Segal and McIntosh 1992). More recently, Jo Brewis and Stephen Linstead have produced an interesting exploration of the temporal organization of sex work in relation to the labour process (1998); and Jackie West has explored the politics of regulating sex work, focusing upon comparative analyses between Australia, New Zealand, the Netherlands and the UK (2000). West's analysis explores the complex intersections between local politics, sex worker collectives and regulatory contexts that are marked by increasing differentiation within prostitution and a blurring of the boundaries between legalisation and decriminalization. There are complex implications for sex workers, including sex worker discourse having substantial impact (but not radical transformative change) under certain conditions – for example, in opening up debates on labour law reform; the significance of sex worker discourse upon local initiatives, such as zoning in Utrecht; and a combination of industry growth and legalization encouraging investment and the links between mainstream leisure industries and prostitution becoming more extensive. West's analysis focuses upon the impact of sex worker discourse and the influence sex worker collectives have on the changing regulation of prostitution. The impact of sex worker discourse is an important and undertheorized aspect of the politics of prostitution.

In the last three years, feminists writing from the perspective of 'pro-sex feminists' have produced works that highlight prostitution as 'performing erotic labour' (Chapkis 1997; Nagle 1997). This work builds upon that produced by sex workers in the 1980s and compiled by the activist Priscilla Alexander (Alexander and Delacoste 1988). Both Nagle's and Chapkis's texts aim to 'help heal the schism within feminism that had developed around commercial sex' (Chapkis 1997: 1).

Two major feminist perspectives are documented in the available literature. First, women working as prostitutes are exploited by those who manage and organize the sex industry (mostly men). Moreover, prostitution and the wider sex industry serve to underpin and reinforce prostitution as a patriarchal institution that affects all women and gendered relations. Second, in contemporary society, prostitution for many women is freely chosen as a form of work, and women working in the sex industry deserve the same rights and liberties as other workers, including freedom from fear, exploitation and violence in the course of their work. Additionally, sex work or erotic labour can actually be a 'liberatory terrain for women' (Chapkis 1997: 1).

Jill Jesson carried out research into the incidence of adolescent female prostitution in the care of a local authority. Jesson published a literature review (1993), in which she explores the following major perspectives on prostitution: structuralist, feminist, and the prostitute's perspective. The structuralist approach she documents has been labelled functionalist elsewhere (Jarvinen 1993). Here, Davis's Durkheim-inspired functionalist perspective (1937) is outlined and criticized from a feminist perspective, and Jesson concludes that 'feminism and prostitution are not easily reconcilable' (1993: 521). Quoting from Fogarty (1982) Jesson states that, on the one hand, some feminists feel that prostitutes are wrong to work, and in the process are being exploited by men. On the other hand, feminists are acknowledging that prostitution may have been a freely chosen form of work in a society that has little to offer women. Highlighting the social stigma prostitute(d) women experience, Jesson goes on to describe how prostitutes have tried to shift the discourse around prostitution away from issues of morality and deviance towards that of prostitution as work.

Johannes Boutellier (1991) develops the legalization/decriminalization debate from the perspective of prostitution and criminal law and morality in the Netherlands, and hangs this upon the involvement of leading feminists. According to Boutellier, a coalition between feminists and bureaucratic powers has changed the public debate on prostitution. In 1985 the government changed the article on brothel keeping (250 bis) which had been instantiated in the 1911 public morality act. 'Brothel keeping was no longer to be prohibited, except for cases of violence, force or overpowering' (Boutellier 1991: 201). The revision of law facilitates prostitution to be perceived as work, but there is concern about the relationship between prostitution as work and prostitution as traffic in women. Currently, feminists in the Netherlands are clear about their stance. 'Prostitute' women should not be blamed; instead, the men who organize them and visit them should hold responsibility. Judicial policy should look towards brothel keepers, *not* the women who work in the brothels. Improving the socio-legal standing of women is central to the feminist cause.

Boutellier documents the shifts in feminist approaches to prostitution, from the coalition with the social purists in the early part of this century to the emphasis on prostitution as a psycho-social problem and the need for rehabilitation to reinforce family ties and male moral standards in the post-war years, and to the current situation, which Boutellier calls 'moral indifference'. The late sixties and seventies are seen as times of the liberation of sexuality. The Melai committee in 1977 warned the government against intruding into the private sphere and pleaded for selective action against exploitation of individuals and nuisance to residents/neighbours. The debate was one that focused upon the management and control of prostitution. Prostitution is a 'technical-juridical problem of public order' (Boutellier 1991: 206). This debate is now being waged in Britain over the legalization (regulation) or decriminalization of prostitution (Matthews 1986).

For Boutellier there are also two major feminist approaches. The first views prostitutes as victims of male sexuality 'and thus male sexuality should be the main subject of concern' (1991: 207). The second, 'subjectivist', position places the experiences and needs of the women concerned in centre stage and views prostitution 'as a legitimate form of labour freely chosen by thousands of women' (1991: 207). Government policy is unnecessary once proper conditions for this work are established. From this approach, for Boutellier, the feminist approach is compatible with the 'morally indifferent technocratic approach absorbed with management and control'. Boutellier explains this shift in part to social changes in what is termed 'moral judgement':

> Until the 1960s moral judgements were part of the encompassing political ideologies of a religious, socialist or liberal kind. Lately, these ideologies – at least in the Netherlands – seem to have lost their importance in defining social problems. This change is often referred to as the 'individualisation' of society. ... Morality today might more usefully be seen as the mediation between individual experience and state bureaucracy.... The prostitution issue is not nearly what it once so much was – an issue of ideologically defined morality – but an issue about the subjective experiences of the persons involved and the bureaucratic necessity of regulations. (Boutellier 1991: 209)

Laurie Shrage (1989, 1994) approaches the issue of feminism and prostitution from feminist philosophy and outlines a very clear picture of the very difficult issues that the debate raises for feminists. On the one hand, feminists want to support the abolition of discriminatory practices which serve to punish and harass prostitutes but which rarely punish the clients or pimps (mostly men) involved in buying sex or organizing the sex industry. On the other hand, feminists cannot support prostitution and the sex industry because 'feminists find the prostitute's work morally and politically objectionable' (Shrage 1989: 347). Ultimately, the sex industry (like other institutions in society) is structured by deeply embedded attitudes and values which are oppressive to women, for prostitution depends upon the naturalization of certain principles that marginalize women socially and politically (Shrage 1989: 349). These principles are embedded within a cultural framework that involves assumptions, behaviours and beliefs which legitimate women's subordination. For Shrage, prostitution and the sex industry simply perpetuate 'patriarchy ideology' and hegemonic heterosexuality. Furthermore, prostitution is a consequence of patriarchal hegemony which forms the foundation of all our social institutions and practices (1989: 360). The answer for Shrage is to challenge the cultural presuppositions that sustain prostitution: 'Prostitution needs no unique remedy, legal or otherwise, it will be remedied as feminists make progress in altering patterns of belief and practice that oppress women in all aspects of their lives' (1989: 360).

Shrage suggests a consumer boycott of the industry. Although she acknowledges that her arguments are consistent with the decriminalization of prostitution, she concludes that feminists have every reason to politically oppose prostitution because it is a practice that epitomizes and supports gender asymmetries which are oppressive to women (1989: 361).

There is a growing body of literature – mostly by feminists working in the sex industry and their supporters – that insists that for many women prostitution is freely chosen service work and that women and men working in the sex industry deserve the same human rights and civil liberties as other workers. This literature locates the debate firmly within 'human rights and civil liberties' and, one could argue, the sociology of work (Jaget 1980; Delacoste and Alexander 1988; French 1990; Drobler 1991; Roberts 1992; Boyle 1994; O'Neill 1996; Jarrett 1997; Nagle 1997; Chapkis 1997) within the context of a postmodern or late-modern society rooted in the ideology of individualism.

Whores and Other Feminists (1997), edited by Jill Nagle, aims to provide a platform for the voices of feminist sex workers, voices that are absent from feminist discussions on prostitution. Nagle's approach to feminist thought on the issue of prostitution echoes the claim of Nikki Roberts: 'the feminist movement has failed the prostitute, and failed her badly' (Roberts 1992: xi). Nagle's book developed from her own exploration of the sex industry 'both as a consumer and a provider'. She, in turn, was 'surprised to find many of my own prejudices overturned' (1997: 2). Nagle distinguishes between freely chosen voluntary sex work and coerced, involuntary, sex work. She calls our attention to the work of prostitute activists around the globe who have been working for over 20 years to improve conditions in the sex industry, and she is critical of feminists who do not include the perspectives of feminist sex workers in feminist debates. Nagle maintains that 'traditional feminist analysis of sexual oppression' is not the only story through which to interpret commercial sex (1997: 2).

Gayle Rubin describes the contributors to Nagle's volume as 'some of the most passionate and articulate feminist activists on the planet' (Nagle 1997). The contributions include essays and personal narratives, some of which are very moving. However, the major problem with Nagle's text is that she does not develop a clear enough description or critique of what she calls 'traditional feminism'. And, in failing to provide this, her aim to try and facilitate discussions between 'traditional' feminism(s) and whore feminism(s) falters. The possibilities for developing a discursive space for feminists working in the sex industry and feminists not working in the sex industry are dashed.

The introduction to Nagle's book contextualizes the contributions within a postmodern feminism that deconstructs binaries of female identity, including lesbian/heterosexual; good-girl/bad-girl; white/non-white; reproductive/non-reproductive. Nagle wants to uncover hidden areas of agreement between feminists whom she calls (a) sex-positive feminists (the whores and other feminists of the title who argue for myriad forms of female and male sexual agency) and (b) stop feminists (whom she calls 'traditional feminists', bound by a 'moral' agenda). She hopes that uncovering similarities will strengthen mainstream feminism: as 'lesbian feminism strengthened mainstream feminism, so will whore feminism' (1997: 13). The book asks some interesting questions, such as: How does working in the sex industry affect the feminism of individual workers? How does whore stigma affect women not working in the industry or working on the borders of prostitution? The collection provides some illuminating personal accounts from women working in the sex industry who are avowedly feminist and who, for Nagle, will together help sex worker feminism change the face of feminism as a whole.

For example, Vicky Funari's contribution focuses upon her work as a peep-show dancer to support her work as a film maker and artist. She writes: 'Most mainstream porn is part of a feedback loop of consumerism; boring, repetitive, quantifiable self-hypnosis. The porn industry has more power to deaden our imaginations and our passions than it has to hurt us physically. Like any distraction porn can be used to the point of abuse' (Funari 1997: 30). Funari's contribution gives voice to the complex business of separating your body from your soul (see Edwards 1993), of managing the separation of the body as the tool of the trade and the psyche (self-identity/self-worth) within the context of good-girl/bad-girl images. Funari also writes about managing the very difficult personal issue of seeing the men you mix with in your local community (supermarket, coffee house, friends of your partner) turn up to watch the peep-show while you 'perform' naked, behind glass in the peep-show booth.

Priscilla Alexander's contribution focuses upon the differences between coerced prostitution and sex work as voluntary, chosen, service work. Alexander argues that the 'stop feminists' Nagle names 'have internalized the universal hatred of women and named the sexually assertive woman, "the whore", as the cause of women's pain' (Alexander 1997: 83). As a feminist, Alexander argues from a human rights' perspective for sex workers' rights and for pro-sex feminism. Alexander argues that we will never be free until women stop being afraid of being called a whore.[1] Furthermore, laws restricting migration and prohibiting prostitution create the perfect conditions for trafficking to flourish (1997: 90–1). Alexander wants sex workers to have the same rights and liberties as other workers.[2]

The contributors to Nagle's book argue that working in the sex industry can be empowering for women, in that they acquire a sense of being in control of their own bodies and are thus able to deal more effectively with harassment (Dudash 1997: 116). Furthermore, some claim that sex workers can help to educate men about women's sexuality and sexual needs in order to address sexual inequalities; some of these men are attempting to 'redefine their own sexual needs in creative and healthy ways' (1997: 114). 'Working in the sex industry has made me even more aware of just how much power I do have in my relations with men that I didn't recognize before' (1997: 117).

Carol Queen does not want to be a 'good-girl' and indeed relishes 'the opportunity' her work provides her 'to learn secrets, to support our clients' forays away from traditional masculine sexuality, to transgress restrictive boundaries and rebel against rigid limitations created by our own fear of sex' (1997: 135). In an essay addressing sex-radical politics, sex-positive feminism and whore stigma, Queen invites mainstream feminism 'into bed with whore feminism', arguing that whores 'are only one of a multitude of groups who do not get an open-minded hearing in mainstream feminism today'. Furthermore, 'whores labour on the front lines of patriarchy' (1997: 135).

The differences between what Nagle calls 'pro-sex' feminism and 'traditional feminism' appear to be so great, with feminist whores or 'pro-sex' feminists taking a defensive stance against 'traditional feminism', that we are left looking into an abyss. Of course, there is no single feminism; if nothing else, postmodern feminist thought and practice has taught us this. Feminists of all persuasions are working from the margins, although some are more marginalized than others, and sex worker feminists are certainly marginalized. In part, the perspectives in Nagle's edited collection provide a picture of two clear poles to the feminist debate around prostitution – contradicting her introductory statement which argues for a focus upon plurality and a deconstructive challenge to binary thinking. In the end, Nagle's text reinforces the binaries, reproduces the polarity. There are two feminist perspectives from the standpoints of women working in the sex industry. Traditional feminism, which is defined as 'stop feminism' (stop the sex industry/stop sexual pleasure), and pro-sex feminism (the sex industry allows space for empowering/transforming gender stereotypes, sexual pleasure, and helps to change masculinities in creative ways). Thus, the aim of transgressing binary thinking and representing the multiple realities of women with a view to developing discourse and collective action against the ideology of individualism, and across the feminist divide, cannot be 'read' from Nagle's text.

On the other hand, the narrative accounts from women who 'chose' to work in the sex industry do provide us with complex pictures of sexuality, identities and the lived experiences of women traversing the spaces between good-girls and bad-girls, between gender conformity and sexual identity, in a consumer society pivoting on the power of the penis and the rights, needs and aspirations of the individual. The narrative accounts also provide a useful understanding of the complex, lived relations of women who work in the sex industry as prostitutes, dancers and strippers; women who identify as bisexuals, butch lesbians; women who support 'mainstream (good-girl) work roles', such as Vicky Funari (film maker) and Tawnya Dudash (student); women who move from mainstream work roles to work in the sex industry, such as Norma Jean Almodovar (from cop to sex worker).

Wendy Chapkis is very critical of this notion of 'free choice' because very few women's lives involve free choice in that we are located in disadvantaged positions in hierarchical structures of sex, race and class (1997: 52). Instead, Chapkis outlines a more pragmatic perspective than Nagle by drawing upon the collaboration between the Dutch prostitutes' rights movement and anti-trafficking activists, both of whom advocate increased worker control and 'self-determination'. Lisa Hoffman, the director of the Dutch Foundation Against Trafficking in Women, states that women make a 'rational choice' to work in prostitution and that free choice is something very few people actually have (Chapkis 1997: 62). For Chapkis, when erotic labour is viewed as a form of service – work, free from an act of man's command over women, and viewed as work, 'it is revealed to be an arena of struggle where the meaning and terms of sexual exchange are vulnerable to cultural and political contestation' (1997: 57).

Live Sex Acts: Women Performing Erotic Labour (1997) by Wendy Chapkis aims to challenge the divisions between 'good-girls' and 'bad-girls' and build bridges across the two poles in the ongoing feminist debates around prostitution. Chapkis, professor of sociology and women's studies in California, is an activist who has collaborated with women working in the sex trade against the closure of massage parlours and against the prosecution of 'johns': 'Perhaps it was my identity as a lesbian that made me wary of a strategy calling for the arrest and punishment of any party to consensual adult sexual activity' (1997: 3). For Chapkis, being 'queer' helped her to identify and admire 'politicized whores'. However, in the process Chapkis found herself defending her reputation and sexuality amid heavy criticism from other feminists in what she describes as 'sex wars'. Her 'perverse' sexual politics and practices came under fire:

> I will say that, in my experience, feminists opposed to prostitution, pornography and s/m [sadomasochism] fight with a passion reserved for the truly self right-eous. It is not only that they know they are right, but they know that the safety of women elsewhere depends on the triumph of their position. Women who disagree are not only enemies but traitors. . . . My own experience as a designated enemy has not only intensified my hatred of war in any context, it has also raised the stakes for me in wishing to see this conflict resolved. (1997: 5)

For Chapkis there are no 'truths' about commercial sex or, indeed, sex; there are different perspectives in what is a complex and contradictory set of issues. Chapkis is pro commercial sex and makes an argument for commercial sex to be defined as 'erotic labour'. For Chapkis, immersion in the debates included training as a massage practitioner and seeing clients in California and Amsterdam; paying 'for sexual services in the form of hands-on sexual instruction from two professional sex workers' (1997: 6); and selling sex to women clients for one afternoon in Amsterdam. For Chapkis, this was not about immersion in the field to achieve 'insider status' but rather about putting her own 'body on the line . . . to reveal something more about my own resistances and fascination with the sale of "intimate services" ' (1997: 6). The core research activity involved conducting more than fifty interviews with women working in the sex industry as call girls, escort workers, pornography actresses, brothel workers, peep-show workers, street workers and window prostitutes – all involved in '"prostitution politics"'. Chapkis stresses that the stories told throughout her book are mediated and that they are stories to be interpreted. Chapkis is very clear about her own position in the debates. Her interviews were conducted largely in California and Amsterdam and were all with women who identify as politicized and as such are performing erotic labour in situations described as 'freely chosen' and are 'empowered' by their work. These voices are a far cry from many of the women I interviewed in the UK, as we shall see later in the book.

There are three feminist positions outlined in Chapkis's book: pro-'positive' sex feminism, anti-sex feminism and sex radical feminism. Chapkis identifies with sex radical feminism and draws on the voices of women performing erotic labour and on the photographic work and training workshops of Annie Sprinkle and a 'sex goddess' called 'Vision' to expound the category or typology.

Pro-'positive' feminism views prostitution and pornography as corrupting practices that undermine 'positive' sex or eros based upon love. Sex is given expression in love and is violently articulated in 'pornographic objectification' (Chapkis 1997:13). Kathleen Barry, Gloria Steinham, Sheila Jeffreys and Carole Pateman are all quoted to define pro-'positive' sex feminism.

> For pro-'positive' sex feminists, then, sexuality may be able to be reclaimed from the patriarchy, but not in forms easily recognisable as sex. Because prostitution and pornography have already infiltrated our imaginations, women's fantasies and sexual activities must be cleansed of their residue. Pro-'positive' sex feminists advocate the abolition of the erotic by the pornographic, and to free women from the sexual objectification of men. (1997: 16)

For anti-sex feminism there is no possibility of reclaiming sexual terrain for women because the very meaning of sex is male domination (1997: 17). Sex is constituted by male domination. Chapkis draws upon Catherine MacKinnon, Karen Davis and Andrea Dworkin to illustrate this perspective. The prostitute can never be perceived as 'sex worker' because she is 'sex object' – woman is constituted as and through sex. 'Catherine MacKinnon insists ". . . men say all women are whores". We say men have the power to make this our fundamental condition' (1997: 19). For Chapkis, by

> constantly reiterating that women are whores, and that whores are no more than objects, such feminists blind themselves to the fact that prostitutes, no less than any other worker, and no less than any other woman, engage in acts of negotiation, resistance and subversion that belie their designation as passive objects. Anti-sex feminism, like pro-'positive' sex feminism, cannot accommodate this reality. (1997: 20)

The only way forward for Chapkis is a radical feminism of opposition and subversion, making subversive use of the sexual order through a radicalism which goes beyond the work of Steven Seidman, whom Chapkis has drawn upon until this point. Sex radical feminism is made up of those individuals who identify with libertarian ethics and politics (Camille Paglia) and others who situate sex within structures of power and privilege (Annie Sprinkle, Pat Califia) (1997: 21).

Sex radicals of the latter persuasion (for example, Sprinkle and Califia) agree that sex is 'deeply implicated in structures of inequality... *and* ... sex is a terrain of struggle, not a fixed field of gender and power positions' (my emphasis; 1997: 26). Sex radicals aim to subvert the cultural order from within, offering a vision of sexual culture that resignifies sexual language and practices. Pat Califia and Annie Sprinkle are drawn upon to show how sex can be used as a cultural tactic to destabilize male power as well as to reinforce it. The entire debate is used to show that the position of the prostitute cannot be reduced to passive object, 'but instead can be understood as a place of agency where the sex worker makes use of the existing social order' (1997: 29–30). The prostitute is a symbol of women's authority and a threat to patriarchy. Chapkis concludes with the statement that the reality of prostitution is far more complex than either sex libertarianism or radical feminist rhetoric gives credit for, and indeed the use of the sex worker as a symbol helps to cloud the real complexity of her life.

But Chapkis has already stated that there is no 'truth' nor a single version of 'reality', so there is some contradiction here. Furthermore, I would argue that the use of symbols and the deconstruction of symbols and tropes can help us to better understand the complexity of the lives and experiences of women working in prostitution, and the many ways cultural texts imagine and re-present 'prostitutes', 'whores' and 'sex workers'. For these images and re-presentations are indices for all women in reflexive modern and postmodern times, as we shall see in chapters 5 and 6.

Additionally, Chapkis tells us that women working in the sex industry operate within the constraints of social prejudice as well as unequal privilege, and these differences produces different experiences of sex work. The biggest challenge, she tells us, is in tackling the structural inequalities that are reflected in the industry but are rooted in society at large.

It is, however, the structural and social inequalities that are largely missing from the stories collected from the women interviewed. Broader socio-structural analysis is missing in an otherwise rich and diverse book which speaks of the complex differences between feminists both inside and outside the sex industry and the autobiographical accounts of some women working in the sex industry in the USA and Amsterdam. One would expect that the stories of women could be used to illuminate and interrogate the larger social, sexual and racial structures and dimensions to women's lives and lived experiences, but Chapkis does not draw the links and connections to wider social issues from the stories gathered here.

The bottom line for Chapkis is that she is on the side of sex workers, supporting sex worker advocacy not only to transform the social conditions under which sex work or erotic labour takes place, but also to improve the status of those performing erotic labour by transforming the cultural meanings attached to prostitution – that is, getting rid of whore stigma. There is for her an urgent need to produce conversations across the divides both within and beyond the trade. This involves building a prostitution politics that is a 'hybrid perspective', that draws upon radical feminists, abolitionists and sex radical feminists. Thus, for Chapkis, feminists can divert their energies away from fighting each other and towards pursuing collective purposes and shared goals.

This 'hybrid perspective' contains: the radical feminists' insistence that injustice should be challenged and not accommodated; the sex radicals' insistence that subversion is a creative means of opposition; the abolitionists' insight that just because something has always existed it is neither inevitable nor unchangeable; and the prostitutes' rights perspective that transforming our lives does not mean a politics of prohibition (Chapkis 1997: 213). The goals of this 'hybrid perspective' are: to work towards a fundamental redistribution of wealth and power between men and women; to work towards an organized and empowered workforce; and to decriminalize consensual sexual activity.

The problem we are faced with here is that, while the goals of the 'hybrid perspective' are commendable, the ways in which we might achieve these goals are fraught with problems of difference involving rights, liberties and the fundamental means through which any or all might be achieved. Chapkis is asking a great deal from a feminist coalition of the three major feminist perspectives, as outlined above. The what, why and how of such a coalition is not predicated on socio-cultural economic contexts and possibilities. And, ultimately, the relationship between socio-economic, sexual and social inequalities, women's lives and the broader structures of power, control and signification is absent from an otherwise provocative and richly detailed mapping of sex work as erotic labour, based upon the wonderfully complex stories from the women themselves. Chapkis presents us with a very powerful interweaving of sexual fantasy and subversive challenges to sexual mores through the work of politicized feminists performing erotic labour and illustrated through the work of Annie Sprinkle. However, this work does not address the very structures of domination.

Julia O'Connell-Davidson's approach (1998) focuses very clearly on the structures of domination. In *Prostitution, Power and Freedom* we find a very thorough analysis of the limits to freedom experienced by prostitutes in their encounters with the clients, pimps and managers of the sex industry. This concept of unfreedom is rooted in a critique of the systematic inequalities of capitalism, including the economic, legal, political and gender dimensions. The problem for O'Connell-Davidson is that, given the unequal power relations involved, there is limited scope for transformative change because of the unfreedom experienced by prostitutes and, by extension, prostitutes' collectives. The future is bleak as far as transformative social change is concerned. The analysis of the limits to freedom is very thorough, but the transformative possibilities for prostitutes' collectives cannot be adequately addressed given the primary focus of the text upon structures of domination. More work needs to be developed on prostitutes' collectives as a new social movement, as discussed by Jackie West (2000) and later in this chapter.

The stories told in Chapkis (1997) offer us a less bleak version of commercial sex than other writers, for example Hoigard and Finstad (1992) and

O'Connell-Davidson (1998). Chapkis admits that in the process of research we often find the stories we expect, and the ones most suitable for our political purposes. One way of countering this is simply to let the stories and narratives speak for themselves and to interpret according to our version of the 'realities' we seek to explore and understand. Another way forward is for us to draw upon the voices, narratives and stories to cast light on broader social structures and processes. What must be acknowledged is that Hoigard and Finstad's study (1992) focused upon street workers, mostly drug-using workers, whilst Wendy Chapkis's interviews contained only 10 per cent of interviews with street workers – and even these women worked behind windows in Amsterdam. Chapkis is concerned that in her text 'the voices of the most marginalized might be overwhelmed by those more favourably positioned' (1997: 212). This is certainly the case, and a comparison with the work of Hoigard and Finstad deserves more reflection and space than Chapkis gives it.

However, the stories told in Chapkis (1997) are insightful, and together with other stories from Nagle (1997), Hoigard and Finstad (1992), Eileen McLeod (1982), McKegany and Barnard (1996), and O'Connell-Davidson (1998) help us to understand the many differing and similar experiences of women from various class positions, races and sexual preferences working in the various facets of the sex industry and also in differing geographical locations. Comparative analysis that seeks to examine the differences and similarities between women working in the same facets of the sex industry but in different countries is very much needed.[3]

The approaches taken by Shrage, Nagle and Chapkis are indeed informative, and indicative of the feminist debates upon prostitution in contemporary Western society. What is clear is that they introduce ideas, concepts and visions that illuminate the complexity of women's experiences and lives. But listening to what 'prostitute(d)' women are telling me and showing me suggests that it is too simple to reduce the feminist approaches to prostitution to these largely two diametrically opposed perspectives: feminists against prostitution but for prostitutes, and whore feminism, which is 'pro-sex' and against or subversive of 'traditional feminism' and sexual oppression.

The situation is much more complex and contradictory as Eileen McLeod identified back in 1982. McLeod published *Women Working: Prostitution Now* following her work with the Birmingham PROS (Programme for the Reform of the Law on Soliciting) street campaign. McLeod was concerned to show that 'prostitutes' are ordinary women and that analysing prostitution may contribute to understanding more general social relations. McLeod developed a feminist perspective that includes the voices of women working as prostitutes as well as the voices of clients, and her work had a great influence on me.

Chapkis, Shrage and Nagle would, I think, agree that we need analyses that recognize the contradictions and resistances women articulate as well as the complexity of their lives in order to work with women to develop better understanding, policy and practice. These feminists would (I guess) agree that it is important to focus upon the personal, small-scale lived experiences, actions and interactions to develop a thorough understanding of routes into prostitution and the sex industry; 'making out'; and the way women sustain and manage the social stigma involved in order to develop practical and political responses to prostitution based upon women's needs and rights.

My point here is that in order to develop a better understanding of prostitution and the sex industry we need to examine the interrelationships between the micrology of women's lives and the meta-conditions of wider society, including historical analysis. This in turn could facilitate the development of work, including policy-oriented practice by women who identify as feminists working in the sex industry and by women who identify as academic feminists, activist feminists or simply feminists. Involving ourselves in action research – working together – is a useful place to start in order to develop analyses that acknowledge the sameness, the difference and the need for collective responses.

Acknowledging the ideology of individualism that marks contemporary culture and politics, and also focusing upon the wider social and economic contexts to women's involvement in prostitution, necessitates *asking women* about personally felt experiences, routes into prostitution, making out in prostitution, and the extent of exploitation and violence against women working as prostitutes, in order to develop a more thorough (complex) analysis. Asking women is of central importance. It is difficult for women in contemporary society to work together to challenge sexual and social inequalities, particularly given the ideology of individualism. Talking to individual women through in-depth ethnographic work could highlight oppositional spaces and resistances in individual women's lives, which may enable or facilitate collective action. At the very least, it will highlight previously hidden lives and add to our understanding of women's involvement in prostitution, difference, gendered relations and women's situatedness within structural and psychic structures, processes and practices.

The strength of the work of both Chapkis and Nagle is that they engage *with* women working in the sex industry through empirical ethnographic research. However, they do not examine women's narratives to explore the specific problems women face within patriarchy, the socio-cultural and economic structures of domination that inform, support and give rise to prostitution and the sex industry. The sex industry is instead taken as a given, a reified social structure, and unlike women's relationship to sex, sexuality, desires, and sex work it goes un-theorized.

However, what we have to realize is that, in part, our particular situation, history, politics and experiences inform our way of seeing and knowing the research we undertake, and both Nagle and Chapkis are very clear about their respective 'positions' in their work. My 'position' is also clear: I am analysing and reflecting from immersion in women's lives in order to develop better understanding and praxis rooted in experiences, meanings and possibilities for social change *with* women. As a sociologist (a cultural interpreter and critic) my vantage point is informed by sociological and cultural discourses (Western

Marxism, feminism, postmodernism, interpretive ethnography) rooted in my understanding, experience and practice of feminism as a way of seeing and knowing the world *and* as a politics for change.

Margaretha Jarvinen's analysis is based upon an interactionist approach. Jarvinen (1993) produced an excellent study of prostitution in Helsinki covering the period 1945–86. Prostitution is defined as heterosexual prostitution known to the local authorities. Jarvinen outlines three theoretical approaches to prostitution: functionalist (Davis 1937; Kinsey et al. 1948; Ellis 1959; Winnick 1962; Benjamin and Masters 1965; Clinard 1968; Verlare and Warlick 1973); feminist (Davis 1971; Gray 1973; Finnegan 1979; Walkowitz 1980; Hoigard and Finstad 1992; McLeod 1982); and interactionist/constructivist (Gray 1973; Bryant and Palmer 1975; Verlade 1975; James 1977; Miller 1978; Foltz 1980; Prus and Irini 1980; Vitaliano 1981; Potterat et al. 1985; Salomon 1989).

For Jarvinen, functionalists, initially Davis (1937), developed an approach which sees prostitutes as deviant, as mentally, sexually and socially abnormal. Yet, prostitution is also normal, universal and functional – a safety valve for society. Feminist approaches developed during the seventies and eighties are rooted in turn-of-the-century feminism, and discuss inequalities, gender relations, the socio-economic power of men, the way prostitution mirrors patriarchal view of sexuality and, hence, woman as commodities. For Jarvinen, normal women choose prostitution from a subordinate position in which they face few attractive alternatives. The social interactionist/constructivist approach that Jarvinen develops in the study sees prostitution as a relative concept. Prostitution is socially constructed through time and society. Prostitution is a career and is related to the relationship between prostitutes and their milieux. The stress is on the interaction between the prostitutes (object) and the (subject of control) relevant authorities.

Working as 'prostitutes', women and young women can and do become enmeshed in the local subculture (Miller and Miller 1972; Gray 1973; Binderman, Wepman and Newman 1975; Janus, Scanton and Price 1984; Jarvinen 1993). Subcultural approaches are documented as male dominated, structured not by prostitutes but by their pimps (Jarvinen 1993). Davis (1971) describes three categories of prostitute: a hustler subculture; a dual-world culture and a criminal subculture. In the first category, lifestyle was structured by prostitution, irregular living patterns, alcohol and drug abuse, and a live-for-today mentality. In the second, women combined prostitution with family life, studies and conventional jobs. In the third, women identified with a criminal subculture and were involved in crimes such as drug offences, thefts, shoplifting. Jarvinen (1993) maintains that these studies show that women's involvement in prostitution is determined by two central factors that bind these women to the particular subculture: their relationship to men (and to a degree other prostitutes) and active socializing with pimps and other men. Prostitution milieux are, therefore, for Jarvinen male subcultures with women playing secondary roles to pimps and clients; women living with partners and children occupy a more marginal position. Thus the interests of pimps and clients are maintained.

This analysis is also reflected in my observations of the social organization of prostitution in the UK. Although I do have a problem about these fixed categories, they seem altogether more flexible in my experience. Some people can be located in all of the three categories, but mostly people seem to move in, and in and out of, these categories depending on life-stage, family commitments, the birth of their children, who the father is (partner or pimp or both) and relationship/friendship group. They are altogether more dynamic than any of the authors listed gives credit for. For some young women and young men prostitution is a temporary business. They move on and out.

Furthermore, I have observed female subcultures centred around the friend-ships of women. These friendships are woman-defined and woman-dominated; they are about supporting other women, assisting other women and, essentially, about peer empowerment. These cultures are very clearly expressed in the work of both Nagle (1997) and Chapkis (1997).

Jarvinen (1993) blends feminist and interactionist approaches, exploring the relativity and control of the prostitutes' career as well as the social relations involved between pimps, clients and prostitutes. This is a thorough and scholarly work making use of much ethnographic data. An important conclusion is reached: that the concept of prostitution is a social construction whose meaning varies from setting to setting; that the line demarcating prostitutes' liaisons from reciprocal sexual relations is determined by a process of social definition. The context of the milieu is an important one. But, in one sense, the central importance placed upon it precludes the opportunity/space to look more widely at the broader social–cultural context.

The growing importance and influence of the international and European prostitutes' rights movements as a new social movement is absent in Jarvi-nen's work. Wider social, economic and cultural contexts are not dealt with in depth due to the focus upon the milieu. The endemic nature of violence against prostitutes (a key aspect of the social relations between pimps, clients and prostitutes) is not really addressed and is not examined. Jarvinen's analysis is very helpful in that it articulates the fluidity of the interrelationship between whore stigma, the labelling of 'prostitutes', and the meaning-giving practices and relationships women engage in with significant others, peers, pimps and relevant social agencies. Taking an interactionist/constructivist approach could free up space for resistance and empowerment through social praxis, but there is a need to define the broader context within which milieux are embedded and sustained. What, then, is the broader social context to the milieu?

The broader social context can be examined and illustrated by looking at both the meta-conditions of reflexive modernity and/or postmodernity and the micrology of individual women's lives – dialectically. In this way dis-sonances and differences between explanations of the micro and macro will be illuminated and can be explored in greater depth. At one and the same time, examination of the micro will throw up pictures of the wider social experience and an examination of the macro will throw up issues to be examined through in-depth work with individuals and groups.

Part of the broader social context is undoubtedly the work of the European and international prostitutes' rights organizations who are currently calling for prostitution to be identified as work, within the context of national and international labour law. They argue that women should have the same rights and liberties as other workers. Many 'whores' who are also feminists or feminist-informed are arguing that the realities of women's lives do not necessarily give them the opportunity to engage in debate about male oppression and the problems related to supporting patriarchy (McLintock 1992). However, many women involved in these organizations and many women working as prostitutes are aware and antagonistic to the involvement of men as pimps, ponces and abusers of women working as prostitutes. Strategies of resistance are developed and shared between women around self-help, support and peer-group empowerment/education. This work is taking place on individual levels and also collectively through the work of the English Collective of Prostitutes, POW! and WHIP in England, Scotpep in Scotland, APRAMP in Madrid, HYDRA in Berlin, HWG in Frankfurt, Cal-PEP and COYOTE in the USA, EMPOWER in Thailand, the UK network of sex work projects and the European and international prostitutes' rights movements across the globe.

On the other hand, argued most notably by Kathleen Barry, we cannot turn a blind eye to the horror of international trafficking in women and children when exploring possibilities, both practical and ideological, for sanctioning the use value for exchange value of women's bodies, or prostitution as work (see also Council of Europe 1991). Furthermore, as Carole Pateman argued back in 1983:

> Neither contempt for women nor their ancient profession underlies feminist arguments; rather, they are sad and angry about what the demand for prostitution reveals of the general character of (private and public) relations between the sexes. The claim that what is really wrong with prostitution is hypocrisy and outdated attitudes to sex is the tribute that liberal permissiveness pays to political mystification. (1983: 565)

For Pateman, prostitution needs to be 'placed in the social context of the structure of sexual relations between men and women' (1983: 563).

There is a great need to examine prostitution from a critical feminist 'woman-centred' position (a version/development of standpoint(s) feminism) that acknowledges the lived experiences of women working as 'prostitutes' within the context of sexual and social inequalities. Such an approach should aim to give sex workers a voice by working with them through participatory action research. This describes the approach taken in this text. The reflexive interrelationship between feminist theory, women's lived experiences and policy-oriented practice articulated through feminist participatory action research is central. Prostitution and violence, prostitution and the state, feminism, prostitution and the political economy and the social organization of prostitution (at a national as well as a European level), the management of female sexuality, sexual trafficking and tourism are all key themes and concerns. Identifying spaces of resistance can become the means through which women-centred change can be developed on a collective scale at local, national and international levels. The emphasis is upon exploring the issues with women working as prostitutes, developing collective responses and, in so doing, both challenging the ideology of individualism and responding to the criticisms of women working as prostitutes towards feminism(s), begun by the work of Alexander, Nagle and Chapkis.

Feminist analyses of prostitution inevitably challenge the ways in which sexual and social inequalities serve to reproduce ideology, partiarchy and the structuration of gender relations. The central ideological problem for feminism is that the exchange of money for sex is taken to be the exchange of equivalents. This is a socially created illusion and is central to the commodification of women's bodies as use objects and our subsequent oppression in society. Both first- and second-wave feminists have fought battles based on this very use value of women and women's bodies. However, feminist thought must acknowledge that for some women prostitution gives a good enough standard of income, relative autonomy and can be fitted in around child care. Prostitution has always been a means for women to acquire an income – economic need is the bottom line.

Furthermore, as Nagle's work (1997) shows very clearly, many women are choosing work in the sex industry as dancers, peep-show workers, lap-dancers, as a response to economic need and limited options. Focusing upon the moral rights and wrongs of prostitution in the UK – the enforcement of a justice model based upon Victorian ideology and Wolfenden (which criminalizes and stigmatizes the whore but not her client) – hides the gender issues implicated in the question: why do men use prostitutes? It is this issue which needs to be given more attention (gender relations and masculinities) while at the same time working with prostitutes' rights organizations, women working in prostitution and the wider sex industry to address sexual and social inequalities.

As the work of Chapkis (1997) shows, feminism(s) and feminists must face up to the contradictions inherent in working with and for women working in the sex industry, and call for the return of civil liberties and the rights of human dignity to people working as prostitutes. There is also a need for direct action from all those agencies working with 'prostitutes', particularly at the level of the criminal justice system, to explore their policies, codes of practice and funding mechanisms in order to develop more woman-centred responses. Feminists necessarily challenge the discrimination and oppression of women. Creating a space for women involved in prostitution to be heard, and, in turn, for feminist research to inform theory and practice around women's involvement in the sex industry, is at the very heart of this approach and can serve to resist, challenge and change sexual and social inequalities via feminist praxis on an individual and a collective level.

We do need to explore the social organization of prostitution in all its complexity. This includes a look at men and masculinities and at the agencies working with and for 'prostitutes', who necessarily affect and are affected by the experiences of women working as prostitutes. Contextualized within a broad understanding of prostitution, social order and social change in contemporary times, we may be able to move towards recommending changes in social policy and developing concerted action to help effect such change. One thing is very clear: prostitution and the broader sex industry is a deeply embedded global institution within social, cultural, economic and political structures. Rooted in capitalism, commodification and, as Pateman (1983) argues, the structure of sexual relations between men and women, it is a major task for feminists to develop better understanding of the complex issues involved and to develop feminist responses (see Kempadoo and Doezema 1999).

Health perspectives

Research on health issues for women working in prostitution has led to innovative responses to the health and welfare needs of women, and also points to the problematic nature of the interest in the health of women working in the sex industry. Originally scapegoated for transmission of AIDS to the general population through unprotected contacts with clients; then perceived as health educators of their client group; eventually prostitutes were perceived as recipients of healthcare and protection in their own right (see Scambler and Scambler 1992). Health-based research and practice has been instrumental in supporting and developing some pioneering work in Britain. The Safe project in Birmingham; the Praed Street project based at St Mary's hospital in Paddington, London; Scotpep and the Centenary project in Edinburgh; the Health Shop and POW! (Prostitute Outreach Workers) based in Nottingham; WHIP (Women's Health in Prostitution Project) in Leicester; Liverpool's Response project; Stoke-on-Trent's Sex Work Outreach project; the Wandsworth female sex workers project; the Cardiff outreach project and the Sheffield AIDS education project are but a few examples. POW! in Nottingham, WHIP in Leicester and Stoke-on-Trent's Sex Work Outreach project are the three I am most familiar with.[4]

Information, education and support around peer education and women's self-empowerment are aspects of the work undertaken at the projects named above. Data collected particularly from the pioneering Safe project (Kinnell 1989, 1991) and the Praed Street project (Day and Ward 1990), as well as by McKegany and Barnard in Glasgow (McKegany et al. 1990, 1992a, 1992c; McKegany 1992), Morgan-Thomas, Plant and Sales in Edinburgh

(1989, 1990), Morgan-Thomas (1990), Plant (1990) and Green (1992), has developed greater awareness and understanding of working women's health, welfare needs and circumstances. Such data was instrumental in debunking the idea in the public imagination of the dirty, disease-ridden prostitute. It became clear that most women working as prostitutes are very self-conscious of their health needs and are taking precautions against the risk of contracting STDs, including AIDS. Health agencies, in particular, have been instrumental in developing research which generates better information about the extent of prostitution and the male client group, but which also develops services to support and empower women working in prostitution. What is very clear is that research on prostitution needs to be understood within the context of the current law.

Prostitution and the law

Research on prostitution and the law points to the fact that the current law relating to prostitution in the UK is made up of 'piecemeal legislation' which criminalizes a 'variety of objectional conduct' (Dingwall 1997: 437). Moreover, this piecemeal legislation is riddled with inequalities, especially in relation to 'punishing the provider rather than the buyer of sexual services' (see *Sex Workers and the Law*; Lee and O'Brien 1995; Kelly et al. 1995; Barnardo's 1998; alongside academic research: Edwards 1997, 1998; English Collective of Prostitutes 1997; O'Neill 1994; O'Neill et al. 1994; Green, Mulroy and O'Neill 1997; Scambler and Scambler 1997; Barrett 1997; Benson and Matthews 1995; Melrose and Barrett 1999).

There is also a general lack of clarity in some areas of the law. For example, what is meant by 'living off immoral earnings'? Moreover, a girl over 13 but under 16 can be charged with soliciting, even though she can't give lawful consent to sexual intercourse. Diduck and Wilson comment:

> The modern history of the common law has shown how legal reforms and procedures, as much as the substance of law, reflects and maintains patterns of difference and inequality in social relations generally. (Diduck and Wilson 1997: 504)

Examples of patterns of difference and inequality include the fact that after two cautions a woman/girl can be defined in law as a 'common prostitute', but there is no such definition in law for a male prostitute. 'Common prostitute' refers specifically to women. The law is very clearly gendered and, as far back as the campaigns by Josephine Butler, Butler and her supporters objected to the double standards involved in the language and operation of the law, which stigmatized, criminalized and punished women but not their clients (Jerrard 1992; Smart and Smart 1978; Smart 1992; Edwards 1984, 1998; Carlen 1988, 1998; Kennedy 1992; Stanko 1985;

Morris 1987). Moreover, there is also an obvious disadvantage for women who carry the stigma of 'common prostitute' when they appear in court. Discriminatory language helps to produce and maintain what has been described by various researchers (Pheterson 1986; A. Murray 1995a, 1995b; McLintock 1992, 1995) as 'whore stigma' and has a long-term, negative effect on equal opportunities for any woman named on record as a 'common prostitute'. Three unsuccessful amendment bills attempted to remove the use of the term 'common prostitute' in 1967, 1969 and 1990 (Edwards 1998: 61–2).

There are many opportunities for interpretation of the law to influence decision making throughout the criminal justice process up to and including sentencing practices (see Carlen 1998; Devlin 1998; Cavadino 1997; Ashworth 1988). For example, what constitutes soliciting in a 'public place'? What constitutes a 'brothel'? A 'brothel' has no statutory definition in law, and decisions in court rely on previous case-law (Diduck and Wilson 1997). It is widely referenced in the available literature that women soliciting for the purpose of prostitution constitutes '*immoral purpose*', but men soliciting the favours of a 'common prostitute' does not constitute an 'immoral purpose' (see Edwards 1998: 64–5).

There is a contradiction in the law around under-age sex, which gives rise to a lack of clarity in sentencing decisions. Having sex with a girl under 16 is illegal, *but* a girl of 13 or over and a boy of 10 or over can be prosecuted for soliciting.[5] Having been proved guilty of having sex with a girl under 13 years of age necessitates a maximum sentence of seven years; if the girl is over 13 but under 16 the maximum is two years. The defining line between 13 and 14 is totally at odds with the Children Act (1989), whereby a child is anyone under 18. This also raises questions about the interpretation and enforcement of young men of 17 and under who either work as prostitutes, live off immoral earnings or could be defined in law as 'pimps'.

The law needs to be very clear about these issues and respond in ways that are contextualized within the Children Act (1989) and the various other relevant European and international instruments. The UN Convention on the Rights of the Child states that primary consideration must be given to the best interests of the child and that states must undertake to protect children from sexual exploitation, taking appropriate measures to prevent the involvement of children in prostitution, pornography and other unlawful practices.

Enforcement of the law differs with regard to the prosecution of women for 'soliciting' and the prosecution of men for 'kerb-crawling'. There are many potential reasons for this, including the greater visibility of women; the difficulties in proving the 'persistence' of men soliciting the favours of women following the 1985 Sexual Offences Act; the resources at the disposal of police force areas; gender bias and sexual inequalities in dealing with female 'prostitutes' and male 'kerb-crawlers'.

A man commits an offence if he solicits a woman. According to the sex offences legislation, a 'woman' includes a female child. The penalty is a maximum level 3 fine of £1,000. Bob Golding (1992) has written about the lack of national standards for fining women. Furthermore, he states that practices and policies adopted by all elements of the criminal justice system are not coordinated. Golding's study (1992) reported that fines vary widely in different parts of the country and in different courts in the same city. In eleven vice areas the average fine was £50; in thirteen areas the average was £100; in seven areas the average was £200 and in two areas the average was £300 and £400. In 1997, under the Sexual Offences Act (1956), 8,901 women of all ages were cautioned and convicted of soliciting; under the Sexual Offences Act (1985) 813 men were prosecuted for kerb-crawling and 68 for persistent soliciting (Home Office Statistics, Research and Development Unit).

Enforcing the law has everything to do with the way the law is interpreted by police officers, as front-line workers, and subsequently by the courts and the Crown Prosecution Service. Whether the focus is upon adult prostitution, child prostitution, pimping, kerb-crawling or trafficking, the *social meanings* (along gender, race and class lines) which underpin or can be 'read off' from the written law need to be uncovered and discussed in any attempt at law reform. Clear anomalies found in the available literature include:

- outmoded legislation which reflects particular bias and prejudices (the predominant focus on the providers of sexual services and not on those who manage/control/coerce);
- treating children involved in prostitution analogous to adult females and males;
- differential treatment of men and women in both the interpretation and enforcement of the law.

In any attempt to update the law along feminist principles, a clear analysis of the anomalies, contradictions and loopholes in the substantive law must be developed, with a view to bringing about a fair, balanced and just response through the legislation within the context of wider European and international instruments.

However, there is evidence that the legacy of prosecuting the prostitute and not the client, carved out by the Wolfenden report (1957), the 1956 Sexual Offences Act, and the 1959 Street Offences Act (but rooted in much earlier legislation), is shifting in the UK.[6] The clients of prostitutes are now criminalized through the 1985 Sexual Offences Act for the offence of kerb-crawling (although some researchers are calling for heavier penalties for kerb-crawlers (see Benson and Matthews 1955). The Kerb Crawlers Rehabilitation Project (KCRP), founded at Leeds Metropolitan University, focuses attention upon men as wrongdoers and in need of re-education concerning their attitudes and behaviour to the women and girls involved in prostitution. Men are referred to the project for 'rehabilitation'. The project is pioneering an approach which focuses squarely on men who purchase sexual services. The men referred to the course are made aware of the endemic violence against women working on street, the backgrounds of the women/girls from whom they purchase sexual services, and the links with drugs, abuse and leaving local authority care. The aim is to deliver an interventionary strategy which persuades or diverts men from purchasing sexual services. The project is rooted firmly in an understanding of prostitution as exploitation.

The project has come under a lot of criticism, particularly from the National Network of Sex Work Projects, which is affiliated to the European Network for HIV/STD Prevention in Prostitution (EUROPAP). The major criticism from the National Network of Sex Work Projects is that it is unlikely that a one-day experience of the KCRP will have any lasting impact on the behaviour of the very tiny proportion of the client population who will be referred for 'rehabilitation'. Moreover, poverty is a global factor for drawing women and men into sex work, and responses that focus upon a minority of men over a short period offer no strategies for addressing levels of poverty nor the reasons why men seek to buy sex.[7] Clearly, evaluation of the KCRP project will throw greater light on the effectiveness of the project over time and provide answers for the critics.

As Susan Edwards (1998) has stated, different ideological constructions of prostitution will have an effect on shaping law and policy. For Edwards, the current schism between prostitution as sex and a matter of privacy and prostitution as exploitation will shape the climate in which the reconstruction of legal prostitution in Europe will take place (1998: 67). As we have seen, prostitution as a matter of privacy and prostitution as exploitation form the two major poles in the international debate on prostitution. These two perspectives support either *the decriminalization of prostitution* (axing all laws relating to the regulation or criminalization of prostitution and focusing upon international labour law) or the *regulation of prostitution* (strengthen existing legislation or maintain an abolitionist approach). One issue is very clear: improving the socio-legal standing of women challenges the illegal, criminal activity that surrounds prostitution and related offences. The work of prostitutes' rights organizations focuses very clearly upon improving the socio-legal standing of the women concerned.

Prostitutes' rights and participatory research

Prostitutes' rights and grass-roots organizations are an important development in recent years – probably *the* most important development. Scotpep and the Centenary project can also be counted in the realms of prostitutes' rights organizations alongside the English Collective of Prostitutes. In the UK, during the last decade, there has been a noticeable development of grass-roots organizations led by women working in prostitution and in the wider sex industry and/or by ex-workers. This is also the case in North America (Nagle 1997: 259–61).

Valerie Jennes (1990, 1993) shifts the debate about prostitution away from discourses of sin, sex and crime and places it within discourses of work, choice and civil rights by focusing upon the work of COYOTE (Call Off Your Old Tired Ethics), a prostitutes' rights organization in North America. It will be interesting to follow the development of prostitutes' rights organizations in the coming years, particularly as they develop their work and advocacy linked to health and welfare agencies, criminal justice agencies and policy change. The European and international prostitutes' rights movements have to date had most impact in Germany, the Netherlands and North America, generating inter-agency support, and campaigning and lobbying for social change. In London, the English Collective of Prostitutes has had some impact upon policy change and, for well over twenty years, has tirelessly campaigned for the rights and liberties of women working in the sex industry.

The impact of globalization on the sex industry and on prostitutes' rights is an important avenue to examine. Kempadoo and Doezema (1999) have produced an edited collection of papers, essays, interviews and reports from sex workers, activists and academics, premised upon the assertion that sex work is intricately capitalized and thoroughly globalized in the late twentieth century.

Sexual labour is defined as a primary source of profit and wealth and is a 'constituent part of national economies and transnational industries within the global capitalist economy' (Kempadoo and Doezema 1999: 8). Prostitution/sexual labour is articulated (drawing upon the work of Wendy Chapkis (1997)) as akin to emotional labour. Understandably, given the particular perspective taken by the authors, they reject notions of sex workers as exclusively 'victims', even in situations where children, women and men are involved in debt-bondage or indentureship. The authors seek to uncover and present the complex relationships between personal agency and resistance to oppressive and exploitative situations and structures 'within the context of both structural constraints and dominant relations of power in the global sex industry' (Kempadoo and Doezema 1999: 8–9).

The authors claim that agency is an integral part of feminism, and that women's agency in prostitution is often rejected by feminists. Many of the papers in the collection are embedded in empirical, ethnographic research and provide a complex picture of agency and selfhood within the context of local/national political economies. We are constantly reminded that one cannot examine prostitution in isolation from economic, political and social factors, for example in relation to: migrant sex workers to Japan from Thailand (chapter 8); Ghanaian women emigrants in Côte d'Ivoire (chapter 7); migrant experiences from the Caribbean (chapter 9); child prostitution and identity in Thailand (chapter 10).

The major themes discussed in the collection include: the specificity of racism; the existence of a 'canon' in prostitution studies; the impact of globalization; the impact of sexually transmitted diseases; the impact of the global prostitutes' rights movement. Racism is examined particularly in relation to Third World sex workers and includes two major dimensions: racisms embedded in the structures of local industries and racisms involved in the cultural imperialism and international discourses on prostitution. The 'canon' in prostitution studies is premised upon constructions of prostitution and the prostitute/sex worker found in the literature of the 'First World', the USA and Western Europe. The 'canon' serves to privilege Western categories, subjects and experiences in the internationalist discourses on prostitution. The authors intend to directly counter the North American and Western European hegemony within contemporary feminist and prostitute writings – hence the focus upon the Caribbean, Ivory Coast, Thailand, Japan and Cuba.

The authors discuss the impact of globalization on sex industries and sex work internationally by focusing upon the development of sex tourism as a major industry. Using Cuba as an example, the authors tell us that sex work 'fills the coffers of countries whose economic survival is increasingly dependent on global corporate capitalist interests' (Kempadoo and Doezema 1999: 16). The excellent chapter by the performance artist Coco Fusco (1999: 151–66) illustrates this point well. Migration is another impact of globalization that is explored alongside the feminization of international labour migration; dislocation; involvement in oppressive and complex situations for some women and children against a backdrop of laws prohibiting or regulating prostitution, migration and trafficking. In some cases, it is the laws prohibiting legal sex work and immigration that can form the major obstacles (Kempadoo and Doezema 1999: 14–19 and chapters 2 and 4).

Within the context of the global prostitutes' rights movement, there is a particular need to create space for the recognition and rights of sex workers in non-Western countries. The authors make a very strong call for the need to address the lack of Third World sex worker representation in the international arena. Overall, the book seeks to define a global sex worker movement from the various situations of complexity. The authors hope that this work will impact upon the women's movement and feminism.

Given the globalization of the sex industry, as witnessed by simply logging on to the world wide web, it is certainly time our analyses focused on the global dimensions of prostitution and on the international instruments we could develop and use to collaboratively address the injustices and inequalities that sex workers face. Comparative analyses that seek to examine the differences and similarities between women working in the same facets of the sex industry but in different countries is very much needed (see O'Connell-Davidson 1998). What is very clear and refreshing about Kempadoo and Doezema's collection is that it introduces ideas, concepts and visions that illuminate the complexity of women's experiences and lives and focuses especially on non-Western experiences, structures and contexts within an overarching understanding of globalization, and on the possibility for addressing some of the problems through a redefinition of prostitution as work.

Moreover, the book brings home to us that it is too simple to reduce the feminist approaches to prostitution to the two diametrically opposed perspectives we find in much of the literature: feminists against prostitution but for prostitutes, and whore feminism which is 'pro-sex' and against or subversive of 'traditional feminism' and sexual oppression. The current situation regarding feminist approaches to prostitution is much more complex and contradictory, as Eileen McLeod identified back in 1982. We desperately need analyses of prostitution and sex work which recognize the contradictions and resistances women articulate, as well as the complexity of their lives, in order to work with women to develop better understanding, policy and practice.

Globalization, post-colonialism, the realities of patriarchy and hierarchies of gender orders are pivotal concepts to interrogate prostitution at the end of the twentieth century and should form the context to responses based upon political action or *praxis*. Such responses could promote the needs and rights of the women, children and men involved in the sex-for-sale industry *with* their help.

This is the strength of Kempadoo and Doezema's book, alongside the fact that it is contextualized within the specific trans-national, socio-cultural and economic structures which inform, support and give rise to prostitution and the sex industry. The response to this book in policy terms should be to seriously explore the recommendations of Bindman and Doezema in their very thorough research report for Anti-Slavery International, *Redefining Prostitution as Sex Work on the International Agenda* (1997).

National and international research has stated that women working in the sex industry deserve the same rights and liberties as other workers, including freedom from fear, exploitation and violence in the course of their work. Bindman and Doezema (1997) argue that the best way forward is to regularize 'off street' prostitution through the International Labour Organization within the context of European and international conventions. The authors argue that limited resources and rigorous policing could then focus upon those who abuse, traffic and are involved in illegal activities associated with the industry.

Working in participatory ways with women working as prostitutes is important not only in terms of having their concerns, needs and voices heard by agencies working with and for them, but also in terms of working together in democratic ways to develop women-centred change. Moreover, it is important to work with and for young people involved in prostitution in order to develop and implement interventionary strategies that help prevent the involvement of young, vulnerable and emotionally needy young people in prostitution, and also to develop strategies of harm minimization for those who will not or cannot stop working as prostitutes (O'Neill, Goode and Hopkins 1995).

At the 1991 European Prostitutes Conference held in Frankfurt am Main, delegates were made aware of the legal and social situations for 'prostitutes' in the sixteen countries represented at the conference. Many of the women and men present were vociferously against the entering into prostitution of young people who were vulnerable, emotionally needy, and not really aware of their own needs around their sexuality (Drobler 1991). The delegates at the congress were strong, articulate women who demanded the de-criminalization of prostitution and the same rights, civil liberties and rights of human dignity as other workers. Indeed the Women's Committee of the European Parliament called on member states to decriminalize prostitution and protect the health and safety of sex workers, pointing out that the 'semi-illegal, shady background against which prostitutes operate actually encourages such abuses as prostitution under duress, degrading working and living conditions, maltreatment and murder'. The women and men attending this 1st European Prostitutes Conference voted upon a resolution to be included in the European social charter calling for the decriminalization of prostitution and for prostitution to be accepted as a profession. Certainly, going back to the need for law reform in the UK, I would not like to see us legalize prostitution and then go down the same road as many other European countries as far as the human rights and civil liberties of prostitute(d) women are concerned (see Drobler 1991).

> German law allows girls to flaunt their wares within carefully controlled areas, such as the Reeperbahn in Hamburg, but while it taxes their earnings at a rate of 56 per cent, it does not offer any form of social security. In France... the law... forbids prostitutes from living with their children once the child is over the age of 18. It even obliges women to inform the police when and where they are going on holiday... The Dutch are actually persecuted by pimps and harassed by health inspectors and the taxman... Soon they are likely to be forced into a registration scheme and obliged to declare their every move, sexual, medical and financial. (Walter Ellis, *The Times*, 9 November 1992)

Working *with* women is important – their voices should be heard and listened to. Standing back from the personal experience and looking at the contexts and structures in which and through which people live necessitates an examination of: the employment, education and training structures and possibilities for women; the system of local authority residential care and the whole concept of 'care'; the freeing up of traditional structures and institutions to allow for greater diversity, choice and plurality in contemporary society; the oppression and domination of women by men illustrated so tragically by the endemic nature of violence against women, but more specifically against prostitute(d) women; and, finally, sexuality and the social organization of desire contextualized within historical analyses.

In working with the complexity of women's lives, feminist research is of central importance to help create the intellectual and practical spaces for women's voices to be heard and listened to and in turn for them to feel validated and involved. We need to engage with the depth and complexity of women's lives in order to better understand women's lives, their spaces of resistance, ways of making out, in order to better address policy change. Key considerations for future work with women working in prostitution are as follows. We need further research directed at:

- developing policy changes around women's employment and the feminization of poverty;
- the violence and abuse of women and children – given the fact that violence against 'prostitutes' is endemic, they are perceived as a throwaway population;
- the relationship between routes into prostitution, homelessness and poverty and leaving local authority residential care;
- the current and future work of the prostitutes' rights movements at national, European and international levels, particularly regarding international trafficking in women and children;
- the benefits of multi-agency working groups which are woman-centred, and have women working as 'prostitutes' represented as key players, in order to develop better-organized networks of support to working women around health, welfare, legal and vocational/employment needs, as well as safety needs such as safe houses, information, knowledge and counselling;
- preventative work with young people at risk;
- and last, but by no means least, law reform, both nationally and internationally.[8]

Engaging with the realities of women's lives within the context of social order, insecurity and social change at an everyday as well as a more global level may enable us to understand the lived relations of women working in the sex industry and envision and work towards better futures for all women. The reflexive interrelationship between feminist thought/research, women's lived relations and policy-oriented practice is a good enough place to start, if it is grounded in the multiple standpoints of women working in prostitution.

The materiality of everyday life and indeed the relationships between ideology, knowledge and power need to be understood within the context of wider structures of signification and legitimation and control (Giddens 1984). Our lived experience, our emotional lives are wrapped up in materiality. Coming to understand in a reflexive and purposeful way the relationship between lived experience and wider social and cultural structures, processes and practices is constitutive of what I call a 'politics of feeling'.

Renewed methodologies (such as ethno-mimesis – dealt with in the following chapter) for social research can counter postemotionalism and engage with the standpoints of women working in prostitution through participatory action research and thus develop interpretive work which produces both understanding/interpretation and spaces for collective action. Such work will hopefully encourage readers to become 'actors and participants not just spectators' (Denzin 1997: 281–2).

2

Feminist Knowledge and Social Research: Ethno-Mimesis as Performative Praxis

One key aim of this text is to examine the transformative possibilities involved in conducting feminist action research with female 'prostitutes' and in so doing to develop the foundations for analyses of prostitution rooted in a politics of feeling. This chapter outlines the methodology used in this interpretive account of feminism and prostitution and defines the methodological approach as *ethno-mimesis*. The chapter is organized into four major sections: an outline of the author's research with women as participatory action research; the postmodern turn in ethnographic research; an outline of ethno-mimesis as a new theoretical construct illustrated through the medium of performance art and photography to re-present and re-tell the narratives of women working as prostitutes; and the importance of critical feminist standpoints in the development of 'feeling forms' through participatory action research.

Discovery-based participatory action research with women working as prostitutes

My work on the phenomenon of prostitution and the rights and needs of women working as prostitutes began in September 1990 when I was commissioned by a Safer Cities project in the Midlands, UK,[1] to examine current responses to prostitution with a view to developing multi-agency initiatives. The brief was to undertake a pilot study on prostitution in a Midlands city and make proposals for multi-agency initiatives. The aim was to interview the central agencies and highlight areas of political conflict, as well as areas of commonality and shared concerns, in order to develop multi-agency strategies. It was hoped that the pilot study would serve as a vehicle for getting the agencies around the table to discuss the research findings, with a view to bringing them together into an integrated multi-agency strategy.

The aim was to develop multi-agency initiatives which would serve to facilitate the empowerment of individuals and groups, particularly women working as prostitutes. I was concerned that the study should aim to look at the underlying factors behind prostitution, examine the wider socio-political issues involved in women entering prostitution and examine the interplay between the various statutory and voluntary agencies concerned with prostitution and the women who work on street. In this initial project the focus was upon street prostitutes/street prostitution. The study was progressed as participatory action research.

The responses to the research by agencies and women working in prostitution were instrumental in developing a Multi-Agency Forum on Prostitution to tackle some of the inequalities and problems that women and young people were experiencing. The Forum was a multi-agency working group made up of women working as 'prostitutes', women representing 'prostitutes' and representatives from statutory and voluntary agencies working with and for female 'prostitutes'. The Forum aimed to develop a more closely organized and hence better network of services to sex workers in the Midlands as well as develop responses to prostitution which were women-centred.

This self-organized working group ran for three years (1991–4) and was instrumental in breaking down some of the barriers and stereotypes around 'prostitutes' and prostitution (including breaking down barriers between agencies). We were able to develop a consensus approach which led to a better understanding of each other's needs/roles/responses to prostitution and also supported the development of an agency run by and for women working as prostitutes. The Forum operated with a revolving chair and revolving venue. In this way, the Forum was owned by the members, not by a single organization/agency.

The initial study, commissioned by Safer Cities, was conducted from a feminist/woman-centred perspective and made three key recommendations in collaboration with a group of women representing sex workers and representatives from the police, probation services, social services, voluntary agencies, health authority, local magistrates and, initially, local residents groups (the latter did not want to be involved in the development of the project but were pleased to be involved in the pilot study). The study recommended that there was a need for:

1 better-organized networks of support for women;
2 a better understanding of and more information and action research on routes into prostitution from local authority care (children in the care of the local authority living in residential children's homes);
3 research to facilitate routes out of prostitution for women who want out and to reinforce the fact that women do have options.

I will take each of these recommendations in turn.

Better-organized networks of support

The initial twelve women I interviewed entered prostitution for financial reasons. All had entered prostitution by association, that is to say they all knew someone, a friend or acquaintance, who was working the streets. They stressed that condoms are always used with clients and that this is stated in the initial business transaction together with the price. All the women in this group had been assaulted by clients in the course of their careers. Two had been violently raped at knifepoint. All had mounting fines, which would necessitate a court appearance for fine default if the fines could not be paid.

I also observed two women being 'processed' by the Magistrates' court. Both were individuals who had left the care system, had been involved with violent men and had suffered a history of abuse and neglect. All of the women were carrying fines for soliciting on street. One woman had just returned from a stay in prison for fine default. One woman was carrying £2,000 in fines, which she could not feasibly pay, and was expecting to be 'sent down'. One woman had 'lost her children' to local authority care during her stay in prison for fine default as she was deemed an 'unfit mother'. Another young woman was evicted from her flat when it became known that she was a 'prostitute', but not before her belongings were taken by bailiffs because of non-payment of poll tax.

There appeared to be a good network of support and advice between the women on street, but this was showing signs of breaking down under the intense policing of the vice area. Vital skills and information were not being passed on to newcomers. The lack of such information could put them at risk with respect to their health as well as to their physical safety.

The participatory research illuminated the need to provide for the self-protection, welfare and education of the women, with their help and the need to work on the attitudes and practices of the various agencies they came into contact with. We agreed that key agencies could provide a more closely organized network of services to address material, economic and social/emotional needs, as well as encourage self-help by coordinating services through a street-level centre for the city's sex workers.

The street-level centre was developed along two distinct models. One was organized by and for women themselves (developed by the women who represented women working on and off street at the multi-agency forum) along peer education lines.[2] The health authority and the multi-agency forum gave important support and assistance. The second agency was developed by the health outreach worker, along the lines of a street level drop-in service for all those who wanted advice and information about sexual health matters. This might include worried parents, young people (gay, straight or bi-sexual) and women working in prostitution – indeed anyone who wanted confidential advice.

Routes into prostitution from local authority care

The initial findings showed that many of the women working on street had entered prostitution when living in local authority care or on leaving local authority care. This second recommendation led to a three-year research project that focused on routes into prostitution from local authority care and led to participatory work with young women working in the sex industry (see O'Neill, Goode and Hopkins 1995; O'Neill et al. 1994). It also, in part, helped to facilitate the women-centred street-level agency to collaborate with social services in order to develop harm minimization work with young women involved in or at risk of involvement in prostitution.

Routes out of prostitution

Women talked about wanting out of prostitution but did not know what else they could do to earn the income they generated through sex work. This led to the submission of a bid (by myself and the street-level agency working with women in the sex industry) to the European Social Fund. The bid was successful, and the agency developed and delivered training workshops and gave advice on employment and education options for women. Some women attended college and were given expenses for childcare. We employed a worker who focused specifically upon encouraging women to see that they did have options through on- and off-street outreach sessions. We also ran two 'training fairs' to show women some of the many opportunities available in the area for education and training if they were looking for alternative ways of earning. Additionally, we put together a booklet, specifically for working women, which documented the many education and training opportunities in the local further education sector.[3]

The pilot study was discovery-based and was conducted from a 'woman-centred' approach, which enabled in-depth understanding of women's experiences within the context of contemporary society, the real and practical relations through which women live out their lives. These relations include the utter complexity of the interrelationships between women and agencies such as the police, voluntary and statutory organizations working with prostitutes, residents and vigilante groups, and aspects of the women's own personal lives as mothers, daughters, wives and lovers. My initial contacts with women were made on street with the help and support of a health worker who was instrumental in the development of the research.[4] It took a long time to develop the trusting relationships that were vital to the further development of the work over the subsequent five-year period of the research.

In taking a woman-centred approach I was concerned to create spaces for the women's voices to be heard and listened to by voluntary and statutory agencies, and for the women to inform the progress of the research. In this way the 'stereotypical subjects of research' became involved in the process and practice of the research through the multi-agency forum and subsequently through the development of community action initiatives funded by the European Commission. The pilot study was the catalyst for developing further work with women working as/representing 'prostitutes' (see O'Neill et al. 1994; O'Neill, Goode and Hopkins 1995), for further immersing myself in the available literature and for considering the relationship between feminism(s) and prostitution.

In the process of the participatory research I became immersed in the relationship between feminist theory, feminist practice and the issue of prostitution in contemporary society, initially street prostitution and then sauna or parlour work. I began to consider the problems and issues of the relationship between feminisms and prostitution; the advantages and problems of doing feminist research with women working as prostitutes; the relationship of theory to practice; and the relationship of all of these points to participatory action research and to possibilities for multi-agency initiatives.

It is through the developing force field (Jay 1993) which informs this work – specifically, critical feminist theory, ethnographic feminist research and community-based action/practice (participatory action research) – that this text unfolds. The pivot around which the work moves is authentic commitment to feminist praxis and the dialectical, change-causing relationship between theory, experience and practice, between individual autonomy and collective responsibility. Following Bauman (1995), this work stresses our collective as well as our individual well-being, and looks towards future possibilities which would 'go a long way towards helping citizens to recover the voices they lost or stopped trying to make audible' (1995: 284).

Listening to women who live at the sharp end of poverty, inequality and oppression raises all sorts of issues to do with feminism and the contradictions of oppression (Ramazanoglu 1989). Feminist research as feminist praxis, as 'knowledge for' (Stanley 1990), can give us a much more accurate picture of the realities we want to transform. Acknowledging that there is no one 'truth', no single 'reality', but that there are shared 'truths', experiences of sameness as well as difference, the collective experiences of the 'realities' of women working as prostitutes resonate through this text. In the process of reading their collective voices, their meanings and experiences will hopefully give us a better understanding of women's experiences of prostitution and of difference; and perhaps motivate us to think and act in ways that support women and develop discourses across the divide between 'prostitute' and non-'prostitute' feminists.

The dynamic interrelationship between feminist critical theory and ethnographic research as socio-cultural knowledge forms the epistemological centre around which the chapters are formed. There is a deep-rooted tradition of conducting ethnographic research – by both feminists and non-feminists – which seeks to uncover and learn from the voices and experiences of those on the margins of our social worlds, for example the Chicago School, the Birmingham School of Cultural Studies (especially the work of Paul Willis), and the work of Beverley Skeggs, of Latin American scholars such as Orlando Fals Borda and of Asian-American scholars such as Trinh T. Minh-Ha. The importance of listening to life-stories is that not only do they give us better access into the complexity of lived relations, the interrelationship between the micrology of our lives and broader socio-political structures of power and signification, but we can more easily engage with the complexities of sub-jectivities, difference and identities. The reflexive interrelationship between the micrology of women's lives and the purposeful knowledge acquired in the process of conducting participatory action research with women working in the sex industry serves to develop and to facilitate feminist praxis.

What is participatory action research?

Orlando Fals Borda has developed participatory action research with communities in Columbia, Nicaragua and Mexico. He describes the existen-tial concept of experience (*Erlebnis*) following Spanish philosopher José Ortega y Gasset:[5]

> Through experiencing something we intuitively apprehend its essence, we feel, enjoy and understand it as a reality, and we thereby place our being in a wider, more fulfilling context. In PAR such an experience, called *vivencia* in Spanish, is complemented by another idea: that of authentic commitment resulting from historical materialism and classical Marxism (Eleventh Thesis on Feuerbach: 'Philosophers should not be content with just explaining the world, but should try to transform it'). (Fals Borda 1985: 87–8)

PAR is therefore a combination of experience and commitment. Certainly, a combination of experience and commitment allows us to see and shape the relationship between knowledge and social change. For Fals Borda, the sum of knowledge from both the participants and academics/researchers allows us to acquire a much more accurate picture of the reality we want to transform. For him, academic knowledge combined with popular knowledge and wisdom may give us a new paradigm. Certainly, renewed methodologies that aim to get at the reflexive nature of human thought and action, and the meanings given, both conscious and semi-conscious, could enable us to better under-stand people's everyday experiences and, at the same time, enable us to better understand broader social institutions and work towards social change.

William F. Whyte (1989) suggests that PAR can advance sociological knowledge in ways that would be unlikely to emerge from more orthodox sociological research. For Whyte, the element of creative surprise (which comes with working with practitioners whose experiences and knowledges are different from our own) is a central aspect to conducting participatory action research and advancing social-scientific knowledge.

Maria Mies's feminist action research (1991) talks about the integration of research into the emancipatory process. In her fieldwork with women in

Germany (Cologne), India and Holland Mies shows how women confronting 'other women' and the reality of their lives raises questions about themselves, the situation of other women and their value systems. She talks too about how in this process an un-learning or critical testing takes place of that which women had previously accepted as 'natural', 'normal' and 'universal' through their socialization; how they saw that the lives of other women do not necessarily correspond to their own institutionally acquired knowledge; how each group of women brought their 'affectedness' (subjectivity and concern) into the research process, further sharpening and extending perceptions and prompting new questions. A reciprocity emerged through women's encounters with each other. For Mies, all this was possible because 'in contrast to the dominant understanding of science, the research situation did not represent a power relationship' (1991: 77–8).

What Mies calls 'partial identification' is a central aspect in my work with women and young people working in the sex industry, as well as with those people working in statutory and voluntary agencies providing services to 'prostitutes'. By this, Mies means 'the recognition of that which binds me to other women as well as that which separates me'. 'Partial identification' for Mies brings the necessary closeness as well as the necessary distance from myself. Indeed, such closeness will only be possible 'when women begin with their own affectedness and concern' (1991: 80). Mies developed the term 'affectedness' in her search for similarities that bound her to the battered women she was involved with in a research project in Cologne:

> 'Affectedness' refers to the victim and object status of oppressed, humiliated, exploited beings who have become the target of violence and repression. That is to say, they have been directly affected at one time by aggression, injustice, discrimination. They are victims. When talk is of the 'affected' in normal usage, it is only usually this level of meaning which is implied. The 'affected' are the 'others,' not me myself (as a rule). From this understanding of affectedness there arises the moralistic and paternalistic fussing with which the 'affected' are often treated by the 'un-affected'. They usually become renewed objects of 'assistance' (social work, development help, Caritus) for which they are expected to be thankful. We, however, had all been directly affected ourselves at some time by male violence. (1991: 80)

'Affectedness' also denoted concern, shock, outrage at women's conditions related to critical self-reflexivity and motivation for action. For Mies, feminist research cannot simply be inserted into or added on to the old scientific paradigm 'which splits up living unities into life and thought, politics (morality) and science, and which implies the dominion over women, primitive peoples, and other races' (1991: 80). Indeed, if we want to arrive at a new paradigm in which these divided and subjugated parts coexist in a more integrated relationship, then we must transcend or transgress the old paradigm.

Partial identification is a process involving self-reflexivity, taking in the concerns and needs of the participants in the research, the women and young people. Women are, I guess, on the whole going to be better equipped for this in the current social order.[6]

I understand Mies's use of the term 'affectedness' as being similar to my articulation of the interrelationship between mimesis and constructive rationality in the research process. The relationship between feeling involvement (mimesis or sensuous knowing) and critical distancing (a reflexive process of interpretation, commentary and criticism) is central to the development of my progress through the research.[7] Mies's description and articulation of this process gave me great satisfaction (and relief) and in a sense corroborated my own tentative moves in this direction. Aspects of power are, of course, present in all our relationships; what is important is how one handles the differing situations in which one is involved in order to facilitate and work towards collaboration involving democratic processes (Fals Borda 1985).

My own experience is of a shared, often unspoken, mutual managing of relationships where we are all working through impression management, through our presentation of self, through our shared narratives of self (Giddens 1992), through our friendships, to minimize notions of 'power over' in a pedagogic or hierarchical sense and enhance notions of 'power to' work collaboratively. Sometimes this is painful, tense and difficult and very time-consuming, but it is also creative and worth while to develop 'good enough' relationships of trust in order to work together.

The participatory action research I was involved in in the Midlands began with the pilot study on current responses to prostitution in September 1990. The pilot study was the catalyst for substantive further study which developed along the three interrelated dimensions described above: the formation of a multi-agency working group; the development of action research on routes into prostitution from local authority care; and, finally, working with women to develop 'options' through raising funds for education and training initiatives.

In conducting multi-agency, participatory action research I was interested in the relationship between knowledge and power in these circumstances. I wanted to know if we could make a difference, improve the services and address the needs of women working in the sex industry more effectively, through a multi-agency forum with women as key players. These three projects (women-centred multi-agency work, which included supporting and facilitating the work of a grass-roots project; facilitating options or exit routes for women working as prostitutes via education and training, counselling and guidance; and action research on routes into prostitution from local authority care) developed out of our concern that academic research should not simply be research 'on' but research 'with' and 'for' – indeed be about feminist participatory action research.

Feminist participatory action research is for me about developing feminist analysis of prostitution and support for women working as prostitutes in ways which are about working with women and which have empowering consequences for all those concerned, not just for the stereotypical 'subjects' of research. The relationship between knowledge and power is an important one in effecting social change *with* the participation of those involved (Fals Borda 1985).

Risks and dilemmas

There are, of course, dilemmas and dangers thrown up by doing such close 'ethnographic' research with any group, but particularly with 'marginalized', 'criminalized' and 'stigmatized' groups. One can become immersed in the intra-community politics as well as the inter-agency politics. One can risk becoming so emotionally involved that it is problematic to work effectively due to relationships being so firmly entrenched and to dependency patterns being in place. Relationships of trust take a long time to build and it feels like walking a tightrope for much of the time. Researchers are sometimes seen as little more than pimps: coming into the field to take, they then go back to their campus, institution, or suburb where they write up the data, publish and build careers – on the backs of 'others', of those they took data from. The problems for the researcher are many and can differ depending upon the subject group the researcher is working with, the communities involved, local issues and, of course, the relationships with other agencies and the role taken by the researcher.

Alison Murray (1995a) has stressed that interrelationships between 'professionals', 'peer workers' and 'clients' are much too complex and too embedded in hierarchies of power to ever reflect the 'ideal type' of peer education and peer empowerment. The complexities and messiness of participatory action research must be acknowledged and accommodated within the work that we are involved in. When conducting ethnographic research along the lines of PAR, researchers *must* write themselves into the multiple perspectives that emerge.

I have no fixed answers to the dilemmas and difficulties faced by the feminist researcher. There are no set answers. In progressing the research I endeavour to take account of ethical and political dimensions in the social construction of knowledge and also validate and facilitate the shared participation of the women I am working with in reflexive ways.[8]

Doing this sort of close ethnographic work with women who work on street does have further implications for the women who are out there working as well as for the personal safety of the researcher. Taking time and experiences/ information from women working on street can have a negative effect on their contact with clients and may also produce potential hassle from pimps. 'Taking' from women may be perceived by the women as another form of pimping, particularly given the way the media has portrayed female 'prostitutes'. Most television documentaries open with a seedy portrayal of the deserted, dark street with the hooker in stilettos, fish-nets and miniskirt. The message is clear and the stereotype is upheld of the dirty, disease-ridden prostitute, irresponsible, immoral and probably feeding a drug habit – the whore stigma in operation. It appears that throughout recorded history prostitution is perceived as a 'necessary evil' (Roberts 1992; Corbin 1987, 1990; Walkowitz 1980). Given the level of stereotyping and the concomitant whore stigma and the stereotyping it underpins, is it any wonder that women working as 'prostitutes' are wary of researchers and research 'on' them?

In the process of the research I do not aim or claim to speak for female 'prostitutes' but rather to speak with them, from multiple standpoints, and to open up intellectual and practical spaces for them to speak for themselves. This work developed from a desire to allow 'participants in the process to put themselves in the place of others without reducing the others to versions of themselves' (Jay 1993: 82). This work as a work in progress aims to create social knowledge as critical feminist praxis located within an understanding of the postmodern turn in ethnographic research.[9]

The postmodern turn in ethnographic research

The splinter in your eye is the best magnifying glass. (Adorno 1978: 50)

Atkinson and Coffey (1995: 44–5) discuss the development of ethnography within postmodernism and the crisis of cultural representation. The outcomes of ethnographic work are no longer accepted unproblematically. The authors deal with a number of issues:

- They question the privileged position of the observer and the ethnographer's ability to produce 'realist' accounts of the experiences of 'others'.
- They stress the importance of feminist research, especially feminist standpoint research and psychoanalysis and the role of the unconscious.
- They explore the importance of reflexivity in the research process, the role of language and the role of experimentation/representations.

The postmodern turn in ethnographic research engages with and leads to alternative forms of re-presenting (fictive, poetic or visual) contemporary society and lived relations. Contemporary society is marked by shifts and transformations in social organization and socio-cultural processes and practices, largely since the socio-cultural rebellions of the 1960s (Harvey 1989; Smart 1992; Giddens 1984, 1991a, 1991b, 1992, 1993; Beck 1992; Beck and Beck-Gernsheim 1995; Rojek 1995; Tester 1993, 1994, 1995; Nicholsen 1981; Seidman 1994a, 1994b). Historical and fictive texts can provide richly woven stories of these very shifts and transformations. For example, *Secret Tibet*, a text published in 1954 on Fosco Maraini's journey to Tibet, illuminates very clearly the enormous changes in affects, sentiments and class relations and interrelations that have taken place since the 1950s. The differences between the social world of the 1950s and now is as great as the differences documented in *Secret Tibet* between Western reason/rationality and Eastern religion, that is Tibetan Buddhism. Maraini's observations and the documentation of his journey provide incredibly rich interweavings of information, sensation and feelings, but overwhelmingly of the humanity, solidarity and empathy between people of differing cultures.

Postmodernity is not a separate period; it does not mark an epochal break but is the development of submerged or marginal aspects of modernity (Jameson 1990; Bauman 1995; Seidman 1994a, 1994b). Adorno writes about the 'hyper-modern' (1984). Values such as choice, diversity, criticalness, reflexivity, agency are modern values preserved, come to the fore in postmodernity. The 'postmodern' embraces plurality, ambiguity, ambivalence, uncertainty, the contingent, transitory, disruptive, critical and oppositional in opposition to uniform standardized culture and history as progress. Moreover, there is the abandonment of any claim to universal standards of truth, goodness and beauty. From a postmodern perspective, human knowledge is always situated; there is no authoritative standpoint, and culture is a major site of social conflict and contestation (Sassower 1995).

For Bauman (1992) postmodernity brings a major reorientation in sociology from a legislative role to an interpretive role. Sociology must take up the mutual understanding of diverse communities, valuing the plurality of cultural traditions and subcultures. The postmodern sociologist aims at 'giving voice' to cultures which, without her or his help, would remain dumb or stay inaudible. Postmodern society renders social differences less threatening, fostering tolerance for diversity, making the unfamiliar familiar.

A postmodern sociology suggests a shift in sociological practice to being more qualitative, ethnographic, interpretive and textualist. This interpretive role involves creative acts of re-covering, re-telling and re-presenting which prioritize certain discourses: feminist critique of psychoanalysis; feminist critique of post-structuralism; feminist critique of 'representation' through cultural and social imaginaries and work on the interrelationships between ethnography and performance arts, including what Denzin calls ethnodrama or ethnoperformance (Denzin 1997; Becker et al. 1989; Conquergood 1992; Mienczakowski 1995; Clough 1994; Trinh 1992; Atkinson and Coffey 1995). This interpretive re-telling should draw upon historical texts alongside fictive texts and ethnographic texts to fully explore and understand the complexity of our social worlds, of our 'lived cultures'.

For many feminists postmodern times and postmodern analysis (with the focus upon situated knowledge, diversity, plurality, the contingent, oppositional and multi-vocality) provide a very good home for feminist thought and practice (Nicholsen 1994).

Feminist thought and practice have developed along a threefold path of largely interrelated perspectives. First of all, what Rosemary Buikema (1992) calls equality feminism, constitutive of second-wave feminism and predicated on writing women into the gaps and absences in various canons, and literature constitutive of modernity. Second, 'difference feminisms', which brings challenges to equality feminism and is linked with radical feminism, which, instead of writing women into the gaps and spaces, develops and creates feminist canons, that in many cases challenge the 'mainstream' or 'male-stream' canons, knowledges and literature. French feminism or *écriture féminine* is one example of difference feminisms. Difference feminisms explore socially constructed difference; criticize the universality of the male subject in contrast to the 'absent' female subject; criticize the category 'woman'; and show that differences between and amongst women preclude the possibilities that we are all concerned with the same social struggles. French feminisms focus upon critiques of subjectivity, difference and language, drawing upon psychoana-lysis to speak of libidinal economies and the relationship between sexuality and politics. Third, post-structuralism or deconstructive feminism, also known as postmodern feminism – or even post-feminism (see Brooks 1997) – which deconstructs the meanings residing in visual and literary texts. Postmodern feminisms are constitutive of hybrid forms of analyses that emerge from critical examination of binary oppositions and an engagement with the complexity of lived experience and lived relations by and for women in contemporary times. Contemporary times, as noted above, are marked by de-traditionalization, post-colonialism, risk, insecurity and greater individual-ization, 'plastic sexuality' (Giddens 1992; Beck 1992) as well as 'that old chestnut' – patriarchy.

Buikema notes that all three approaches produce different strategies and theoretical positions within feminist debates and practice. My own approach, the approach developed in this text, is to acknowledge the interrelations between the three perspectives in order to explore the complexity of women's lived relations in late-modern or postmodern times, whilst approaching the issue of prostitution and feminisms from a postmodern perspective. The key point here is that 'modern', 'late-modern', 'postmodern' times are not to be read as periodizing concepts. On the one hand, clear shifts and transforma-tions have and are taking place that need to be 'named' (for example, increas-ing globalization, cyber technology, de-traditionalization); on the other hand, there are continuities that also need to be acknowledged, for example, socio-cultural and economic inequalities of class, race and gender embedded within rationalization, instrumental reason, patriarchy, racist ideologies and hege-monic heterosexuality. As Graham Murdock states, 'understanding change requires us to grasp inertia as well as dislocation, to recognize the resilience of basic structures over long loops of time as well as the breaks signalled by specific events' (1997: 190).

Working in participatory ways with women involves blurring boundaries, questioning the notion of universal knowledge and the division between knowledge and power. Such work is in many ways indicative of what Bauman sees as characteristic of postmodern sociology: 'a clarifier of interpretive rules and facilitator of communication: this will amount to the replacement of the dream of the legislator with the practice of the interpreter' (1992: 204). This interpretive sociological work is rooted in Marx's dictum that as philosophers we should not only aim to understand and explain the social world but should also seek to change it, to transform it. In order to understand the world we need to engage with lived experience as well as explore structures and practices that serve to enable and/or constrain our actions and meanings and practices (Giddens 1984).

As a researcher, interpretive ethnography grounded in the standpoints of the co-creators of the research (participatory research with the stereotypical subjects of research) and rooted in critical theory is my chosen method. This method privileges women's voices and triangulates their voices with cultural texts re-presenting and imagining women, and aims to provide a feminist analysis of prostitution through 'feeling forms' (Witkin 1974). There are endless possibilities for the many ways in which fictive texts such as film and literature can speak to us as 'feeling forms', as examples of the sedimented 'stuff of society'.

For example, in exploring the role and experiences of women working as Saloon girls in the (Wild) West, film and literature can speak to us about the role and position of women, of differences between the sexes, of differences between the cultures that peopled the West, and also the ways in which the movie/film mocks the surfaces of the land, the landscape, the mountains, the endless skyscapes. Exploring fictive texts as 'feeling forms' alongside historiography can help us to better understand the labyrinthian nature of experience, reality, 'truth', of lived experience and lived relations. An understanding of fictive texts alongside detailed historical work can lend itself to possibilities for immersing oneself in the social and psychic processes that these frontier people would have experienced, inhabited, produced and reproduced. The isolation and the loneliness; the development of social organizations such as laws, schools, workplaces; the interactions with others; the transcendent and transgressive possibilities; and the process of Western colonialism developing amidst the construction and reproduction of communities and societies are all documented through diaries, journals, letters, newspaper items and census documents (see O'Neill 1998: 117–30).

The importance of triangulating cultural texts (film, literature, poetry, photography) with ethnographic life-stories is to re-cover and re-tell lived experiences in order that we might better understand the multiple, varied experiences, the hybrid identities, the differences and similarities in our social worlds. More specifically, this project aims to re-cover and re-tell the stories of women working in the sex industry in order that we might better understand the many issues involved. What we must always remember is that the autobiographical mode involves a re-telling of 'experience', not of a pregiven reality; rather our life-stories are the discursive effect of processes that we call upon to construct and reconstruct what we call 'reality' (Brah 1996: 11). But, more than this, writing or speaking our biographical history can 'bring new forms of selfhood into being' (Steedman 1997: 123).

The main ethnographic work re-covered and re-told in this book took place between September 1990 and January 1996 and involved working with women in two geographical sites in the UK. Subsequent work took place in 1997 and 1998, drawing upon the ethnographic data and including the work of performance artists to provide alternative re-presentations of the life-story interviews with women. The author's 'activist' work, rooted in feminist responses to female and juvenile prostitution (focusing upon women and young people), began in 1990 and is ongoing. This work pivots around renewed methodologies for social research.

Ethno-mimesis: a renewed methodology for social research

In exploring renewed methodologies for social research I seek to develop a methodological model rooted in feminist thought and practice from the multiple standpoints of women working in prostitution. In so doing I draw upon the critical feminist theory of Jessica Benjamin (1993), the critical theory of Walter Benjamin (1992) and Adorno (1984, 1997) and what Denzin (1997) describes as the sixth stage of ethnographic research:[10] 'Ethnography's sixth moment is defined in part by a proliferation of interpretive epistemologies grounded in the lived experiences of previously excluded groups in the global, postmodern world' (Denzin 1997: 54).

The task of renewed methodologies is to re-cover and re-tell through micrology, through storytelling, both the continuities and the transformations – the complexity of 'lived relations', of 'lived cultures' at the end of the twentieth century (postmodern times) in transformative, change-causing ways. Thus countering what Stjepan Meštrović calls postemotionalism: 'intellectualized, mechanical, mass produced emotions' (Meštrović 1997: 26).

Renewed methodologies are therefore central to what Cornell West (1994) calls the new cultural politics of difference. Ethno-mimesis (the combination of social research and the re-telling or re-presenting of the research data in artistic form) is an example of renewed methodologies which show, tell, enable us to experience the complexities of lived experience and lived cultures (O'Neill et al. 1999).

Adorno's and Benjamin's concept of mimesis is pivotal. The research process is, for me, framed by a background immersed in the socio-cultural work of Adorno and Benjamin. While planning and gathering in-depth qualitative data with women working in prostitution, I reflected upon the interrelationship between social theory, social research and social action/practice. Social theory is constructed from knowledge/understanding of the social world. Social theory as ways of knowing can be developed from listening to the micrology of people's lives. Life-stories provide narratives of people's engagement with their everyday worlds and their wider social worlds. They tell of what is personal and meaningful to them, of experience personally felt. As such they can also act as ciphers for the metaconditions of society, for relating the particular to the general.

My methodological approach to gathering life-story narratives is illustrated by Adorno's account of coming to know the work of art and my previous work on feminist aesthetics. Coming to know the work of art (for Adorno), or coming to know a life-story (for myself) involves immersion, identification and subsequent objectification embedded in interpretation, commentary and criticism. Adorno's theory contributes to my project through my understanding and interpretation of the dialectical relationship between mimesis (emotion, sensuousness, 'spirit') and constructive rationality (instrumental rationality, the 'out there' sense of our being in the world). We can use these terms to articulate the relationship of mediation (tension) between emotion, sensuousness, feeling, on the one hand and reason, constructive rationality and the materiality of life on the other.[11]

But what exactly do these terms 'mimesis' and 'constructive rationality' mean in the context of my research? By *mimesis* (influenced by Hegel), I mean sensuousness, feeling, emotion, related to subjectivity, to experience personally felt. The mimetic faculty is the 'capacity to both produce and perceive resemblances' (Nicholsen 1997: 140; Taussig 1993). It is exercised in human experience, illuminated through narratives of experience. Adorno's use of mimesis (which I am re-functioning here) is expressed for him within the structure of art. For Adorno, to know the work of art is to grasp the process which renders it 'spiritual'.[12] This is akin to what Witkin (1974) defined as 'feeling form', subjective, reflexive feeling involved in experiencing art works. Taussig understands 'mimesis as both the faculty of imitation and the deployment of that faculty in sensuous knowing' (1993: 68).

Mimesis is the process whereby we assimilate the self to the other (artwork or ethnographic encounter) through the mimetic faculty. We engage in a dialectic process of immersion and construction (making sense of what we are immersed in, experiencing the enigmatic quality of the work or the 'field') through cognition, construction, objectification, interpretation. Giving oneself over to the piece must be accompanied by philosophical reflection. These are not two separate activities – mimesis and theoretical reflection – but are both halves of the same whole. The 'enactment and assimilation of the other that constitute mimesis are inseparable from but also distinct from the rationality of philosophical reflection' (Nicholsen 1997: 151).

In order to understand the individual/society relationship it is crucial that we engage with subjectivity, feeling, emotion, what Adorno alludes to as 'spirit', the 'unsayable', and what Benjamin (1992) alludes to as sensuousness. In this sense, ethnographic participatory research can 'get at' aspects of lived experience which are unspoken, or unsayable or non-conceptual in a similar manner to the way enigmatic artworks and philosophy 'speak' for Adorno. The function of art and aesthetics, for Adorno, is to reveal the unintentional truths of the social world and to preserve independent thinking.

By *constructive rationality* (influenced by Kant) Adorno is talking about the relationship between the Enlightenment and technical knowledge (Adorno and Horkheimer 1979: 3; Adorno 1973: 320). Reason is constituted by a 'petrified and alienated reality' (Adorno 1984: 28–31). This alienated reality is reflected in Meštrović's postemotional society and is indicative of a loss of feeling and compassion fatigue. I interpret constructive rationality as 'instrumental reason' within contemporary social relations. Instrumental reason is reproduced through the continuous structuring of psychic and social structures and processes. Constructive rationality forms the 'out there' sense of our experience *of* and being *in* the social world, which we, both intentionally and unintentionally, reproduce through our very actions and practices. In this process ('reproducing lived cultures') we are influenced by social and cultural institutions (for example, the media), practices and processes and, in turn, help to produce and reproduce these very institutions and practices.

For example, instrumental reason is centrally involved in the management and hierarchies of organizations and workplaces that operate on the principles of male hegemony, of male rationality (J. Benjamin 1993: 184–216). The subordination of the values of private life (of recognition and feeling) to the instrumental principles of the public world is, for Jessica Benjamin, a consequence of the ascendancy of male rationality. Abstract, calculable, depersonalized modes of interaction and the ideal of the autonomous individual are representative of instrumental reason. The structure of gender domination is thus 'materialized in the rationality that pervades our economic and social institutions' (1993: 187). Instrumental reason helps to reproduce sexual and social inequalities.

Engaging with (or mediating) the critical tension between mimesis, experience, feeling, emotion *and* materiality, reason, constructive rationality as instrumental rationality, can help us to better understand the 'micrology' of women's lives within the metaconditions/structures of our lives. This can, in turn, help us to better understand the individual/society relationship and the wider sexual, socio-economic, cultural and political implications of our actions/interactions – thus, possibly, cutting through ideology or ideological effects by better understanding the relationships between psychic and social processes, structures and practices, feeling and reason or mimesis and constructive rationality. Seeing the inter-relationship as a mediated, dialectical relationship rather than as a polarity/binary, or in a reductionist way (one existing at the expense of the other), enables us to 'know' the complexity of 'lived cultures', of 'lived relations'.

For example, in Sara Giddens's performance work (see below) mediation occurs in the gaps between the performance and reception as critical interpretation. The performance/live art form demands critical reflection. The viewer assimilates the self to the performance, internally traces or mimics the work, which is akin to embodying the work in a 'quasi-sensious mode' (S. W. Nicholsen 1997: 148). Nicholsen writes that there is an active experiential reproduction of the work by the receiver and (for Adorno) this must be supplanted by philosophical reflection on the work (1997: 150). Critical reflection on the enigmatic quality of the work requires the distance achieved by what Adorno calls constructive rationality.

Shierry Weber Nicholsen tells us that cultural critics such as Susan Sontag, Herbert Marcuse and Frederic Jameson have discussed the ways in which we absorb image-commodities in states of habitual abstraction and have concluded that such environments make it increasingly difficult to maintain critical distance and 'genuinely felt involvement' (1993: 13). Moreover, environments of socially constructed images tend to directly shape our experience and opinions without the necessary critical analysis.

Through cultural texts – be they film, art, dance, literature or life-story narratives – we may be able to get in touch with 'reality', with our social worlds, with the lived experiences of others in ways which demand critical reflection. For Shierry Nicholsen (1993) photography (despite the potential for aestheticizing social problems) has the potential to help us develop a broader, more compassionate and accurate consciousness. The photograph is an index, a direct trace of the real rather than a representation. Debates over the deconstructive potential of photography versus the aestheticizing of social problems reflect the critical potential of artworks, and it is this critical potential to 'pierce us' and to 'grasp reality in its otherness' within the context of the image society (which attempts to tame and inhibit critical reflection) that gives photography its critical potential.

Nicholsen's argument for photography is very useful to show the critical potential of producing alternative ways of re-presenting research data. The concept of 'mediation' is crucial to the development of 'ethno-mimesis' – the intertextual mediation between life-story narratives/ethnographic research and ethno-mimetic texts, such as photographic work/live art. The work illustrated in the next section (the performance work of Sara Giddens) presents us with a direct trace of the real, and in so doing has the potential to 'pierce us' and 'get at' women's lived experiences as prostitutes through ethno-mimesis as 'feeling form'. This mediated, constellational form is one example of an ethno-mimetic text and a feminist response to prostitution.

Case study: ethno-mimesis as performative praxis

By focusing upon life-history work with women working as prostitutes and by experiencing women's stories re-presented through live art, we can further our understanding of the complexities of sex, sexualities, desire, violence, masculinities and the relevance of the body – the gendered body, the imaginary body, the performative body, the social body – within the context of postmodern times, de-traditionalization, and what Stjepan Meštrović calls 'postemotionalism' and compassion fatigue. This section is illustrated by stills from a video/live art performance, *Not all the time... but mostly* performed by Patricia Breatnach, choreographed by Sara Giddens, sound by Darren Bourne, video produced by Tony Judge and photographs by Simon Howell. The video/live art performances (there are now a trilogy of performances) were developed as a response to transcripts of interviews with women working as prostitutes and fuse dance, text, sound and video.

Given the crisis of representation in ethnography, texts produced and represented as the outcome of ethnographic fieldwork are no longer accepted unproblematically (Atkinson and Coffey 1995; Denzin 1997). The self-reflexivity inherent in the ethnographic process, coupled with the deconstruction of conventional discourses, are lending themselves to demands for experimentation in the representation of data which are able to transgress gendered and racialized genre-specific boundaries (Trinh 1991; Ugwu 1995). Experimentation has focused upon visual re-presentations, in this example through performance art.

Visual re-presentations

The visual in feminist research has generally not been used intrinsically for interpreting and representing ethnographic data and culture. A notable exception is the work of Trinh (1989, 1991). For Trinh, stories and storytelling are spaces for women's liberation, and transformation. She weaves psychoanalysis with stories of lived experiences from women, with representations through film-making. 'Writing and (film-making) are built on the representations and experiences' (Denzin 1997: 85). The key point here is that Trinh accesses the multiple realities of women through their stories and sees herself as producing visual epistemologies. Trinh claims to work between spaces as a 'hyphen', an Asian–American woman, a writer–film-maker, a woman–a woman of colour, negotiating the spaces between cultures of the First and the Third World – both inside and outside.

Trinh challenges the notion of a single standpoint from which an overriding vision of the world can be written. There are instead multiple realities, multiple standpoints, multiple meanings for 'woman'. Trinh seeks to undo the realist ethnography project; for her there is no real – reality is something already classified by men, a ready-made code (1991: 136). This gendered code allows writers and film-makers to produce texts as film and documentary which look real because they conform to rules concerning what the real looks like. Trinh's films deconstruct the classic documentary film. She provides a counter-documentary text that is reflexive, a site for multiple experiences for seeking the truths in life's fictions. As I argued earlier, by triangulating women's narratives with cultural texts, such as literature and film, it is possible to speak/show the sedimented aspects of lived experiences and explore the relationships between the fictive and the 'real' through hybrid texts.

Hybrid texts

Renewed methodologies are a response to the fragmentation, plurality and utter complexity of living in postmodern times. Such conditions motivate as well as require renewed methodologies to take account of 'new times'. Indeed,

following Alasuutari, Gray and Hermes (1998) hybrid theorizing and reflexivity are crucial to better understand contemporary culture and society,
especially when we consider the ways in which such hybrid research can
'understand culture as a process of meaning making, and give attention to
the power relations that set boundaries to those processes' (1998: 9).

The point about renewed methodologies is that they deal *with* the contradictions of oppression *and* the utter complexity of our lived relations at the
close of the twentieth century – within the context of technologization,
globalization – indeed within the context of what Paul Piccone calls 'the
permanent crisis of the totally administered society' (Piccone 1993: 3), which
is marked by conformist political theory, the transformation of the liberal state,
mass society, pseudo-culture and New Class dominations (1993: 7–9).[13]

The new ethnographies can help to transform our social worlds because 'a
text must do more than awaken moral sensibilities, it must move the other
and the self to action' (Denzin 1997: xxi). The interrelationship between
research and praxis is fraught with tensions. Renewed methodologies, which
incorporate the voices of citizens through scholarly/civic research as participatory research, can not only serve to enlighten and raise our awareness of
certain issues but could also produce critical reflexive texts which may help to
mobilize social change. To repeat a point made in the introduction to part I:
the complex dynamics of this work rooted in PAR are re-presented in the
tension or mediation between a modernist ethos of resistance and transformation through participation as praxis (working with, not on or for); and a
postmodern ethos of hybridity, complexity and inter-textuality (anti-
identitarian thinking, re-presenting the complexity of lived experience
though performance art).

Ethno-mimesis as performative praxis aims to speak in empathic ways with
women, re-presented through the performance text in ways that counter postemotionalism, valorizing discourses, and the reduction of the Other to a
cipher of the oppressed/marginalized/exploited. The photographic stills
below are from the video performance *Not all the time ... but mostly*.[14] We
agreed to focus upon the narratives of women working in prostitution to set in
motion possibilities for alternative re-presentation (ethno-mimesis) as a pilot
study before developing this work with women themselves.

Throughout my research I have used a life-story approach in order to
document the lived experiences of women working as prostitutes and to
develop participatory action research. Stories are powerful learning tools/
experiences, whether they be individuals' stories of their personal journeys
through life, whether they be from the imagination of a storyteller who has
collected the 'stuff' of social life (through immersion, feeling and observation)
and woven it into stories for our pleasure and education, or whether they be
told for a purpose to explain an event or action.

For Walter Benjamin (1992) (whose influence on Adorno was considerable
and from whom Adorno developed his work on mimesis) the most extra-
ordinary thing about focusing upon the telling of stories is that the psycho-

logical connection of the event is not forced upon the reader or listener and it is left up to the reader/listener to interpret the way things are understood. Indeed, in this way, the narrative achieves a greatness that information lacks. A fragment of a story of a life can tell us so much more than one hundred pages of information about a life. For Benjamin, the relationship between listening and memory is seen to be of central importance to the power of stories. The 'traces of the storyteller cling to the story the way hand prints of the potter cling to the clay vessel' (1992: 91–2).

Listening to women's stories relates to a 'politics of feeling' in that the 'greatness' of the narratives, their 'power', the memory of their trace, can inspire thinking, critical reflection and shifts in consciousness, if not practical action. The fragments of women's stories reveal that prostitutes are indices for all women in reflexive modernity/postmodernity. The significance of their words, what they reveal, are the psychological connections between harsh life experiences, the management of self and self-identity, the embodied experience of selling men access or entry to their organic bodies and societal expectations for women of their age, class, race and lifestyle. In their 'otherness' they are perceived and experience themselves as always being outside of mainstream society.

The live art performance as ethno-mimetic text engages with women as human beings, not as 'stand-in political subjects' and in so doing re-presents the ambivalence of prostitution and the situation of the women involved, located as they are between and within discourses of good and bad women. Such discourses and their dynamics can help, in part, to 'name', 'police', 'survey' all women. As Gail Pheterson's (1989) pioneering work has pointed out, 'whore stigma' serves to keep 'other' women chaste and if they are not chaste, they may be, or must be, prostitutes. 'Prostitutes' are 'paradigm signifiers' of the postmodern condition (multiple lives/voices/experiences both inside and outside mainstream society, acting out men's fantasies for a price, living in the spaces within the fictive and the real). Focusing upon life-story interviews with women working as prostitutes provides a good exemplar for exploring possibilities for alternative re-presentation as ethno-mimesis.

Ethno-mimesis as the intertextual relation between an ethnographic life-story and performance as live art represents a re-covering and re-telling of lived experience as embodied performance. Thus, it recovers the tellings of the oppressed and marginalized, whom Denzin and Trinh describe as being on the borders/borderlands/margins (Denzin 1997:95), as well as the tellings of resistance to disempowering sexual and social structures, practices and processes.

The performance text focuses our attention on the performing body, the embodied woman/prostitute, the unfinished body, the fragmented body, the fetishized body and, at one and the same time, the commodified body. The narrative voice speaks throughout the 'performance', and in the space between voice and image we can connect to the flesh and blood 'woman', to her imprint in the text (see figure 1).

You know how a lot of women talk about having managed to split their emotions from actually doing sex and like every woman does it and you don't actually want to do it and you don't . . . feel like doing it but you just go ahead with it anyway . . . erm and that's sort of splitting isn't it . . . but if you do it for a long time . . . and . . . and it makes you feel . . . it makes you feel hard and cold. . . .

Figure 1

The motifs in the re-presentation of women's narratives through performance art and video re-present the *fragmentation* of the body experienced by the 'prostitute' in her interaction with the 'customer', for example, her hands in figure 2 (which she uses to hold her children and give hand relief to her customers) and her eye in figure 3 (she is aware of the fascination and fetishization involved in presenting as a fantasy woman for her clients, but remains alert to potential danger from 'dodgy punters', and is always 'looking, looking, looking').

The body is *fetishized* in the performance text through the use of tight-fitting garments (lycra and leather) emphasizing breasts, stomach, buttocks, legs. In the first performance video, the audience never sees the whole body; rather the camera focuses upon particular (fetishized) aspects of the body: eyes, hands, hair, belly, thighs, legs, and shoes (see figures 4, 5 and 6). The focus of the camera lens and the framing of the body fragments at close range enables the audience to 'see' the fragments of the 'prostituted body' through both the gaze of the customer/client and also from the experience/perspective of the woman ('prostitute') herself. The latter becomes possible through the inter-relationship between narrative voice and performance.

The performance text embodies the ethnographic text, making visible emotional structures and inner experiences which cast light upon wider social structures involving gendered relations. As Stanley and Wise (1993) argue, our very materiality/physicality is an important aspect of social theory and should not be positioned at the level of language or discourse alone. For we

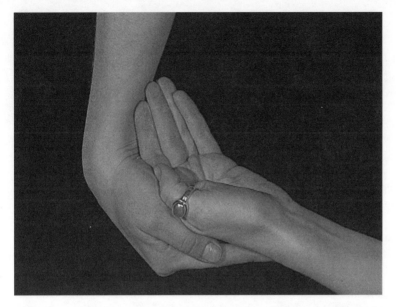

Figure 2   So...if you don't want a baby...you just have to wear one of those special plasters.

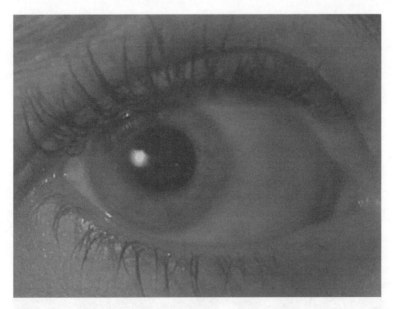

Figure 3   But I can't say how sooner or later it must start, it does start, to affect you....So we stop seeing people, like, for people, we start seeing them as [pause] prospective clients....So all the time you're looking, looking, looking....

Figure 4 He knew one of his daughters ... he knew ... er his daughter was going to be a prostitute. ... He didn't realize it was going to be me ... his little princess.

Figure 5 But I just couldn't see what walking around a classroom with books on my head and learning to pronounce words properly was ever going to do for me.

Figure 6

cannot deconstruct binary categories at the level of language alone; we need to change them at the levels of practice and experience: 'the body has indubitable experiential importance that cannot be reduced to the linguistic alone' (1993: 200). The importance of the body, embodied experience, can be re-presented via mimesis or, in Taussig's (1993) words, through the 'sensuous knowing' contained in cultural texts developed from or grounded in lived experiences. The video stills help to create an understanding/awareness of 'sensuous knowing' in the relationship between the body (body surface, eyes, hands, feet) and the narrative voice – the interrelationship between physicality, emotion, experience. The relationship between the body and narrative is important in making visible emotional structures/experiences in the gap between seeing and listening.[15]

The prostitute(d) body is always already *unfinished*. There is no closure. The body-object of the prostitute is, of course, an unfinished body; it has a presence in the relationship between the real flesh-and-blood woman's body and the imagined body, the 'fantasy' body. The narrative voice in the performance/video is clearly that of an 'ordinary' woman. The narrative voice in relation to the images and motifs enables the viewer to 'feel' and be 'moved' – not in a sentimental way but to participate in the performative text through sensuous knowing. For example, at one point in the video the narrator tells us how, in the process of doing prostitution, she begins to look at all men as potential clients, so that when the gasman calls she thinks how easy it would be to turn a trick for him and make him become a regular client. The viewer can understand through 'sensuous knowing', through ethno-mimesis (the interrelationship between narrative and performance) how it could be to live this way, see the gasman in this way and maybe even turn a trick for him.

> So we stop seeing people, like, for people, we start seeing them as [pause] prospective clients, do you know what I mean? You know what I mean if you meet somebody... a gas bloke comes and mends your meter and you think you can look at him and you can tell, I think, if you used the right tactics [pause] he could become a regular... So all the time you're looking, looking, looking.

The combination/configuration of movement/performance and narrative facilitates the self-reflexive feeling-involvement of the audience, not in a gratuitously emotional, or sentimental or simple voyeuristic way, but in subtle ways which we can speak of through the dynamic tension between mimesis and constructive rationality. We can 'feel with' the lived experiences, lived moments of the woman narrator through the ethno-mimetic 'perform-ance'. At one and the same time, through the tension between the narrator's self-reflexive voice and live art/performance, we can access the lived experi-ences of the sex worker *and* maybe the customer/client.

The point here is that our potential 'feeling-involvement' in the ethno-mimetic text erupts from the tension between the mimetic (sensuous know-ing) and the rational/constructive moments in the interplay between move-ment/performance/motifs and narrative voice, and from the interplay between audience immersion and the critical distancing necessary for interpretation, commentary and criticism. An evocative tension is created between what is played out on screen and the relationship the viewer or audience has with the 'performance'. One is left feeling in some cases 'stunned',[16] but in others able to grasp reality in its 'otherness'; 'feel' emotional structures and inner experi-ences; experience the traces of the 'prostitutes' work within the context of a life, albeit for some a damaged life. In this sense, the ethno-mimetic text is able to 'say' the 'unsayable', the 'outside of language', undercut identity/ identitarian thinking and in the process facilitate a space for the viewers to approach a genuinely felt involvement (see Nicholsen 1997: 12) which demands critical reflection.

The complexity of women's lives are resonant in the interrelationship between voice and visual image. This interrelationship also highlights the 'authenticity' of the re-presentation of women's social worlds and their situatedness between the real and the fictive involved in doing/performing prostitution, being men's 'fantasy' women, and the very real dangers and risks involved. Multiple meanings are generated through the combination of narration and dance/movement through time and space. The performance text 'embodies' the ethnographic text – the life story. Thus, constructing alternative dialogical re-presentation, which hopefully generates new ways of seeing, raises new issues to be addressed and makes visible emotional struc-tures and inner experiences which cast light upon wider social structures involving gendered relations, power, signification and control. Seeking the 'truth' or the 'real' in life's fictions necessarily involves the deconstruction of taken-for-granted ideologies and stereotypes surrounding the prostitute, the whore, the fallen woman – whore stigma. The performance engenders a sense of empathy through the relationship between the narrator's voice and the image and movements of the body.

The ethno-mimetic text will hopefully challenge taken-for-granted meanings around the body object of the prostitute(s) and help us engage with the woman in the text as subject-object through a recovering and visual re-telling of her life story narrative(s) presented in a variety of contexts to varied audiences. The mimetic moment is transgressive, subversive, linking immersion in the story of a life, lived experience, with the fragmentation, blurring of the (presence of) the prostitute(d) body through the performance as text.

Conclusion: Feeling forms, multiple standpoints, 'mediation' and the role of critical reflection

In the process of this intertextual research it is not the aim or claim to speak for the people I interviewed, but rather to speak *with* them, from multiple standpoints, and to open up intellectual and practical spaces for them to speak for themselves.[17] This work, as a work in progress, aims to create intertextual social knowledge as ethno-mimesis, and can help us to avoid accepting reified versions of 'reality' and re-present the complexity of lived experience and lived relations in postmodern times. The interrelation between thinking, feeling and doing (Tester 1995) is crucial to counter postemotionalism in the administered society. The interplay between ethnographic work and artistic praxis is one source of resistance to and transformation of the disempowering and reductive social and psychic processes that Meštrović speaks about so clearly in his work (1997).

> In order to respond reasonably one must first of all be 'moved' and the opposite of emotional is not 'rational', whatever that may mean, but either the inability to be moved, usually a pathological phenomenon, or sentimentality, which is a perversion of feeling. (Arendt 1970: 64)

The importance of 'feeling' in this text is threefold. First, it relates to Arendt's quotation in that the importance of the interrelationship between being 'moved' over an issue and responding resides in the tension (mediation) between feeling and reason. Second, this tension or mediation is inherent in Adorno and Walter Benjamin's use of 'mimesis'. Mimesis is, for Adorno, about behaviour: I assimilate my self to an other through mimetic behaviour. Mimesis is also contained in works of art, within the actual creation, within the objective form. Mimesis is, therefore, an activity *and* part of a product/ object. Mimesis is inherently involved in dialectical tension or mediation

with reason through 'cognition, as construction, as technique, as spiritualiza-
tion, as objectification and so on' (Nicholsen 1997: 148). Finally, mimesis is
expressed in 'the language like quality of art' (1997: 148). For Adorno,
mimesis in art must be supplemented with philosophical reflection, with
critical interpretation. The enigmatic gaze of art (a painting, an installation, a
play, performance art, live art) invites or incites critical reflection. I interpret
Arendt, Adorno and Walter Benjamin as proponents of the necessary mediation between emotion/mimesis/sensuous knowing *and* reason/critical reflec-
tion/philosophical interpretation.

In summary, this tension or mediation in hybrid/ethno-mimetic texts
could help to transform ideology and ideological effects by generating different ways of seeing, experiencing/feeling and knowing our lived experiences,
for example, seeing and feeling racial, sexual and social inequalities as socially
constructed inequalities through performance work (Ugwu 1995):

> Live art's very resistance to categorisation and containment, and its ability to
> surprise and unnerve, makes its impact far-reaching. Growing numbers of black
> artists are engaging in live art practice viewing it as one of the few remaining
> spaces available to express complex ideas of identity. (Ugwu 1995: 55)

Ideology is the representation of sectional interests as universal or 'natural'
interests. Ideology and a related concept 'hegemony' (see Gramsci 1971),
meaning the ideological and cultural domination of one group over another
through engineering consent, are deeply embedded and integrated in our sign
worlds, our understanding and ways of seeing the world, our behaviours and
practices, our institutions and our very social and sexual encounters.

Our sexual encounters can be read through Jessica Benjamin's powerful
psychoanalytical analysis of feminity and domination. Benjamin shows how
masculinity and feminity become associated with the postures of master and
slave, in part through our relationships to our mothers and fathers, and how
the developing opposition of girl as object and boy as subject distorts the very
ideal of the individual. Benjamin shows how this is reflected in the broader
culture, thus preserving structures of domination: 'I will argue that the
principle of rationality which social theorists since Weber have seen as the
hallmark of modernity – the rationality that reduces the world to objects of
exchange, calculation and control – is in fact male rationality' (J. Benjamin
1993: 184). The subordination of all aspects of life to instrumental reason
subverts other values, such as the values of private life and what she calls
'maternal aspects of recognition', nurturance and attunement (the recognition
of feeling) (1993: 185).

Indeed, it appears that the structure of domination is anchored so deeply
into the psyche that it is impossible to envision mutual reciprocal relationships, whereby both individuals are subjects, and broader relations and interrelations where equality and reciprocity are possible. The answer, for Jessica
Benjamin, is to critically analyse psychoanalytic thinking from a feminist

approach *and* analyse the structures of domination represented by the master (subject)–slave (object) relationship. Feminist analysis must not shy away from analysing submission, fearing our own participation in domination; nor must we construct the problem of domination as a problem of male aggression and 'female vulnerability victimised by male aggression' (1991: 9). Nor must we idealize the oppressed 'as if their culture were untouched by the system of domination, as if people did not participate in their own submission' (1991: 9) – for such simplifications reproduce structures of gender polarity while seeming to attack them. We do, however, need to be prepared to deal with mystery, uncertainty and contradiction within relationships, and we need to deal with the tensions between emotion, fact and reason. Jessica Benjamin draws upon the quality Keats demanded for poetry – negative capability – and insists that a theory or politics that cannot cope with contradiction, or with the irrational, or that tries to sanitize the erotic components of human life cannot visualize an end to domination.

Therefore, 'feeling' is used here as a political, theoretical construct (not as sentimentality, not in the romantic sense of 'the prostitute' exemplified in the Hollywood film *Pretty Woman*, starring Julia Roberts, which is a perversion of feeling), as an analytic experience which uses both the heart and the brain (Rose 1983). Ethno-mimesis as a theoretical construct, as an example of a postmodern interpretive methodology, gives voice to the critical, multiple standpoints of women working in the sex industry through alternative means of re-presenting their experiences, meanings, voices, lives.

Part II

Interpretive Ethnographies: Life-History Work

This text provides a feminist socio-cultural analysis of prostitution in changing times and gives voice to the utter complexity of women's lives at the turn of the century. Feminist theorizing and research are problematized, and the text recommends that more participatory and hybrid ways of doing and re-presenting research are developed with women and young people involved in prostitution. It is suggested that the concept of mimesis as 'sensuous knowing' involved in doing participatory action research, re-presenting interpretive ethnography, can help social researchers say what cannot be said through print-based analysis alone.

The interrelationship between epistemology (ways of knowing) and methodology (ways of finding out, underpinned by a particular way of seeing the world – in this case interpretive ethnography and participatory action research) is particularly instructive in the development of 'ethno-mimesis' as a concept (both descriptive and analytical). Conducting interpretive ethnography, and particularly life-history work, with the participants helped me to appreciate more the ways in which women's and young people's lives are framed and the importance of our emotional as well as material resources. Conducting ethnographic research helps us to problematize the categories of 'prostitute' and 'prostitution' and highlight the self-reflexivity of the women and young people involved.

Some of the interviews documented in this section were emotionally wearing, particularly those involving young vulnerable women from local authority care who gave me narratives which were profoundly sad, whether or not they were working as prostitutes. Janey, for example, was not working in prostitution but her mother worked on street. Where prostitution is *experienced* as a lifestyle choice – or an occupation, a work role – and women feel comfortable with this and themselves, the interview process is so much easier. Where prostitution is experienced as the only option, or something the women and young people have to do to earn the money for their pimp, or if they drifted into prostitution at tender ages, or if they are suffering systematic violence from 'boyfriends' or recent violence from punters, the interview process can be emotionally wearing.

The quality of the ethnographic material is due in part to the levels of commitment to the research by all concerned. Working in partnership over such sensitive issues demands care, consideration and trust.[1] The material presented in chapters 3 and 4 is primary data from my own interviews, supported by secondary data from the available literature. Life-history interviews are documented alongside material gathered from outreach sessions on street, from off-street hand-written interviews, or from taped group discussions with the women involved in life-history work. Two of the interviews are with young women who entered prostitution from local authority care. These were both conducted in 1994. One of these interviews evolved into an article for *Childright*, the journal of the children's legal centre (O'Neill, Goode and Hopkins 1995). Both interviews developed out of my relationship with two voluntary agencies, one focusing on outreach work for women and young people, the other focusing on crack use. Both are street-level voluntary agencies working with women and young people working on and off street and/or individuals using drugs.

The narratives presented in this section are necessarily uneven due to the stages in my relationships with the women working as prostitutes. Initially, women were not happy about meeting and talking to me off street. As trust developed, women were more willing to meet and talk but not be taped; later still women agreed to talk about their life-histories and that these narratives be taped (1992–8). All names have been changed. No life-history is presented in its entirely. Some of the women I spoke to on street take 'draw' to help them cope with the 'realities' of street work. Other women I met sniff gas or take amphetamines, heroin and/or crack. Three of the women had histories of crack and/or heroin addiction. The life-history narratives are non-directive. The women and young people direct the discussion/narrative. There may be aspects of their lives they do not want to disclose. The non-directive method helps them to maintain control.[2]

3

Women's Voices, Women's Lives

The splinter in your eye is the best magnifying glass.

Adorno 1978: 50

This chapter explores the emotional, social and economic basis for women's involvement in prostitution, as told through their participation in the research. The interrelationship between psychic processes and social processes, materiality and ideology embedded in lived relations are illustrated in women's accounts of their lives and their working lives. My aim in this particular chapter is to show that immersion in women's lives, working *with* them can produce micrology (fragments of women's narratives or artistic re-tellings of their narratives), which may throw light on broader social and cultural processes. The key points and issues arising from their voices addressed in this chapter are: relationships to pimps and punters; routes into prostitution; managing male violence; 'making out' in prostitution; and routes into prostitution from local authority care.

> women's oral history is a feminist encounter because it creates new material about women, validates women's experience, enhances communication among women, discovers women's roots and develops a previously denied sense of continuity. (Rheinharz 1992: 126)

Listening to women's narratives highlights the fact that economic need is the bottom line for entry into street prostitution. Some of the women represented here (and reflected in the available literature on prostitution) have experienced problematic childhoods, breakdown in families, entry into local authority care, problems around being in the wrong crowd at vulnerable times and ages.

A profile of the 'prostitute' cannot be built up, as Nagle's and Chapkis's accounts show – specifically Tawnya's and Jean Almodovar's narratives in Nagle (1997) and Jo Doezema in Chapkis (1977), discussed in chapter 1. Nor is there a category or type of woman suited to prostitution. Different life circumstances, different experiences, getting involved in exploitative relations with a man at a vulnerable age or point in one's life, association with other workers or in the scene which helps to legitimate selling sex, coupled with desperate financial circumstances and a will to change the situation by any means, can serve to facilitate an entry into sex work.

The women involved in the research are mostly white, from working-class backgrounds and aged between 14 and about 54. All the women I have spoken to during the nine years of conducting research in this area say that they entered prostitution for financial reasons. Many began working in the sex industry through coercion and/or association with friends working as 'prostitutes'. With one exception, all of the women I have talked to had entered prostitution by association, that is to say all but one knew someone else who was working the streets or engaged in prostitution and eventually explored this option in order to earn enough money to live a 'reasonable' existence. For some women, access to prostitution was made through contacts made in certain pubs and clubs frequented by pimps. The women were coerced into prostitution in the course of their developing relationship with a pimp. They were 'chatted up', their drinks bought, a few trips were made to the town centre for window-shopping, looking at expensive items. Sometimes the relationship developed as a 'romantic relationship', and the women were subsequently 'persuaded' to 'do' street work in order that their lifestyle could continue to be 'reasonable' – because he (the pimp) did not work and had little possibility of paid work given the economic climate and high levels of unemployment in the area, or it wasn't worth his while earning because he would have to pay too much of his salary in maintenance (if he had children from past or current relationships).

Women tell me that we do have to be very careful to try and separate the 'male domestic partner' who supports his partner practically and emotionally (he may not, of course, but it is very difficult to draw clear boundaries around the interrelationships between people, and many women not engaged in prostitution may find resonances in their own lives here) and who may be unemployed from the 'pimp' who manipulates and coerces. Many of the relationships I have discussed (with heterosexual women) include degrees of support both practical and/or emotional in tension with degrees of emotional, sexual or physical coercion. Where it is accompanied by emotional and/or practical support, exploitation is experienced to a lesser extent and is sometimes articulated within an understanding or acceptance of taken-for-granted male/female relationships. Many women do not accept that their domestic partner is a pimp. Other women (a small group) see the pimp/prostitute relationship at one end of a continuum in heterosexual relationships, with lesser degrees of exploitation and coercion at the other end, but nevertheless still marked by degrees of power and control. Some women are quite clear that their relationship with men known as pimps is plainly a coercive relationship based upon their use value as prostitutes and their earning potential.

SAM: There are parallels with other relationships, the wife or mistress, relationships between women and men in general. There is more of it with the prostitute –pimp relationship. The exchange of money is the main feature. Main (*major*) relationships wouldn't entertain a prostitute. The emotional bond is the main thing behind main relationships. Women are so giving. A lot of relationships (*with pimps*) wouldn't be happening if she wasn't a prostitute! A lot of women feel they are not worth much. Also it is the security of having a relationship. There is a lot of pressure on us to have relationships [my emphasis].

There is a distinct lack of literature on the subject of the pimp as well as of the clients (Kinnell 1989; McKegany et al. 1990, 1992a, 1992b, 1992c; McKegany 1992; Hoigard and Finstad 1992; O'Connell-Davidson 1998). I use the term 'pimp' in the sense of a man who coerces and maintains a woman in prostitution and where the relationship is a destructive one. Many men termed as pimps are often partners supporting women practically and emotionally, if not materially, and sometimes sharing her income to pay for drugs. The interrelationships between women working as prostitutes and the men whom we call pimps are complex (see O'Connell-Davidson 1998 for an excellent account and analysis of the 'patterns of pimping').

Women working on street have told me that most women and young women on the beat are being pimped, and if they are not currently it is because they are 'new' to the scene and they soon will be pimped. From my own experience accompanying outreach workers on street (particularly during the last couple of years) and also talking to outreach workers in some of the major cities in the UK, it is clear that many of the 'pimps' are boyfriends/ partners who hang around the street casting a 'protective' eye over their girlfriends while waiting for money for drugs. These men/boys will also take a welcome coffee and condoms from the outreach workers. Clearly, a feminist analysis of prostitution must take into account the complex emotional, sexual and social relationships between the men who are pimps, clients, partners and the women working on or off street.

My experience of sitting through thirty cases in the Magistrates' court for kerb-crawling offences supports the evidence in the literature (Hoigard and Finstad 1992; Kinnell 1989; Jarvinen 1993) that the average client is married, in his middle years and often employed in a professional capacity, although, according to the women, 'clients come in all shapes and sizes'. What is clear from the narrative accounts of women in my research is that the gendered relations operating between prostitutes, clients and pimps/partners are complex, and woman do engage in resistances to hegemonic heterosexual masculinities through language, discursive practices and actions/behaviours (see O'Connell-Davidson 1998 for a very clear analysis of the relationships between clients and prostitutes developed from her empirical research on sex tourism).

Women working as prostitutes are the end stop in discourses on 'good' or 'honest' woman (Clark 1980). They are indices for women more generally in conditions of reflexive modernity/postmodernity. This first section will explore women's lives by focusing on themes arising from their life-history narratives: routes in, making out and male violence.

Routes into prostitution

Routes into prostitution are varied. Women make independent lifestyle choices due to the realities of economic need in an economic climate of recession, inadequate benefits, unemployment and increasing debt. Women sometimes drift in through association with friends already working. An option not thought of before presents itself and a decision to try prostitution is made.

> SAM: There is all different reasons why you go into prostitution....I went into it through choice and if I decide to stop it might happen this year or the next, but I can't see it because I am not ready to. I have good clients and I am not prepared to give up them dollars for love or money...I have always known I have high self-esteem because I have other skills and I don't think every prostitute has got low self-esteem because every prostitute hasn't...Once you start stigmatizing prostitution girls start having low self-esteem; once a woman starts believing in herself she can decide for herself...go back to college or work in the co-op....How may women prostitute themselves in relationships they don't want to be in but stay in a marriage for financial gain....If it wasn't for financial gain how many women would walk out of that relationship?

Ann, on the other hand, did not feel she entered prostitution through choice, but rather drifted in within the context of her experiences of sexual abuse perpetrated by her sister's husband. When I interviewed Ann in the summer of 1991, she was working in three part-time jobs, had been alcohol-free for five years, separated from her husband (a heavy drug user) for one year and had given up all drugs. Ann was also paying for adult education classes. Her involvement in prostitution lasted for three-and-a-half years, beginning in her fifteenth year while living at home and ending when she moved away from her home town. Ann left home when she was 15 and went to live with friends who supported her through a difficult period. Her friends were working as prostitutes.

Ann was sexually harassed and then assaulted by her sister's husband between the ages of 13 and 15. Her sister and her sister's new husband moved into the family home when Ann was 13, not long after her father died. Ann developed avoidance strategies, such as not being left alone with him and telling her Mum she would be leaving friends' houses much later than she actually was in order that she could avoid the lift home in his car. Ann had jumped out of a moving car and had thrown ornaments through a window in her home in order to escape and attract attention to her plight.

The central problem for Ann was that her Mum did not listen to her (the central problem is clearly the experience of abuse). In fact, her Mum thought that Ann was the 'problem' – not her son-in-law. The family began rationalizing Ann's behaviour: she was lying; seeking attention; making trouble. Understandably, Ann began to exhibit 'extreme' behaviour in response to what she saw as 'lack of trust' and was 'devastated at her Mum's response'. Ann was labelled a 'delinquent' and 'out of control'. She left home to live with some friends about six months after she first began to work as a prostitute. A woman who lived in the local area acted as a madam and organized visiting massage/sexual services for men living in the local area. Ann was taken on to work for the agency at the age of 15. Ann received a lot of emotional support from her friends and they 'looked out for each other' while they worked: for example, taking it in turns to wait outside clients' houses in case of problems. Ann maintains that she did not 'choose' prostitution. Prostitution brought freedom, money, fun and the ability to leave home. For her, 'choice' and 'control' were exercised by leaving prostitution. She experienced prostitution as a damaging form of work, 'trading off sex for the spending power of men'. She talked about wanting her self-worth to be more than it was, she felt 'passive' and 'done to'. Prostitution was about being used and she was vociferous in her insistence that money and spending power cannot buy self-esteem.

> ANN: Everyone should have the right to form relationships without having to pay for it. Everyone should have the right to relationships which are about give and take. This is good for self-respect and self-esteem and confidence.

Young women can drift into prostitution through peer association and peer pressure. Coercion from pimps is not uncommon. Many young and vulnerable women enter what they think and feel is a romantic relationship, only to find later that their 'boyfriend' is their pimp and will control and manage their 'work' through 'violence', 'love' and sometimes drugs.

Jane fell in love with a man who subsequently groomed her for sex work. Twenty years later she was able to reflect on the relationship:

> deep inside I felt so much anger to that one person...he knew that I was younger...he knew that I was vulnerable. He was a lot older than me...mentally I felt that he manipulated me so the anger is to me as well for letting someone do that to me....When my daughter is sixteen I don't want no man to come and manipulate her....My anger is not because of me but at him and men like him....A man like that could be around when my daughter is older...as the years have gone on I have got stronger and stronger...you can't tell people it's wrong to be a prostitute...the authorities have failed for years...you can't tell people what to do with their lives you just can't.

The meanings and associations we have regarding romantic love are particularly powerful ways of maintaining asymmetrical power relationships between women and partners/pimps. Jane describes the power relationship in the boyfriend/pimp relationship and suggests one way of breaking through what is effectively the ideology of the 'love' relationship she had with her boyfriend:

> The woman makes her money from clients...Perhaps her boyfriend visits once
> a week and she hands over some money...they might have sex or go out for a
> drink. A reverse thing happens here. The woman is the client without even
> realizing. He is paid for his company, his car, his clothes. Getting women to see
> themselves as clients might be one way of breaking the cycle. This is an
> instrumental relationship. He is a user.

Mary speaks about the damaging effects of 'love' relationships, premised
upon the exchange of her body to earn money for her boyfriend, and how
awareness of this comes with the wisdom of age/experience:

> Infatuation is stronger and short-lived. You can take just about anything from
> them in the infatuation stage. Women have to gain the strength to say 'No, this
> is not good for me'. It also comes through age, through learning, through
> feeling more in control with your life.

For Moira, financial independence from her boyfriend is a very important
dimension to the relationship:

> I admire smart men...I stayed five years with someone who battered me because
> of security and money...but now I have power and I need my boyfriend for
> emotional security...I don't need him for anything else...I sort myself out,

Structures of domination are deeply embedded within social and psychic
processes and practices, as much of the literature on gendered relations highlights. The quotations above are a far cry from Giddens's concept of 'confluent
love' (1992). Relationships between young girls and men acting as 'pimp/
boyfriend' speak very clearly about sexual inequalities, and what looks like
relationships built upon the dominance and power of men and the submission
and obedience of women to help maintain masculine 'identities'. These
relationships also speak of the ideals women associate with romantic love
and the madness or blindess of love that Freud talks about. For Freud, love is a
form of madness, a madness that follows certain rules.

> The basic rules can be put quite simply: here, instead of the normal under-
> standing of reality according to specific demands of the reality principle,
> there is a misperception of the love-object, the main characteristic of which
> is an excessive overevaluation of the loved object, especially a sexual over-
> evaluation, accompanied by its idealization. Subsequently the person who
> misperceives identifies with this overvalued, misperceived object. (Theweleit
> 1994: 6)

The search for love is a crucial part of our lived experience. Love choice is an
affect (emotion/feeling) that follows psychic laws. Theorists, such as Theweleit (1994), J. Benjamin (1993), Giddens (1992) and Bertillson (1996),
writing on love show us very clearly that mutual recognition cannot be gained
through submission or obedience nor through identification with the

other person's power, as illustrated through the fragments of narratives told above.

Routes into prostitution are also related to making the money to support one's own or another's drug habit, or to sustain involvement in drug cultures (McLeod 1982; McKegany and Barnard 1996; Hoigard and Finstad 1992). Mary told me:

> When I was in the drugs...I looked terrible. I had nothing in my house...and people came in and took over my house...I was so weak...the drugs did it...I can't blame anybody else but myself....I went into prostitution not because I was forced...I wanted to make my bloke look nice...although I've never had a penny off him...I might not be rich but I've learnt a lot...I could have died...I could have got kidnapped...I've always done what I've wanted to do...If someone says 'don't', I'll do it...there is only one thing...I wished I never went into the drugs.

Certainly, the links between drifting into prostitution from the context of living in or leaving local authority care and drug use/abuse need to be more thoroughly researched. Louise said:

> I left care and...I stopped taking drugs for a while but I started sniffing again...and I started injecting...I got in with the wrong crowd and I got introduced...well I was told that prostitution was the in-thing and I never could see myself as a prostitute. I thought it was dirty and I just started doing it with my friend....It was dead easy money £250 a time or sometimes you got more....At first I felt dirty because a dirty old man is lying on top of me...I have had punters that said to me 'you remind me of my daughter' and I said 'God don't do this to me' and the punters told me this and it's like they wanted to have sex with their daughters....They probably rape their daughters and they scared me sometimes when they do that...then I started taking crack...and then ended up selling my body for rock...just doing it for the rock.

The following narrative is from a young girl who works as a 'prostitute' while in the care of a local authority. This raises a number of issues around sexual violence for those in the care of the local authority, for example: the extent to which 'carers' perceive sexual violence as 'deserved' and 'deserving'; sexual violence as the 'effect' of an 'immoral lifestyle'; and sexual violence as 'outside' their 'control and ability to care'.

Sarah is 14 years of age. Between the autumn of 1990 and September 1992 she had been in five different care institutions. She was put into voluntary care by her mother at the age of 8 because of family problems. The family split up, her father left, her older brother went to live with her gran, she and her brother went into foster care. Sarah had three foster care placements, each lasting approximately six months, between the ages of 8 and 10. In the first placement she remembers 'crying a lot', 'feeling lost', 'unable to understand why she was there', but generally it was a 'good placement'. The second she describes as 'horrible' and the third 'not nice'. Sarah was returned to her mother for a short time, as was her younger brother. It was during her time at home that she first started to 'work'. Sarah met some girls with whom she became friends. She ran away with them as she was not happy at home. She lived with them near the regular beat and soon met a man and a girl for whom she was later forced to 'work'. She was picked up by the police and returned to her Mum. However, this didn't work out and she was put into care again. She was subsequently kidnapped from care by the two people she met; they told her she must 'work for them' and gave her some 'draw'. The girl accompanied her with every client. Sarah was very scared. She was 'slashed and beaten' for trying to run away and she 'wasn't fed properly'. After one week she was picked up by the police, told them what had happened and was put back into care.

While in care she decided she would work for herself. She wanted to buy 'draw, cigarettes and clothes'. Sometimes she would sleep at the clients' houses, sometimes a man would drive her to another city to work for about one week at a time. Sarah was introduced to crack by a man she met at a blues party. He showed her how to take it using a coke can. She became frightened, ran away and found a police station. She was returned to care. Sarah felt that she was moved around so much from care institution to care institution because she was perceived as encouraging other girls to try prostitution. Unhappy, not attending school, chain-smoking, Sarah soon ran away again and lived for five months in a rented flat. At this time she was working in prostitution, drinking, taking crack and 'draw'. Later she began to take heroin and was not eating, 'only packets of crisps'. She was picked up (because her Mum saw her out on the beat) and returned to care. After this she had a trial period at home with her Mum. But the relationship was difficult, 'lots of arguing', and she was put back into care. Of her mother, she said: 'I love her deep down, but disrespect her for all the messing about.' Once again she began to work as a prostitute, taking heroin and coke, but the person supplying her stopped. With the help of a prostitute self-help group and social workers, she is currently off heroin and crack and trying to remain so. She is in a community home which is not very comfortable, 'always cold', with 'worn-out' furnishings, but she likes it and feels relatively at home.

At first Sarah felt 'rotten and disgusted with old men on top of me'. She talked about how she used to physically and emotionally hurt but that she doesn't now because she had 'cut off her feelings'. She said 'it wasn't too bad at first because the first punter just wanted to look at my breasts'. At the home 'they don't understand why I can't stop, they think I should stop – just like that! £2 per week is not enough; I am a smoker, and I am in the circle now.' Sarah has had one abortion, and her social worker took her for a hepatitis B injection. She 'couldn't stand school' and describes herself as 'a loner'. Often, she goes 'out to work when I get bored, there is nowhere else to go'. Sarah has been 'beaten, slapped, punched and forced to have sex without a condom' – raped.

Violence and intimidation from pimps and punters is an endemic feature of women's experiences and life-history narratives. This aspect is well supported in the available literature (McLeod 1982; Hoigard and Finstad 1992; McKegany and Barnard 1996; O'Connell-Davidson 1998; Phoenix 1999; Sanders 1999; Cawthorne 1999).

ANGELA: In three years it has got a lot worse...it's going to get a lot worse....I don't like even going out to the shops at the moment...and at the moment I am getting a lot of hassle from a few people....I pressed charges against this guy who was taking my money...he got sent down....I went to court about eight times....I was getting abuse from his family...you are dealing with the wrong people when you lock these people up....He has robbed loads of girls but no one has been brave enough to do anything about it.

MAGGIE: You have hassle from those wanting to rob you...then you've got hassle from pimps and there is the crack link...then you've got the hassle from punters.

ANGELA: You've also got hassle from the police and the vice....They nick you when they see you and give you a fine and you have to earn money for your boyfriend as well as your fine....Then you get nicked again and your fine goes up...and you're out there more and you get hassles from punters and hassles from other girls...loads of hassle....Younger girls get hassle from the older girls...and they are robbing each other....The older ones can't stand the younger ones....Some are charging low for drugs...any money for any thing ...and the beat prices go lower....When I was first out there it was £30–£35 a time now it has gone down to £15–£20 and sometimes a tenner...and you can't really say anything to that girl, what she does is her life....If I see a young girl I would talk to her...most other girls would beat her up or rob her or kick her off the beat....It's weird when you're out there....It all boils down to one thing though, if you are a working girl you are targeted by all the blokes on the beat...they all watch her...they all think there is a working girl you can rob her...threaten her...she won't go to the police...the police came to me....They said he is a very dangerous man....Girls are so scared at locking up pimps because you get more and more stress....They have families...sisters... brothers...cousins...often they are well known people in the area....You can imagine all the crack dealers...you locked up my run-ins....Now I have to walk around on my own....They all know too many people...you lock one up and you think you have to lock them all up...but I couldn't keep taking what he was giving me...and I am still scared of walking the streets....I've moved area....I don't enjoy my life that much. I have to go to pubs well out of the area....I know I will have to move again....Nowhere is safe....In some ways I am glad I locked him up but in other ways I am not....What do I do when six of them come up to me or someone points a gun at me or tries to inject me with drugs...or kidnaps me?...I have a police alarm.

Routes into prostitution appear to be centrally related to:

- economic need;
- association with the area, with other women working, with men or friends or family who are involved in the subculture or the industry;

- drug use/abuse;
- vulnerable young women and also young men either in local authority care or living 'independently' with little or no support in the community.

These 'reasons' should not be seen independently, for the realities of women's lives are complex. The socio-historical and cultural backdrop to street prostitution is an important contextualizing dimension. Falling 'in love' with a pimp and subsequently working for him may be the reason why a woman enters prostitution, but poverty, drug use and/or being part of the 'scene' may keep her there. Indeed the concept of 'love' needs close attention here, particularly as it relates to 'prostitute identity/identities' and the 'prostitute role'. All of this needs to be contextualized within structures of domination, economic need, rising debt and lack of employment opportunities for young vulnerable people. Added to this, an understanding is necessary of the spaces of prostitution (see Hubbard 1999 for an excellent analysis of sex, prostitution and the city) and of the subcultures or milieux which help to maintain and reinforce involvement in prostitution.

> JANE: It becomes such a closed circuit...because it is not a job you can go out and admit to the world....You have the friends you work with...and they become the friends you go out with...so in the end you stay within the one circuit. Society looks down on prostitutes morally like it's wrong, and it's not wrong....Well it is exciting at first...seeing all that money...it is unbelievable...especially at fifteen and you have things you want to spend it on and you have this man that takes you out once in a blue moon and makes you feel like a million dollars...and at fifteen all you're looking for is that knight in the white shining armour to take you away and make you feel loved...and then after a while you begin to see what prostitution is really about...but imagine a fifteen-year-old having that kind of money.

Making out

How do women 'make out' in prostitution, specifically street prostitution? Women working in prostitution suffer social stigma and social marginalization. Women manage to make out in prostitution with the support of other women, or by leaving temporarily when they are experiencing problems in maintaining 'major' relationships. Women manage to make out by separating their bodies from their souls (Edwards 1993), by 'performing' the 'prostitute' role/identities within certain times and spaces;[1] this can, however, affect women's feeling worlds. In contrast to Chapkis's notion of performing erotic labour as liberatory and subversive, for some women it brings a coldness to their relationships and interrelationships and/or a desperate need to be loved for 'themselves'.

> IMOGEN: But after a while it does become a job....If I have a really bad time at work and I'm really stressed...I mean...actually...I was under the

psychiatrist for stress from work....I can't go home and talk to my boyfriend ...he'll think...if it was just a job...she wouldn't be acting like this....I stopped talking to her...because I felt she wasn't on the same wavelength...she wanted to talk about the here and now...I would say...I don't want to talk about the here and now I want to talk about my problems...that have happened...and why I'm feeling this way...everything was 'the here and now'...I had this letter from the psychiatrist department...and it was like have you been abused...did you wee the bed...what age did you stop....It put me off straightaway...you do need to talk to someone who will sit and listen who will hopefully...understand...it's not an easy job to do...far from it...like I know I have to go to work tonight...and I know I have to put the stockings on and all the slutty stuff...and strut it about....You know you think...I don't even want to go....I don't even want to go.

MAGGIE: This woman I know said...'it's really hard...I've done twelve guys at work and then I've got to keep him happy at home'.

IMOGEN: You see, that to me...that is good...after a busy shift if I can go home and have sex with my boyfriend...it's real...it's intimate...it's pure sex...I mean you fuck the men at work...you do all sorts don't you...but when it...I mean I like a lot of love and attention...and if I can get that at home it perks me up...that little bit higher...we all get like...but I like to get home and feel wanted...after the days I've had...it makes you feel like shit...you want to come home and be loved...and you know...you're worth more than you've just done...even if it's just lying in front of the fire having a massage...blah blah blah stroking you up and down...you feel it differently don't you?

Imogen's coping mechanisms centred upon having a love relationship which helped her value herself, helped her to feel 'you're worth more than you've just done'.

JANE: All working girls feel the coldness and feel used...and you can cope if you opt in and out over the years....Your whole life becomes part of prostitution...you need to learn to separate and that it isn't just your body being used....You come home from work and your man wants to be kept happy and you've been at work all day pretending and you can't be bothered and sometimes you have to pretend with your man....I'm still coming to terms with my life, always look for the good in people but when I was working in prostitution I stopped doing that...I lost it.

For Jane, it was difficult to maintain a love relationship with her boyfriend and she felt that working as a prostitute affected her feeling life to the extent that she stopped 'looking for the good in people', she 'lost it'. Mary, on the other hand, describes her coping mechanisms or ways of making out by maintaining control over her body and, by extension, over the encounter with the client.

MARY: I used to have hang-ups about my body but not any more....I don't care a shit....What they want is my body...it's not what is there on your body...but the clutching and the holding....The thing that made me turn was this one punter....I was massaging him for an hour and a half and when I finally...he ripped me off I'll never forget it....I took my clothes off...and sometimes you never got your money until the end...and he looked at me and he said where is your front to your back...and I just looked at him and said 'you're an arsehole...get up...get off my bed...I know you're not going to pay me...you've had my body'...and from that time I switched....I said hang on you're right because when I wasn't in control of my body he was in control of me...and from that day...I'm a working girl...I work with my body...you know....I went through a bad phase when a condom broke on me...and after that I just kept tightening up with every client...tightening my womb....We couldn't go on the bench because it squeaked and we had to think of the other customers...so I would do it on the floor but my back would kill me....After that I thought OK I am going to stop doing intercourse...so I brought in body to body...the majority of men like boobs but I thought well I'm flat-chested... what you've got is what you've got...so I put oil over my body and massaged the cock with my body....I loved the sauna work.

Indeed, Mary derived a lot of job satisfaction from her role, especially the sauna work whereby she provided a service to the businessmen who became her regulars:

I used to love the sauna work. I loved...communicating, drinking a cup of tea with them. That was my type of life. And I thought this is...you know...it was really 'cos they were really nice women as well. I liked the girls. Yeah. Well, we used to have a jacuzzi as well and we used to do a jacuzzi with the gentlemen and if you got in that jacuzzi that gentleman would pay seven pounds extra but you wouldn't see that. That was brought out for [the manager] to give him a boost...I used to love it. It was seven pounds for this jacuzzi or two pounds if the gentleman wanted to drink...and I was drinking champagne....Oh I was the star. I had a journalist...and he used to come every week for me....So adjusting from the street at first I was frightened....It was like going into a different world of prostitution. I was really frightened. I'm not going to be able to do it. I'm not going to be able to communicate. But on my first day, I'll never forget it, communication with a customer was absolutely fantastic. And I always have time for them 'cos they're my bread and butter. That's the way I used to look at it. They're my bread and butter...so I've got to look after them in the best way. If you look after them they're going to come back. And if they enjoy what they have they'll come back. And that's how I've carried on from that day....I don't care if I get thirty pounds off one and a hundred off another. I would still class each and every one as the same. You know I enjoy going out for meals and I enjoy not just a person coming for my body. Because at the end of the day that's what they're wanting...but I used to say you know whatever's going to happen whether you go out for a six-course meal...or a three-course meal and I always say whatever's in their pocket I'm going to have without stealing, without taking it, they're going to give it me willingly [laughs]. And I have to thank [the sauna manager] for that, for showing me a different world in prostitution. Which is more enjoyable. More satisfying.

MAGGIE: Did you feel it was more like work...did it feel better because you were safer and it was an official business?

MARY: Yes, and your mind was working all the time...is this a good punter or is he going to be a tight punter...and then at the end straight down the road to the casino...lose my money...have a couple of drinks...go home have a sleep and get up again for work....We see a lot...is it the type of life I live...or is it the way I live I see such a lot of heartache...but also I've seen a lot of laughs.

At the 1st European Prostitutes Conference (see Drobler 1991) women working as prostitutes and who were also feminists spoke about the managed and controlled relationship they fostered with clients and the thrill and status their earning power gave them in society. These women experienced their earning power as power and control: 'I say to him what he can do and when he can do it...you can put a clamp on my left tit, but not on my right one....I live in a very nice apartment...I can always pay my bills...eat good food...I am never short of money...never...this gives me power and status in this society.' Certainly, as described by Mary, an emphasis upon 'taking control' and using the body as labour power is a common theme in the impressions and personal experiences from the narratives, in my conversations with sex workers and ex-sex workers and in the available literature.

However, not every sex worker experiences or talks about 'control' and 'choice' in this way. This is inevitable given the complexity of women's lived experience; given the many ways in which we negotiate issues of 'power' and 'rights', 'needs' and 'choices' in the interplay between ourselves, others and the material and emotional resources that are available and not available to us in the context of our lived experience; and, finally, given our experiences of the contradictions of oppression.

'Making out' also includes managing violence and 'gentling' men to prevent violence.

MOIRA: But some of them are right bastards....I took him back to the house and I'd done the business and everything...and coming out of the door I said, 'drop me back at the beat'...and he said 'NO and you ask you don't tell me'....I said 'no drop me back'....It's part of the agreement you see unless they is paying you extra to catch a taxi....So I just punched him in his back and I said 'don't talk to me like I'm shit because you think you're better than me but you're worse than me because you have to pay for sex...I don't have to...I get your money.'...I wouldn't get back in the car after that...it could have got nasty...some of them are alright though.

MARY: Sometimes I think there are certain women picked out from when they are growing up to do certain roles in life....I never thought I would be a girl on the beat...for years and years I used to scorn them....I have never let a customer come on top of me...I am always in control....My second client asked me for oral...I screamed. He offered me £5 and I said I am not doing that...then I had a client who took me down an alleyway and he stabbed me...I beat him and stole his money...it was only a little stab...he could have had my eye out...and touch wood that is the only one....You can see a Jekyll and Hyde...you can feel it...I think that is why I am so interested in what makes people tick....When I was out there I don't care if I make no money...I won't go with anyone...that person can switch, I've seen it happen....If you have that little time to suss them out the best way you can...but also keep that gap...get inside their heads, but keep a distance and keep alert...because if they do switch, you have two paces to get out.... You have to use your initiative to calm this one down...humour him...keep in control....I always have my head clear to work...I've got to be alert....Two of my friends died through prostitution. One of them was stabbed, the other had her nipples cut off...we had done doubles...she used to see the way I worked and I used to sit down and talk to her...but she used to take chances...because she was in the drugs...she needed the money...I loved her so much and she was only 17 or 18....Those thing stick...they will never go away...everybody takes risks...but you have to cope with the risks....He cut or bit her nipples off and he got eight years....I used to say one day you are going to come across someone you will not be able to control...she had a problem and I could not reach it...she needed the drink to make her OK for work and she lost her sixth sense.

Making out not only involves rationalizing the role of 'prostitute' in relation to other roles for women and in the context of possible poverty but also involves managing the relationship between the separation of self/emotions and the body. The body is the tool of the trade. The self is for one's family, partner and self. Actions that facilitate this separation are: not kissing; the speed of the encounter – women on street talked about an average of seven minutes per punter; insisting on condoms with clients but not with partners; creating the situation where the client thinks he is having penetrative sex when he is not; putting a condom on a 'difficult' client with the mouth whilst he thinks he is having oral sex; using an assumed name; rolling or skanking punters (stealing); changing your mind once you have the money. For some women, never getting personal or giving the punter information about private lives was a way of managing. For others, friendly, regular clients were a bonus because they were a known quantity and were described as friends: 'I get my Christmas shopping...a new coat...and presents for the kids...every year after we've been up to London to see a show and stopped over.' Keeping a mental distance is a common strategy: 'I often think about the shopping and what I'm giving – for tea...and one time I remember doing a double with Sam and I was mouthing 'fucking hurry up'....She was in hysterics...and then I went into my 'YES...YESS...YESSS' and when he came I shouted 'EUREKA'....She nearly pissed herself with laughter.' One woman described a client who fell for her and wanted her to stop; he suggested paying for her flat if she would stop, 'but it wouldn't have worked...it was his fantasy really'.

Preferred clients are older men, definitely not young men, 'older married men…everyday clients'. Lola told me she didn't like businessmen; they treated her too scornfully, in patronizing ways; they made her feel like they were paying for her. She preferred older clients, working-class men who would be nice to her, treat her respectfully, have a laugh and a joke with her.

MAGGIE: How do you cope to distance yourself…shutting your eyes…what other coping strategies have you got?

CHERIE: If they're being nasty to you…you talk to them…calm them down…you know if they're being funny…you weigh them up, what sort of person is he.

IMOGEN: Yes…working women are good at that…and you also get the ones like you massage them first…you don't just…you talk to them first…don't you…of all this…'and what do you do for a living?'

CHERIE: And I had one right…said to me…why don't you just shut up and concentrate on the massage?

IMOGEN: And then you're stunned aren't you?

CHERIE: And then they expect you to have sex with them with a smile on your face…when they have spoke to you like you're just a piece of shit that they've you know…and then you want…to punch them…how dare you…I am a human being.

On experiences of working and separating the body from the self, women talk about managing their emotions and managing the client's emotions. Emotional labour is a central aspect of the women's 'relationship' with the client and involves them in manipulating, suppressing and falsifying their own feeling life in order to do the intimate work of fulfilling clients' sexual needs/desires and manufacturing care, concern, consideration and, indeed, a devoted stance to their clients (see Hothschild 1983). In dressing up and performing the role of the 'prostitute', exceptional control of inner worlds is necessary to manage and 'make out', 'survive' as a sex worker. This includes managing your own inner worlds and, as we shall see (below), attempting to manage the inner worlds of potentially violent clients. The issue here is: how do women 'make out' in conditions where they must separate body from 'self' to do the intimate work of fulfilling clients' sexual needs/desires and, at one and the same time, how do they manage to suppress their own feeling life and manufacture care, concern, consideration for their clients? This is one issue which could be taken further and explored *with* women.

Clearly, making out in prostitution is a temporary and difficult business with huge costs to the women involved. Many do not make out, and male violence is endemic. The context to women's involvement in prostitution includes being marginalized, criminalized and stigmatized; having to manage 'male violence' and abuse; bringing up children, often alone, as single-headed households; and at the same time 'managing' 'prostitute status' or 'whore stigma'. Racism and racist ideologies are an additional problem for black women and also black boys/young men. Coping with the 'love' of children, partners, clients; coping with poverty; and coping with involvement or non-involvement in drug subcultures are additional concerns. The earnings of women are dependent on how many clients are available in a particular area – which in turn is dependent upon how the area is policed – as well as on their involvement with pimps and others who feel they can 'take' (rob) money from 'prostitutes'. Making out involves:

- being able to separate one's feelings from the use value of the body and view the body as a tool;
- developing distancing techniques;
- being hard and strong so as to avoid as much abuse and incivility as possible;
- developing skills of sussing out clients to avoid and minimize problems, particularly violence.

Male violence

> Some of them are violent some of them aren't…it's all mental…it's all mental.
> (Moira)

Women working the street are likely to have suffered violence and abuse from clients as well as from pimps and domestic partners (Hoigard and Finstad 1992). It is clear that sexual violence against women working as prostitutes is endemic. Clients, pimps and domestic partners account for most of the violence against women, although sometimes other women or assailants unknown to the women are involved. The violence women have talked about includes rapes and beatings. The overwhelming extent of violence against women is violence from clients and from pimps. Women have recounted various experiences to me ranging from verbal abuse and threats to extreme and brutal violence: being punched and kicked and battered with the heel of a man's shoe while desperately trying to escape naked from his flat; being kidnapped, raped and imprisoned; and, for one under-age girl, being kidnapped from local authority care and starved and beaten into working for two people, a man and a woman.

Some of the women talk about how they have experienced very few physical assaults and attacks due to the fact that they are good at 'gentling' men, at 'negotiating' and 'counselling'. Further to this they talk about the violence they experience or have experienced in a very matter-of-fact way. Hoigard and Finstad also talk about this aspect of women's working lives: 'I often felt that the women talked about violence in a strange way. Bluntly, without any special dramatization, they could relate kidnappings, confinements, rapes, and death threats as if these were almost normal occurrences' (1992: 63).

Angela experienced the problem of violence when she told her boyfriend she didn't want to work any more:

> At first my bloke had something over me and it was only last year when I thought why do I do this....After that he became violent because I didn't want to do it for him...and I realised he only wanted my money....I was scared of leaving him because of all the hassle I was going through...but he never helped me and I thought I'm going through this on my own, I might as well be on my own...he's just into his money....I think I am better off without him...it's weird.

One of Angela's clients, who had become a friend, helped her out:

> Some of the men have been really nice...some of them take you out for meals...buy you clothes...some of them have helped me...look after you make sure you are alright...decorated my house and bought carpets for my house....I've met loads of nice ones...I've still got one now...he was once a punter...but now we don't do business now...he's like a granddad to me now....I'm his granddaughter...part of his family...he helps me if I have got a problem...he comes and sees me everyday guaranteed....He sorts out all my bills for me if I get stuck...he's brilliant...picks me up everyday...comes to my house and stays with me until he goes home....At weekends he comes over and I cook him dinner...he is old...about 64...his sister is dying in hospital at the moment...he has only got his sister and me....I met him through another punter...took me round to his house to cheer him up....Before then he was in his house for twenty years...would not leave his house apart from going to work...since then he comes around here....When I was going through bad times with the bloke I was going out with...he said...'you ever lay one more hand on her it won't be her locking you up it will be me'.

Louise was three months pregnant when she was violently attacked and left for dead in the middle of the road. Ironically, a regular client driving by picked her up and took her to hospital.

> That hurt me when I got raped that time...but some men have abused me but it doesn't bother me....But a few weeks ago I got attacked and I went to a place where he wanted to do it and he got a knife out and it was on the beat and he wanted to go inside and he wanted oral so he pulled out a knife and cut my throat, well I moved my chin so he cut my chin. I had six stitches, then he beat me up and made me go down on him and then threw me to the floor and I said 'don't I'm pregnant'....I ended up biting him and that did not do anything and he strangled me twice and I remember lying there when he was strangling me and I was struggling all the time, I never gave up...and I remember hard bricks coming down on my head.

Pauline recounts problems caused by the effect of alcohol on clients:

You get a few...the only problems you really have is the drink...that's us biggest enemy...if anything is...drink....But if they look too drunk you don't even let them in...but if you haven't got no money and a drunk comes to the door you haven't got much choice....I did one...he came to the door, it was about half past eight and I'd been there since half past four...so you are not guaranteed to earn any money anyway....He wanted a jacuzzi...so we booked him a jacuzzi....I took him into the room and told him I wanted me money up front...he took his trousers down and he'd pooed all down his trousers...horrible...and he only had £10 on him....He says 'can't you trust me for the rest of the money?'....I said 'NO...you can go and get the rest and come back'...and he did...and I had to do him in the jacuzzi....I put him in the jacuzzi first...because he was caked in it...and then when we was finished...he put his trousers back on....He didn't even come...'cos he was that drunk...he couldn't have made it....I felt sick...but...I had to do it because I needed the money...it was the only one I had that night...it was either do him or do nothing...things like that stick in your mind....The working-class man is better...the middle-class men...business men treat you like they are paying for it...but the working-class men they talk to you have a laugh and that makes it a lot better....You have to be able to talk to them in the room to break the ice...if they don't talk to you...you feel...you feel...like what you are....If they talk to you they make you feel alright...it's a lot better....You get your regulars mind you don't see them sometimes for weeks on end...some of them tell you they love you...and I don't like that...I think...leave me alone...but I always make it quite clear...I say I'm married.... Some girls get phoned up wanting to take them out...someone always ends up hurt...he may never come to see you again...if you're straight with them in the beginning it's a lot better.

Cherie still shudders at the hatred in her client's eyes as he 'came' on top of her:

This one guy...he would come in and always have sex and like...he insisted that he was on the top...so you're like trapped underneath...and he had his arms above my shoulders...and you always shut you're eyes don't you...you can't look at them...'cos you'd be sick...can you...and I opened my eyes once...and he was like that [gestured] at me....I felt my heart go into my throat...I thought he was going to kill me...he's gonna kill me and I couldn't move...he had hate...he wanted to kill me...I couldn't move...I could see it...and I was so frightened...and then what he did was say 'I don't want it this way, get off the bed...get off the bed'. So he wanted it so I was sitting on the edge of the bed...and he was ramming it in...and I said ...'you're being too rough'....He said 'I'll be as rough as I want' so I just finished with him...got him out...and when I came out of the room...you saw me...I was like...I thought he was gonna kill me...have you ever done that...it was horrible...piercing eyes...he looks at you and wants to rip your head of....He wants to kill you...it's horrible.

The 'violence' recounted above is physical, material and psychological. It is misogynistic. It is about the 'power' of men and men exercising control over women, taking sexual frustrations out on women working as prostitutes. It is about the enactment of male perversions (see Kaplan 1991). It is also about damaged individuals damaging others. It involves undermining and marginalizing, and because of the lack of state action against violence against women, and the lack of an outcry and direct action against the way prostitute women are seen as 'deserving victims' (see Bland 1992), reifies the 'throwaway status' of women working as prostitutes. These are the same women who are seeking to earn the best they can for themselves, their partners and their families. They are women for whom prostitution is work. Some of the women have been abused, have come out of care institutions inadequately prepared for independent living, are emotionally needy and vulnerable and/or are seeking a group, a subculture, where they feel they 'belong'. This is further complicated by the fact that not all clients are 'dangerous' and out to harm women, as Angela's account shows.

It is worth nothing that at the October 1991 European Prostitutes Conference (Drobler 1991) many 'whores' were vociferously against the entering into prostitution of young people who were vulnerable, emotionally needy and not really aware of their own needs concerning their sexuality. The women at the congress were strong, articulate women demanding the decriminalization of prostitution and the same rights, civil liberties and rights of human dignity as other workers. Indeed, the Women's Committee of the European Parliament calls on member states to decriminalize prostitution and protect the health and safety of prostitutes, pointing out that the 'semi-illegal, shady background against which prostitutes operate actually encourages such abuses as prostitution under duress, degrading working and living conditions, maltreatment and murder'.[2] This fits in broadly with those feminists who are concerned to follow an approach involving decriminalization as 'harm reduction' rather than as sanctioning the use value of women's bodies.

> MOIRA: I have lost friends, they look at you totally different...it bothered me...I thought fucking hell I am a prostitute....I am but I'm not...I have two different lives...work and me....My boyfriend's friend sat watching the telly and said look at them dirty prostitutes...and I said just remember I am a prostitute and this is my settee paid for by prostitution and my TV and my carpet and everybody looked at me horrified....I was so frightened (in the beginning)...the first punter just wanted to look....I had these durex and I wasn't even to sure how to put it on properly....I had real horrible nightmares that night...and I just counted my money that was my comfort.

In *Coming Out* (1977) Jeffrey Weeks writes about the 'coming out' process related to homosexual identities and the activities of homosexuals in countering hostilities. In some of the narratives women tell of their 'coming out' processes and reveal the ways in which they experienced and countered the processes involved in 'whore stigma'. Useful information about the formation of 'prostitute identity' as a temporal phenomenon and of 'role management' is given, contradicting some of the taken-for-granted ways of seeing prostitutes and countering some of the stereotypes (see also Phoenix 1999 for a useful analysis of the prostitute role and identity as a result of extensive fieldwork with women working as prostitutes). Similarly, what Mary McIntosh terms the 'homosexual role' is analogous to the 'prostitute role': 'the creation of a specialised, despised and punished role of homosexual keeps the bulk of society pure in rather the same way that the similar treatment of some kinds of criminals helps keep the rest of society law abiding' (Weeks 1977: 3). This is also, I argue, the reason why, in part, it has taken various institutions like the media – alongside feminists, researchers and activists – so long to seek to demystify or demythologize the category of 'prostitute' and the 'prostitute' role. These categories serve to maintain the boundaries between good-girl and bad-girl – saint and sinner – to keep the bulk of women 'pure', but they also serve an important function in the male imaginary. Tarts, hookers, whores, slags – highly sexualized women who 'love their jobs' – give sexual services to men and 'love it'.

Drawing upon Nancy Chodorow, contextualized within the work of Freud and the Frankfurt School, Jessica Benjamin points to the process of 'differentiation' as key to understanding erotic structures of male domination. The necessity of separating from the 'other' (usually mothers in our societies) in order to be confirmed as a separate person and as a male person, sometimes prevents the boy from recognizing the mother as a separate individual, as a subject, as an individual. In breaking with the dependency on and identification with the mother the boy risks losing the capacity of mutual recognition, for his independence is predicated on 'I am nothing like she who cares for me' (1993: 76). He can accept the separation at a cognitive level but, at a feeling level, identifying with the bodily connection and empathy with the mother threaten his sense of self-identity. The female other is related to as an object. Rationality substitutes for affective exchange. Rationality bypasses real recognition of the 'other's' subjectivity. This Benjamin calls 'false differentiation'. Male identity emphasizes only one side of the balance of differentiation (becoming separate from the parents – becoming I), and difference is prioritized over sharing; separation over connection; boundaries over communion; self-sufficiency over dependency.

Violation and denigration through erotic domination and submission of the other is one expression of false differentiation in the male. The association of femininity with masochism persists in our culture (J. Benjamin 1993: 81). The symbolization of male mastery through the penis emphasizes the difference between subject (male) and object (woman). It denies the commonalities between men and women that could prevent him from violating her, and it reinforces the dialectic of control, represented for Jessica Benjamin in the master–slave dialectic (1993) which underpins rationality as a structure of domination. Taken together, 'false differentiation' and the structures of erotic domination serve at the very least to maintain the role of prostitute as the role of 'thing' in the male imaginary, a thing who gives sexual satisfaction to her 'master' and 'loves it'.

The 'prostitute role' helps to show and control legitimate or 'right' behaviour and practices from illicit or 'wrong' behaviour and practices. The 'prostitute role' also serves to separate out deviants, women who transgress from the rest of the population of 'good-girls'. The prostitute as wrongdoer has through time been medicalized – for example, defined as 'rivers of infection' – and the bodies of prostitutes have been examined, treated, restrained, locked up and brutalized. *What they do* becomes *who they are* – 'lazy', 'good for nothing', 'careless', 'dirty', 'disease-ridden', 'bad mothers', 'greedy'. The 'identity' of the prostitute is wrapped up much more closely in her bodily functions than is the case with the rest of the female population, and, as Gail Pheterson (1986) has pointed out, the label of the 'whore', the 'prostitute', serves to keep all other women chaste, and if they are not chaste they may or must be prostitutes.

Some of the women I have worked with talk about living multiple roles and managing the contradictions between them all. The role and identity of 'the prostitute' is sometimes denied; when accepted it is sometimes used to confirm the woman's identity as a prostitute in a positive sense – for example, see the excerpt from Moira where she defines herself as a prostitute against the derision of her boyfriend's friend. This very clearly represents a 'coming out' story. I do not claim that the women's narratives are indicative of most women working on street. However, there will certainly be resonances in these stories for many women.

'Coming out' and 'prostitute identity/identities' are areas that could be developed further with women working as prostitutes. Additionally, work on the services that 'ordinary men' ask for/demand/take would prove a very useful insight into gendered relations and the structures of sexual practices in later modernity/postmodernity. Equally, such 'stories' could illuminate sites of resistance to hegemonic heterosexuality. One thing is clear from the narratives above: the care-giving role is deeply implicated in the psychic and social interactions between women and their clients and pimps.

How can the voices of women articulating multiple needs, experiences and meanings be addressed by women-centred research? My answer is by collective responses through action research, through participatory action research, through ethno-mimesis, through working with and for women working as prostitutes. Developing alternative forms of re-presenting women's lives is important to better understand the complex issues involved, to show the usefulness and importance of academic involvement in the public sphere, and to facilitate new ways of re-presenting multiple standpoints in postmodern times. The self-reflexivity inherent in the narratives contained in this text show women and young people working in prostitution as subject–objects, countering their 'otherness', their status as object, as commodity, as commodified 'other'.

Summary

The experiences and meanings of women documented here and the way they narrate the stories of their multiple realities speak of resistance and awareness and an understanding of the role and shape of male domination, male hegemony and human suffering. Engaging with their feelings, their 'realities', helps us to get a deeper understanding of gendered relations, of sexualities, of sexual and social inequalities. Certain themes have arisen in the course of examining the available literature and listening to women working as prostitutes:

- the many ways in which women are marginalized, stigmatized and develop 'prostitute(d)' roles/identities and the ways they perform those roles/identities within the structures of male domination;
- the importance and centrality of gendered relationships and what this says about gendered relations in wider society;
- relationships between love, desire and work;
- relationships between love, sex and violence against women;
- for some women economic need and entrance into prostitution revolve around patterns of consumption and the care of their children.

Doing participatory action research is for me about a politics of feeling – both in the research process, in the critical feminist standpoint approach and in the outcomes of the research – as feminist praxis. I learnt so much more than there is time or space to express here. The interviews further developed my own sense of solidarity and empathy with the women I worked with, some of whom became my friends, and with whom I worked to develop community action responses to the needs of women and young people. The narratives represented here are clearly stories of resistance to domination and oppression from women working in the sex industry and illustrate both their strength of spirit and the complexities of sexual and social inequalities at micro and macro levels.

4

Adolescent Prostitution: Runaways, Homelessness and Living in Local Authority Care

In this chapter I will discuss young people's experiences of 'doing' prostitution while in local authority care, on leaving local authority care or from situations of being homeless and/or 'runaways'. The ethnographic work with young people that informs this chapter was conducted over a three-year period with young people working predominantly on street (O'Neill et al. 1994; O'Neill, Goode and Hopkins, 1995; Green, Mulroy and O'Neill 1997).

These groups of young people are reflected in the literature on juvenile adolescent prostitution (A. H. Nicholsen 1981; Lowman 1987; McMullen 1987; Jesson 1993; Barrett 1997). This does leave out the young people who work from home, after school or instead of going to school. There is some anecdotal evidence that this is happening in some localities.[1] However, my impression is that in the UK these young people are very much a minority compared to the young people working from situations of being in care, having left care, being homeless or abandoned by their families and/or the state and/or living in situations of dire poverty. Forty per cent of young homeless people are care leavers.

A report by The Children's Society, *The Game's Up* (Lee and O'Brien 1995), highlights the criminalization of young people involved in prostitution and their pathways through the criminal justice system, emphasizing the need for child protection from sexual exploitation and abuse. Further to this, the report highlights the links between involvement in prostitution and running away, unemployment, school problems, neglect, sexual abuse and living in or leaving local authority care. The risks to young people include violence, murder, rape, sexual assault, involvement in pornography and organized prostitution. Associated risks are sexually transmitted diseases, HIV/AIDS, drug and alcohol abuse, depression, self-mutilation, attempted and actual suicide, physical injuries, problems in sleeping and failure at school (Lee and O'Brien 1995: 15). The report recommends the need to operationalize legislation that is currently in place to protect and prevent the involvement of young people in prostitution, and to develop harm-minimization practices on behalf of young people involved or at risk of involvement in prostitution.

Taken together, the Children Act (implemented in 1991), the United Nations Convention on the Rights of the Child, the Council of Europe and criminal legislation – which includes the Sexual Offences Act of 1956, the Street Offences Act of 1959, the Indecency with Children Act of 1960, the Sexual Offences Act of 1967, the Local Government Miscellaneous Provisions Act of 1982, the Criminal Justice Act of 1982 and the Sexual Offences Act of 1985 – combine to carve out the legal framework that could provide more positive responses to child/juvenile prostitution based upon protection, prevention and harm-minimization. Moreover, the authors of the report recommend that this framework can be used to 'create coherent and effective local and national initiatives designed in consultation with young people and professionals…to provide practical support for children and young people to help them leave the street' (Lee and O'Brien 1995: 67).

Currently, children and young people are more likely to have this legal framework used against them. They are more likely to be perceived and treated as 'criminalized' than to be exploited (Barrett 1997). Two pilot projects under way in the UK are being conducted by police forces in Wolverhampton and Nottingham and are supported by the work of The Children's Society and Barnardo's. Young people involved in prostitution are treated as 'victims not villains' and the clients are dealt with by the law as child abusers. It is too early to tell how effective these measures are in diverting young people from prostitution and the criminal justice system, or how effective they are in prosecuting the clients of juvenile prostitutes. One key criticism of this approach is that treating children and young people as 'victims' is not necessarily going to engender positive outcomes; and the 'hard to reach' young people will still end up in secure environments, in the care of the local authority or in the criminal justice system. Analogous to the literature on domestic violence, treating young people as 'survivors' rather than 'victims' may be a better approach.

Juvenile prostitution is an area which is under-researched in Britain. Jill Jesson (1993) argues that we need to know more about the reality of young people's lives before we can offer a meaningful response. The research on child and adolescent prostitution is about better understanding the reality of young people's lives in order to offer more meaningful responses (O'Neill, Goode and Hopkins 1995; Green, Mulroy and O'Neill 1997).

The available literature on female prostitution sees prostitution in terms of a social career divided into three dimensions: beginner, occasional prostitute and professional (Jarvinen 1993). Female prostitution has also been analysed around HIV, drug use and runaway children, which tells us about the role of commercial sex in their lives but not about the young women categorized as prostitutes (Pheterson 1990; Silbert and Pines 1981; James 1977; Earls and David 1989). Female prostitution has also been analysed around the fecklessness and deviance of women who are either too mad or bad to know better (Davis 1937, 1971). It is time women and young people working as prostitutes were heard and listened to (Jaget 1980; Nicholsen 1981; Sereny 1984; McMullen 1987; Lowman 1987; Pheterson 1986, 1989; Delacoste and Alexander 1988; Kinnell 1989, 1991; O'Neill 1994, 1995; O'Neill, Goode and Hopkins 1995; Green, Mulroy and O'Neill 1997). It is time we developed a better, clearer understanding of the male adults who pay for sex, who pay to live out fantasies with under-age girls, with children, with young women.

Male prostitution has been explored in relation to HIV, drug use, homelessness and runaways, (McKegany 1992; Waldorf and Murphy 1990; Gibson 1995; West and de Villiers 1992; O'Mahoney 1988; Philpot 1990; Lloyd 1977; Lee and O'Brien 1995), and has been described as a 'survival mode for runaway youth' (Nicholsen 1981: 2). Issues of sexuality, whether or not the boys offering services identify as homosexual, heterosexual or bisexual, have been raised in connection with male prostitution. Indeed, the focus has been predominatly upon the boys, *not* on the clients or 'punters'. Nicholsen remarks that whilst:

> the issue of a youth's sexual preference ought not to be the basis for providing or denying social welfare services, there are some agencies that provide to youth according to some invisible criteria of 'most deserving' *but some agencies have a problem with young people beneath the age of consent* [my emphasis]. All youth in this category are viewed as ultimately being consignable to some adult parent. The 'parent' in such cases may be the youth's natural parents, the state, a judge, or some appointed adult owning 'limited rights of their citizenship' so that they cannot legally obtain work without someone's permission, be absent from school, be on the streets without some address to go to, and most importantly, youth in this category cannot obtain help on their own from many social service agencies...except for placement in a detention hall, or a one-way bus ticket back home. (Nicholsen 1981: 4–5)

It is time we turned our attention to the 'law-abiding', 'normal', 'everyday' men, usually married with children, who pay children and young people for access to their bodies, their body-objects, for sexual services. At one and the same time we need to better understand the roles and relationships young people have with the 'adults' occupying positions of power and authority in their lives as well as the issue of young people's citizenship rights in contemporary Western society (see Evans 1993).

Judith Ennew (1986) explores prostitution within the context of the sexual exploitation of children, pornography and the wider sex industry. My own work explores prostitution from a feminist perspective (O'Neill 1997) and examines the role of the state and 'women-centred' multi-agency work (O'Neill 1994), female prostitutes' experiences of violence (O'Neill 1995), responses to juvenile prostitution from a youth service perspective (Green, Mulroy and O'Neill 1997), and masculinit(y)ies in relation to pimps and punters. Judith Green (1992), working for the National Youth Agency and funded by the Worshipful Company of Weavers, carried out an analysis of current practice and an examination of the issues involved in work with young women involved or at risk of being involved in prostitution. Green highlighted good practice and a range of projects operating nationally with and for young people involved in prostitution, particularly in the youth service.[2] There is a substantial and growing body of literature on young people's experiences of care and leaving care (Berridge 1985; Fisher 1986; Bonnerjea 1990; Garnett 1992; Biehal et al. 1992; Stein 1990, 1991; Porter 1984; Lupton 1985).

The types of prostitution young people become involved in are usually street work; bar and club pick-ups; organized groups who provide young people to clients for a fee; transitory or part-time prostitution for a bed andor some quick money. Nicholsen (1981) provides a typology of prostitution existing in large cities:

- call services, both agency and private individuals;
- female streetwalkers who work for themselves;
- female streetwalkers who work for pimps;
- amateur streetwalkers who hustle part-time for themselves or boyfriends partners;
- boy street-hustlers;
- weekenders working for excitement or enough money to party for the weekend;
- professional hustlers between the ages of 19 and 22 who have been working for a couple of years and who may be involved in pornography;
- survivors under the age of 18, boys and girls who have run away or who have been 'pushed out' (see McMullen 1987), who lack education, work skills, skills needed for independent living;
- survivors under the age of 14.

The latter group consider themselves fugitives and view their survival as being 'outside both law and society' (1981: 9); they are totally distrustful of adults. Finally, Nicholsen talks about child opportunists who are runaways, throwaways who trade sex for food, a bed, a roof andor love and affection.

One clear difference in the social organization of male and female prostitution is that young men tend not to have pimps and certainly, on street, women and young women do. However, as West and de Villiers say, this is not always the case:

> There was one case in the sample (*50 young men* [my italics]) where a boy's first contacts were made for him by a pimp on a commission basis....He had no money and was hanging about Victoria Station on his first day where he met a friendly man in his sixties who asked if he would like to make some money. He was told all about the rent scene and he agreed to a meeting fixed by telephone

with a punter who came to a nearby café. He handed over a share of the takings
to the man the next day. The arrangement ceased as he learned to find his own
clients. (West and de Villiers 1992: 77)

The difference here is that this young man had a relationship with the pimp
based upon mutual need. When he no longer needed the man to seek his
clients, the exchange relationship ceased. Women living with and/or working
with pimps have very different experiences, as we found in chapter 3.

Barbara Gibson states that most of the young people she has worked
with have lacked most of the basic needs children require, as defined by
the NSPCC: 'love, trust, respect, physical care, attention and praise'
(1995: 154).[3] Having experienced unhappy childhoods and been deprived,
neglected and mistreated, they lack self-confidence and self-worth. This has
also been my experience in working with and talking to young women and
young men involved in prostitution – the sex for sale industry. There are
common themes running through the lives of the young people I have talked
to, and these themes are also present in the work of, for example, Gibson
(1995), Nicholsen (1981), McMullen (1987), Sereny (1984), West and de
Villiers (1992), Ennew (1986). These themes are discussed below.

Destructive interrelationships with adults

First of all, there are destructive interrelationships with adults: 'profound
confusion in their relationships to adults', particularly men – 'men are seen as
abusers...men cannot be trusted' (Gibson 1995: 155). Further to this, there
are 'emotionally intense, albeit seemingly neglectful, relationships' with
mothers. Gibson feels that mothers were, for some of the boys, 'put on a
"pedestal" and "idolized"' (1995: 156). Violence, sexual and/or emotional
abuse marked their relationships with adults. Paul said: 'I got beaten up
lots of times. I was forced to have sex and I was ripped off. People had sex with
me while I was asleep, I was abused loads of times' (Gibson 1995: 163).

Jessica[4] was put into local authority care because of abuse by her mother
and her father. In the children's home she was befriended and subsequently
sexually abused by a full-time 'carer':

> Before all this came out I was waiting for the trial of my father...which was
> going to court, and it was a year I had to wait, a year before it went to trial and
> then I had to wait another half year....I went and of course it caused me a great
> deal of pain because I could see my mother...whom I love dearly...like I don't
> hate her now...but I seen her and she used to laugh at me and things like
> that...and my brothers....He had got all these witnesses and there was my
> medical records against...and I was in the witness box for about four hours
> one day and two hours the next day...I had got a screen in front of me but
> knowing that he was behind the screen is scary....They dragged up a lot of
> things...my diary and I had to read it...photos...it was pretty horrific to go

through and I was amazed that I managed to get through it with the hammering they was giving me in that court....In the end he got found not guilty anyway...no one would tell me why...my key worker told me he had got let off...I couldn't handle that....My solicitor...who wasn't my solicitor until that day didn't really tell me enough information about what was going to go off...I was pretty shocked when they started throwing all this stuff at me that I didn't know....My solicitor phoned my key worker up and like, saying no one knows why there was this outcome....But I wanted to appeal but no one explained why I couldn't...so he ended up walking free and I actually seen him on the last day...they let him out the same time as me and I crossed the car park...it scared me...I suffered a lot of pain knowing he had got away with it....Now he is married and has another lot of kids so I am afraid for them...he got away with that...

Labelling and stereotyping: 'delinquent', 'mad' and 'bad'

Disruptive behaviour both in and out of school leading to being labelled as delinquent is common. Absence from school, and a growing sense of 'not fitting in' as a consequence of lengthy absence, serves to prevent young people acquiring good enough literacy and numeracy skills. This, of course, leads to one obvious outcome – poor employment chances. Being labelled and seen as bad, 'other', for some of the young people I talked to, led directly to their being placed in voluntary care. Janey felt that the 'disruptive' behaviour that led to her foster parents placing her in care when she was 14 helped her to survive being in care:

> When I was took there...by this time I had an attitude problem...I was frightened but I didn't let it show...I plonked all the things in the bedroom...all the girls come round to see the new girl...I said 'does any of you smoke'...Course they all said yes....'Let's go for a fag then'....They thought I was going to be OK...We went down for a smoke and they all lit up...I didn't...They said 'what's up haven't you got any fags?'...I had a bad attitude problem....It helped me in there....If I'd gone there as an insecure...vulnerable little girl I would have hated it....Because I had this attitude problem which made me strong...I liked it.

Jane's experiences were similar as she was placed in care by her Mum because she was 'out of control':

> I was always praised in the junior school and I got my eleven plus and when I got to the comprehensive school the classes were too big and my Dad died and I think it sent me doolally....I was entering adolescence and my Mum was entering the change so you had two neurotic females in the house....I really did miss him...I still miss him desperately. I would love him to see my babies....I stopped going to school and got in with a bad set...and I had a knock-back when I was put in the middle grade in the third year...and ended up in care....I was put into voluntary care for six weeks but then they decided

not to let me out....A psychologist at the assessment centre asked me to put bricks together. I said 'no' and they took that as hostile...and they said it was better that I stayed in care.

Being labelled as 'other', as 'delinquent', also follows the disintegration of young people's families by death or divorce, or follows being abandoned by their families or a significant parent/carer. Once in care they have to face up to the realities of living in care: bullying; no continuity of care (due in part to multiple placements but also to the fact that the culture of care usually precludes becoming attached to one person, putting trust in one person); harassment around their developing sexuality and sexual preferences (particularly for boys beginning to identify as homosexual and girls beginning to identify as lesbian); physical violence; loneliness and loss of the familial situation (no matter how bad their experience of 'home' was, there is an attachment to 'their' home, 'their' family, 'their' Mum and/or Dad); continual assessments and record-keeping, reports about them; experiences of seeing 'trashing' (wrecking) of the home or being involved in 'trashing'; becoming involved or being intimidated into involvement in crime (TWOCing/theft/ burglary); and prostitution.[5] Of course, for many, being in care also means being in a situation that is less harmful than the familial situation: they are not being beaten up by fathers or mothers; they are not being sexually abused by fathers, uncles, brothers and, sometimes, mothers. Inevitably, the loneliness and dislocation – even 'shock' – associated with the move into care colours their feelings towards being in care.

Experiences which have been expressed by all the young people I have interviewed who are living in residential care or who have now left the care system and are living independently include:

- physical, sexual and emotional violence against them or their mother by their father or stepfather;
- the fear and loneliness of moving in to care;
- problems around fitting in, especially learning who is 'top dog' in the home;
- fitting in with other young people and 'going along' with the group, even if it means prostitution, TWOCing (taking without owners' consent), burglary, robbery or drugs;
- lots of moves between homes or from foster care to residential care, from residential care to foster care, sometimes with a spell of time at home;
- lack of privacy, for their experience is that their lives are lived out in public, with lots of people having access to their personal lives, their personal experiences;
- daily harassment, abuse, incivilities;
- problems of leaving care – not being adequately prepared, living in temporary accommodation, not being able to find or keep a job, not being able to get on or maintain a college course.

Indeed, all the young people I have spoken to have had problems maintaining their place at school once they moved into care. For some young people the experiences of living in care were expressed in profound and distressing terms:

> ALICE: I was in hospital because I wouldn't eat a lot...I had problems with eating a lot...when I was younger...when I was a baby...I had things with feeding...so I don't know what it is....Sometimes if I am grumpy or something I won't eat...sometimes if I do it for so long it becomes a habit...sometimes I don't realize....Because I was so upset and wondering where my Mum was and all that I wasn't thinking about food, know what I mean....when I was younger because I was so unhappy all they wanted to do they said...they wanted what was best for me...they wanted to choose for me...they wouldn't let me choose...it made me really unhappy....When I was 13 I slashed my own wrists...I am lucky I haven't got any scars...but I did that with a broken milk bottle....I have done a lot of stupid things in my life...I have been unhappy in lots of places...I've not really wanted to be in care my whole life really....When I was in the secure unit...that's where I went when I was 12 until 16...you wasn't allowed to go to the park...you weren't allowed to go and get some food when you wanted something or go out to the shop...you had to have someone do that for you....You couldn't choose what you wanted to eat...couldn't go and like – you know how parents do sometimes with their children – you couldn't have a normal life like that....They did things for you and tried to help...to me they were like trying to put me into a mental person...do you know what I mean...you know a problem. And that wasn't me...they made me feel like I was an ill person with mentally ill behaviour, do you know what I mean...they half way got me ill....I tried to get out of it...all I needed was a bit of care...I never got that...all I got was worse....They were like holding me and things like that...using my arms...I never thought I was really, like, because they were getting me so mad...they were trying to get me mad...they were making me mad...they used to lock me in a room on my own...just brick walls and a metal door....When I came to [the residential unit]...I thought it was going to be different...you could go out when you wanted to and all that stuff...but you had to come back at a certain time...I just felt at 16 I had to live on my own and that was that. I was happy...when I was in [the residential unit] it was like...you should be in a pink dress...do you know what I mean...they were trying to make me perfect when I wasn't a perfect person...nobody is....They was like...trying to make me into a little girl with pink shoes...white socks...all that and there was the secure unit trying to make me mad...I was like trying to figure out for myself.

Sexual abuse

Young people talk of being sexually abused at young ages. The meanings associated with sex, with love and affection are often coloured by these early experiences of abuse. Alice was abused as a baby and as an infant she was hospitalized and taken into care:

> I have been abused and all that stuff...I have never had parents who actually cared, never had like lots and lots of money given to me...and like presents given to me...do you know what I mean?...When I was two I went into care...I nearly died because I was so abused...I stayed in hospital for a year.

Mostly the young people talk about early experiences of abuse as harmful and damaging, but some young people experience their abusers as affectionate and talk about the relationships in warm and friendly terms. Two of the boys Gibson writes about experienced their sexual abuse positively as 'love', as 'affection', as bringing rewards such as money and adventure. Others, however, are clearly damaged and experience these early sexual experience with adult men as abuse of self and self-identity.

> I'm dead against prostitution. I got into it because I thought sex was about love, and underneath it all I was looking for a Dad (I found out who my Dad was a few months ago, he won't have anything to do with me). A few years ago I thought it was a good way to make money, but it's not worth the price. I've lost all respect for myself in doing it. I wouldn't recommend it to anyone...Then when I found out about my HIV for sure, I felt like topping myself loads of times. (Paul, in Gibson 1995: 86–7)

Associated with the latter point is the fact that being given rewards (affection, care, consideration, money) for the sexual abuse between adult and boy or girl encourages the children/young people to associate prostitution later in their young lives with a mechanism for gaining rewards – the things that they need, the things that matter to them. Money, as Gibson says, is 'power' to the boys: 'It's straightforward – unlike their experiences of the currency of love. The "dance" in getting the money is often a devious and dangerous game. The highs and lows are addictive. It is a gamble and an adventure, in which the stakes are bodies and minds' (Gibson 1995: 162). Power 'over' the client, getting the client to hand over his (or her, but mostly his) money is, as Richie McMullen (1987) says, 'part of "the game"'.

The 'game' has terribly high stakes: murder, rape, torture, slavery, pornography, sexually transmitted diseases, health problems, drug use and abuse, violence, intimidation, bullying and many forms of racism. Racism consists of the language and terms that are used in the interactions between client/punter and prostitute. Racism is embedded in the performances expected or demanded by clients, related to symbolic associations of blackness with increased sexual prowess, slavery, animal passions or passive femininity (see Fanon 1986; Young 1996). The risks are high, the feeling of 'power over' lasts only so far as the boy or girl or woman can manipulate the client into thinking the power lies with them. The relationship between all of this and a stable sense of self-identity is fraught and chaotic, the costs both emotionally *and* physically are high.

> I enjoyed the life, the adventure. You never knew what was going to happen. Going off with a stranger, closing your eyes and 'jump', see what happens. You

risked your life every time you stepped out there. You didn't know where you were going to end up. You might get attacked, killed, arrested, anything could happen....I couldn't do it now. I remember everything, and think, is that really my past? I think I must have protective spirits to have got through what I have. (Adam, in Gibson 1995: 151–3)

Violence

Violence is a common theme – in their young lives before working in prostitution and in their current personal relationships and work relationships. Violence against 'prostitutes' is endemic and related to this is the fact that violence is a taken-for-granted aspect of their lives. Some of the young people, both young men and young women, I have talked to feel that they are to blame for their lifestyles, for their problems, and that they must just endure the consequences. They don't expect help, support or protection. Carol feels that because her Mum always told her she was no good and that she would never get anywhere in life that she won't. Carol feels a sense of doom attached to anything she really wants to do or be. Pat feels that everything that happened to her – sexual abuse by a neighbour, being put into care, the separation of her mother and father, becoming a prostitute – is all her fault. Pat feels that she is somehow responsible for things that happened to her and also for the problems between her Mum and stepfather.

Racism: 'exotic others'

Young black people have specific problems, for racism is a central aspect of their lived experiences. Whether they are living in care and/or living independently and doing prostitution, racism comes from peers, police, clients, passers-by, indeed, the people closest to them, the social worlds they live in and through. The psychic alienation this causes is sometimes literally 'maddening' and a career involving mental health services ensues; or the psychic alienation is 'unbearable' and the young person takes their own life or gets involved in a no-escape, risky situation which leads to loss of life. The stereotypes of young black stud, or passive, fragile, feminine homosexual Eastern prostitute abound. Punters want to play power games with these young people, power games that symbolize slavery, humiliation, myths of black sexuality. Black youth need to conform and play out these stereotypes in their encounters with the mostly white punters, who are often married with children of their own.

When I was with a punter I had a problem in being in control, taking charge, I couldn't talk to them. They always were in control. I think what made it worse was I felt so vulnerable and used. I should have just dictated what I was going to do or what was on offer, and not let them get away with anything else. I shouldn't have let them do anything I didn't want them to. I think that's what made it worse, I just felt so dirty the whole time....Punters want black boys to be slaves. They want to whip and beat them up, and make them wear slave collars. They want to totally degrade the boys. They think all black guys have got big cocks. That's why black guys are supposed to be so popular...I went into this room full of straps and equipment. He really punished me. What scared me most was that I didn't know what he was going to do next. (Ryan, in Gibson 1995: 129)

I just thought life weren't worth living. I was doing a lot of self-harm, cutting my arms. There were times when I cut my arms I'd just cry...90 per cent to die and 10 per cent to be found. (Simon/Simone, in Gibson 1995: 92)

Young black women working as prostitutes are often seen as 'exotic', the punters want to try a 'bit of the "other"'. Anxiety about the 'other' and gaining control over this 'other' marks black women's experiences with clients. These men are also often married with children of their own.

Runaways, throwaways, and outlaws

Running away from familial situations which became unbearable, including living in social service care, is a common theme. Young people are often driven 'underground' or, as A. H. Nicholsen (1981) states, become 'outlaws' to avoid the system of care which either puts them back into care or returns them to a familial situation they cannot bear. There is no legal source of income from the state in the UK for 16–18-year-olds unless the young person is on a youth training scheme or has left care. Lacking accommodation and not knowing the system can lead to a situation where young people do not claim or are denied benefit and drift around squats, surviving as best they can. Prostitution, for some, is an obvious answer – the body is their only commodity. Pauline began to work when she was 17 to make extra money for her boyfriend and herself. Pauline was on a youth training scheme and was unaware that she could claim benefits: 'I was eighteen months on street – it was my idea to go out...to make some money for a drink...my boyfriend used to get £64 per fortnight – not enough to live on.' Later on she found out that she could have claimed during this time because she had been in care.

MAGGIE: How long were you in care?

PAULINE: I was in care from when I was 12...I understand now why I was there....My Mum didn't believe me...she tried to sweep it under the carpet ...so she didn't have to face it...so that's what's made me the way I am.

MAGGIE: So, did she put you into care?

PAULINE: Well first they put me into hospital [laughs] when I was 12…a mental hospital…she thought I was disturbed, but now I think about it I'm not surprised with all that happened.

Pauline was 12 when she told a teacher at school that she might be pregnant by a neighbour who was sexually abusing her:

> I lived with me Mum and stepdad…and stepdad and me Mum's daughter….I always felt different…my sister was always spoiled….She had new clothes and I had second-hand clothes…and he [the neighbour] told me he loved me…and that's all I wanted…I just wanted someone to love me….I was only 11 when it started and it went on for nine months…until he told me I was pregnant…. When I was 12. I didn't fully understand how you got pregnant…except that when you were pregnant you were having a baby…and that frightened me…so I told a teacher at school. My stepdad come to the police station with me…I didn't realize it but it was their wedding anniversary…the day I told the teacher….They thought I was trying to upset things. The Police told us that they had found a diary and I wasn't the only one, but because me Mum wouldn't stand by me…they didn't think they would have the evidence…so he got to walk out of court….She said at the time…because there had been this film on a few nights before – about this girl whose father got – she told me I couldn't watch it, so I went upstairs. I only watched about ten minutes of it…so I turned it over. She said I had seen this film…but I didn't see it…my stepdad believed me. He was crying himself when I gave me statement, but my stepdad loved my Mum more than anything so he'd always side with her…well he just kept out of it…I didn't really know what was going on, I was more worried about being pregnant.

Many young people experience rape, but these young men and women do not feel they will receive sympathetic responses from the police and criminal justice system because of their involvement in prostitution. What they 'do' becomes who they are, they are outside of mainstream society and so do not feel eligible for the same protection as their non-prostitute counterparts. They frequently do not report crimes perpetrated against them, but, as Pauline's account shows, even if they do report them there is no guarantee that the case will be supported, by parents, guardians or the Crown Prosecution Service. The added problem for young men is the issue of the age of consent.

McMullen (1987) states that we don't know whether girls or boys are more at risk over the issue of violence. The impression from the available literature suggests that there are more girls than boys involved in the sex industry. Add to this the well-documented literature on male violence against women, contextualized within patriarchal capitalism and hegemonic heterosexuality, and young women would appear to be more at risk from male violence. Over the years more girls and young women have been murdered by 'prostitute' killers than boys and young men.[6]

Violence against women, as Liz Kelly (1988) has shown, is experienced along a continuum from incivilities and verbal abuse to murder. Male violence against women is endemic, it pervades our entire lives; we are not free from it in the 'private' sphere of family life, nor in the public spaces and structural institutions we inhabit in the course of our working lives, leisure pursuits and day-to-day travels. Patriarchal capitalism involves deeply embedded male violence against women. The biggest problem in looking at the issue of male and female prostitution in terms of who faces the biggest risk is that this will inevitably lead to who should have the biggest share of resources available for research, support projects, policy initiatives. Feminists have fought, and are still fighting, long and drawn-out battles to ensure that resources are available to meet the most basic needs of the victims of male violence; and to attempt to shift public attitudes and the ways we socialize our male children to accommodate sexual and social equalities.[7]

What we do know is that the social organization of male and female prostitution is both different and similar. Differences include: the age of consent, ideologies around 'homosexuality', Clause 28 and the way the criminal justice system deals with young men involved in prostitution. McMullen states that he was 'reliably informed...by a magistrate that when such young people come before the bench – girls are invariably fined, whilst boys are sent for psychiatric reports' (1987: 37). On the other hand, there is evidence to suggest that girls who are in the care of the local authority are more likely to be sent to secure units and seen to be in need of moral guidance (Sobey 1994). These young women will not usually be fined if they are under the age of consent andor in the care of the local authority. They will instead be returned to local authority care to be dealt with there.

The social contexts in which prostitution takes place, given that our social world is constituted by patriarchy and capitalism, are marked by the fact that male and female 'prostitutes' are available for men who can and do pay for sex. The experience of doing prostitution for young men and young women combines both economic and emotional neediness, psychic and social aliena-tion. 'I act "bad", I feel "bad", I am "bad", I'm no "good", what I am is me, and I'm stuck with "it"' (McMullen 1987: 37).

Criminalization

Young people (technically above the age of consent) can be fined for impor-tuning for immoral earnings or for soliciting. They may still be under social service care; since the 1989 Children Act social services can look after young people until the age of 21. Non-payment of fines can lead to spending time in a youth detention centre or, depending upon their age, in prison. Simon/ Simone was sent to Feltham Young Offenders' Centre four times for non-payment of fines: 'If the police can't get you for importuning, they'll get you for highway obstruction. The fines mount up at £50 a time, £30 a time and in the end they mounted up to £800. I refused to pay them. I had to go to prison four times altogether, for different fines' (Gibson 1995: 101).

The Council of Europe Report (1993: 17) acknowledged that exploited and abused children are situated in a twilight zone. They are characterized by a high degree of invisibility and mobility. Moreover, the problems involved tend to be overemphasized by the media and underemphasized by the criminal justice, welfare and educational agencies. In Britain many researchers and children's campaign groups and charities believe that the legal system has failed to respond effectively to the men and women who use, abuse and 'control' children, and has instead criminalized and stigmatized young people (Children's Society; Barnardo's; Association of Chief Police Officers; Barrett 1997; Scambler and Scambler 1997; Edwards 1998). The laws surrounding children under 16 are very unclear. For example, a girl over 13 but under 16 can be charged with soliciting, even though she can't give lawful consent to sexual intercourse. Research by Susan Edwards (1998: 56) highlights the criticisms inherent in the fact that the penalty for indecent assault was increased to ten years in 1985, but no such increase was made to the maximum sentence for unlawful sex with a girl under the age of 16. The maximum penalty for unlawful sexual intercourse with a girl aged between 13 and 16 is two years. Moreover, it appears from the available literature that the men who engage in sexual activity with children involved in prostitution are rarely charged with anything more serious than kerb-crawling.

In response to this situation, in February 1999 the Home Office and Department of Health issued guidance for the police, social services and all other agencies working with children involved in prostitution. The HO/DoH guidance sets out a multi-agency approach based on local protocols to address the problem.

Home Office figures show that between 1989 and 1996 in England and Wales 4,495 young women under 18 years were convicted or cautioned for offences relating to soliciting (Home Office Crime and Criminal Justice Unit (RDU)). Following the campaigns on juvenile/child prostitution headed by the Children's Society, the Association of Directors of Social Services and the Association of Chief Police Officers issued statements saying that child prostitution should be dealt with as a child protection issue under the Children Act and not as a criminal offence. Wolverhampton and Nottingham anti-vice squads responded by launching pilot schemes treating under-17s involved in prostitution as victims of child abuse. What this means is that the young people are directed to social service support services and the men who buy sex with young people, or who procure and 'pimp' young people, are targeted by anti-vice officers. Results in both Nottinghamshire and Wolverhampton are very encouraging. In Nottinghamshire, social services provide the lead agency (with a dedicated lead officer) in multi-agency collaboration with police and key voluntary agencies, but most importantly with POW! (Prostitute Outreach Workers).

The legacy of prosecuting the prostitute and not the client – carved out by the Wolfenden report, the 1956 Sexual Offences Act and the 1959 Street Offences Act (but rooted in much earlier legislation) – is shifting in the UK.

There is a lot of ongoing work in both England and Wales which focuses upon the inequalities in the law, especially in relation to 'punishing the provider rather than the buyer of services' (*Sex Workers and the Law* 1997; Lee and O'Brien 1995; Kelly et al. 1995; Barnardo's 1998; alongside academic research: Edwards 1997, 1998; English Collective of Prostitutes 1997; O'Neill et al. 1994; O'Neill, Goode and Hopkins 1995; Scambler and Scambler 1997; Barrett 1997; Benson and Matthews 1995; Melrose and Barrett 1999).

Health and related problems

Isolated and vulnerable, some HIV positive, others living on street, in squats, as 'outlaws', children and young people suffer health problems such as asthma, bronchitis, rashes, crabs, dental problems, with little or no support from friends and relatives. *Somehow* they survive, and show amazing initiatives in gaining basic necessities to survive and develop resilience to the traumas and hardships they undergo:

> One day I think the effects of my past are going to come out. I'm going to have a breakdown. I want to postpone it until I'm more secure and better able to deal with it. I know I haven't dealt with the problems in my head. They keep piling up. I have a lot of pressure inside of me. (Adam, in Gibson 1995: 153)

What surprises me most in this work is not so much the terrible, harrowing histories they tell me about, or that we can find in the literature, but the fact that so many are survivors, that they come through all their physical, emotional trauma and are 'together' people – friendly, trusting, good people with a sense of hope for the future. Some, as one would expect, are not survivors.

In the process of taking an ethnographic approach to explore the needs of young people in care (with specific focus upon prostitution) I have become acutely aware of the following issues that have unfolded from listening to young people:

- the effect of pre-care familial experiences, particularly physical, sexual and/or emotional abuse by the father, stepfather or mother's partner or abuse of the mother by the father, stepfather or partner;
- routes into care;
- 'making out' in care;
- peer-group pressure and the 'culture of care';
- male violence and peer abuse;
- the feelings expressed by young people of abandonment, hopelessness and the need to 'belong'.

Finally, the stories of young people who are effectively runaways and living in temporary accommodation throw up issues to do with problematic and abusive familial backgrounds, lack of care, lack of continuity in their lives and, ultimately, lack of love. For some of these young people prostitution was presented as a means to an end, a means of escape from one appalling situation – poverty, living on the street – into another, the means to earn enough money to 'sort themselves out', or as part of a developing love relationship with a 'pimp' or client.

Psychic processes and social processes

McMullen offers us a two-pronged analysis of youth prostitution. First of all, in relation to emotional neediness, young people experience a 'poorly experienced and underdeveloped sense of personal power...a deep feeling of being inconsequential to anyone or anything' (1987: 39). Second, they experience a lack of economic power. For McMullen, the interconnection between lack of personal power and lack of economic power forms the 'motivating agent' for entrance into prostitution. Indeed, for him, the lack of economic power is unlikely by itself to be a motivating force, for otherwise why aren't many more young people becoming involved in prostitution? The two conditions must be present.

A poorly developed sense of personal power combined with childhood sexual abuse may be insufficiently motivating, but may motivate self-harm, or suicidal behaviour, with prostitution becoming a slow form of self-torture. Combine economic need, living in a squat, no money for basic food and drinks, the opportunity to 'do' prostitution – a hand job at first, or simply a look at her breasts for money – with a 'poorly developed sense of personal power' or 'psychic alienation' and the result is a potentially powerful combination of motivating factors.

The young women I have talked to entered prostitution on street and in parlours, primarily, they told me, because of dire economic neediness, debts, the risk of becoming homeless. These very women's lives are also marked by damaging relationships with men, violence, fear, abuse and lack of personal power in relation to these dominating men. This is usually combined with coming to know someone who is working, who suggests that they 'try' prostitution as one answer to their situation.[8] This is not to make a case for factors that are solely present in the lives of women who 'prostitute'. This would simply feed the representation of the prostitute as 'other' to us 'good-girls', as somehow existing so that we can define ourselves as 'better' than they. Many women in 'mainstream' society experience and have experienced abuse by powerful men and sometimes by women in their lives, so too do they experience economic neediness, debts, homelessness. The additional factor is the *opportunity* to try prostitution. The influence of the social/environmental context can be the deciding factor.

Bruno Bettelheim made a very important point in his account and analysis of the consequences of living under extreme fear and terror. The external symptoms of neurosis and psychotic breakdown (rooted in the inner difficulties of man) reflect back the nature of society, showing up 'what ails all of us in some measure at present, and warns us of things to come...they can also inform us about which forces an age looks to for solving the difficulties it is failing to master' (1991: 52). The point I am making here is that we need to address psychic processes *and* social processes in trying to understand juvenile prostitution and in trying to find ways of caring for, respecting and supporting the needs of young people both in and out of care. I am talking here about our most vulnerable children and young people – all the evidence points to the fact that our society is failing them.

The usefulness of trying to better understand psychic processes is what these processes reveal about the social conditions; and, the reverse, the usefulness of trying to better understand social processes is what they reveal about psychic conditions and processes. In accessing the interrelation between psychic and social processes through life-stories, we can develop better analysis and understand the very social worlds we must all of us aim to change. Hence the vital importance placed in this text upon the interrelationship between what Zygmunt Bauman calls autonomous individuality and collective responsibility.

> To put it in a nutshell: the chance of counteracting the present pressures towards draining intimate and public life from ethical motives and moral evaluations depends at the same time on more autonomy for *individual* moral selves and more vigorous sharing of *collective* responsibilities. (Bauman 1995: 286)

The obvious contradictions between the two are for Bauman illusory, and acceptance of the illusion is merely part of the problem, 'a product of tendencies which need to be rectified' (1995: 286).

Clearly these young people have been denied possibilities for developing autonomous individuality and have also been let down, failed, by the lack of collective responsibility for them on the part of parents, the state *in loco parentis* and the very communities they live both within and outside of as 'outlaws'. How can feminist interpretive research as feminist praxis address this?[9]

Feminizing theory

Feminist critical theory is, for me, about:

- understanding and analysing lived relations embedded in sexual and social inequalities;
- exploring the ways in which socio-economic structures mediate action/practice/feelings;

- exploring the relationships between the personal/experiential and the materiality of lived relations;
- working towards renewed ways of 'being', thinking and articulating lived relations through collaborative work, through action research (a politics of feeling).

Work such as this is inspired by feminist critiques, by ways of seeing and knowing, and is directly related to the urgent need to develop interventionary strategies based upon collective responsibility. We need to focus our attention on the gendered social organization of the sex industry, structures of male domination, the social organization of desire and male violence as well as on the men who want 'sex' with children and young people (see Ennew 1986). Feminist critical theory and interpretive ethnography can together renew methodologies for social research and reconstitute social theory.

I have found that through life-story work with young people we can explore the ways in which socio-economic structures mediate cultural practices within an understanding of the necessary inter-relationship of psychic structures and processes and social structures and processes. Socio-economic structures do not mediate cultural practices in a deterministic way; the relationships are much more complex and reciprocal. Our experiences of the social world are marked by plurality, fragmentation, diversity and difference but also have unifying tendencies. The standpoints of young people must be acknowledged and listened to, and advocacy networks must be developed to operationalize their voices.

Questions of methodology are of central importance here. Methodologies underpin choices, decisions, why we conduct certain research and, of course, the research tools we use. In this instance, ethnographic, qualitative research helps to develop critical hermeneutic analysis and critical understanding. A key issue for me is the relationship between the general and the particular, the minute aspects of everyday lived experience, the relationship between experience personally felt and the wider cultural/social structures, processes and practices. Emotion and feeling, care and concern involved in doing action research with women and young people are experienced in tension with reason, rationality and the material/practical aspects of lived experience. Frigga Haug's approach is a useful one:

> In our view, the form that individual life-processes take can neither be predicated, nor can it be deduced from economic laws; it is itself a question for empirical investigation....The number of possibilities for action open to us is radically limited. We live according to a whole series of imperatives: social pressures, natural limitations, the imperative of economic survival, the given conditions of history and culture. (Haug 1987: 42–3)

Feminist critical theory is *not* about writing women in or adding women on but about reconstituting social theory via feminist thought, feminist analysis of the social worlds – social knowledge. Critical social theory helps us to understand and explain the social worlds in which and through which we live and, in turn, we help to reproduce. Recovering and re-telling women's and young people's subjectivities, lives and experiences is central to better understand our social worlds with a view to transforming these worlds. Such work reveals women and young people's resistances, strengths, humour and knowledge, as well as the reflexive understanding of the legitimation and rationalization of male power.[10]

Women and young people's voices speak for themselves. Critical feminist theory can take up these multiple voices to describe, illuminate and challenge:

- the conditions of and for women and young people in contemporary society;
- relations between genders;
- relationships between the particular and the general, between personal experience and wider society, between sexuality and desire;
- indeed, the structural, cultural and political contexts in which and through which we develop social knowledge.

Putting young people's voices in the centre and listening to them is vital. Ethical and moral considerations are also important.

Ethical/moral considerations: autonomous individuality and collective responsibility

> Just as there can be no understanding which is not situated in some historical context, so there can be no 'moral standpoint' which would not be dependent upon a shared ethos, be it that of the modern state. (Benhabib 1992: 25)

The sharing of collective responsibilities is a moral imperative in current times. Bauman tells us that moral life is a life of continuous uncertainty and that to live a moral life one needs strength and resilience to engage in jointcollective responsibilities:

> To be responsible does not mean following the rules; it may often require one to disregard the rules or act in a way that rules do not warrant. Only such responsibility makes the citizen into that basis on which a human community resourceful and thoughtful enough to cope with the present challenges can be conceivably built. (Bauman 1995: 287)

For both Benhabib and Bauman there exists a critical tension (mediation) between autonomous individuality and the sharing of collective responsibilities. Benhabib outlines Arendt's interpretation of Kant's theory of reflective judgement, seeing in it a model for inter-subjective validity where judgements have to be submitted to the public realm. Judgement involves certain narrative and interpretive skills which together constitute the capacity for an 'enlarged mentality'.

> Enlarged mentality involves and is in part the effect of representing to oneself the multiplicity of viewpoints, the variety and perspectives, the layers of meaning which constitute a situation. This representational capacity is crucial for the kind of sensitivity to particulars which most agree is central for good and perspicacious judgement. (Benhabib 1992: 53–4)

For Benhabib, macro-institutions of polity, politics, administration and the market, on the one hand, and culture, on the other, interpretations of the good life, projections of happiness and fulfilment, socialization patterns 'form the larger ethical context of which morality is always but an aspect' (1992: 55).

In locating narrative and discourse in the centre of her feminist ethics of care, Benhabib is committed to the 'spontaneity, imagination, participation and empowerment that Arendt saw to be the mark of authentic politics whenever and wherever it occurred' (1992: 95). Here:

> 'to think from the standpoint of everyone else' entails sharing a public culture such that everyone else can articulate indeed what they think and what their perspectives are. The cultivation of one's moral imagination flourishes in such a culture in which the self-centred perspective of the individual is constantly challenged by the multiplicity and diversity of perspectives that constitute public life. (1992: 141)

There is, therefore, 'a fundamental link between a civic culture of public participation and the moral quality of enlarged thought' (1992: 140). In looking towards a public culture of shared collective responsibilities, this text is first of all committed to creating the spaces for the voices of people who are marginalized and 'other' in our society, but also urges that we listen to their voices and act upon them, *with* them. The central problem we face at the turn of the century is fragmented communities and loss of cohesion. Moreover, increased emphasis upon consuming/consumption for its own sake, as a pastime, as a leisure pursuit, for the 'self', to enhance the 'self' to make one feel 'good' about 'the self'. The loss of collective action is reinforced by certain agencies of social control; for example, the actions of the police and legal system in upholding the latest Criminal Justice Act effectively prevent collectives and communities from travelling our roads and gathering in our rural spaces (see Hetherington 1996).

Seventeen years of Conservative government has left in its wake decimated communities that were once thriving localities based around employment in the mining, fishing, shipbuilding and steel industries. This has created in its wake a generation of people who have never known what it is like to be fully employed, to share in the world of shopping in malls, to buy *new* consumer goods and *new* clothing, to have credit and credit cards, to have a share in consuming and consumption for its own sake.

In this chapter the voices, the narratives of our most vulnerable children and young people have been presented. They illuminate most clearly the lack of 'care' in our local authority residential care institutions, in social institutions and in structures funded by the state to deal with the very people whom Steve Box (1983) described as being perceived by the state as either 'social junk' or 'social dynamite'. The narratives illuminate most clearly the endemic nature of male violence against women, children and young people. They also illuminate the 'phenomenal' ways in which these young people triumph over diversity, surviving sometimes in the most horrendous conditions with enough semblance of 'self' and 'selfhood', to 'make out', to carry on living 'reasonable' lives. They are also a very strong indictment against the depthless consuming culture that Galbraith (1992) labelled the 'culture of contentment'.

For Frigga Haug, taking a Foucauldian analysis, child sexual abuse is 'intimately mixed up with the social construction of the family, with sexuality, with the entire experience of childhood, and with the acceptable limits of public jurisdiction' (1995: 1). On the one hand, the family's role is to 'anchor sexuality and provide support'; on the other, 'the family is the most active site of sexuality, where sex is constantly being solicited and refused, where it is an object of obsession and attraction, a dreadful secret and an indispensable pivot' (1995: 2). The ways in which silence is forced upon the child and the mother has to be revealed and changed. For Haug, it is urgent 'that women locate their own public space with its own language; because calls for justice and new laws, the search for guilt, victims and "beasts" is not in itself a policy of liberation' (1995: 2). The 'confession', revealing, talking, narrating, does, of course, bring aspects of surveillance into the lives of these children, young people and women, but it is also the 'necessary liberatory step in the process of making public the *truth* of the family' (1995: 3), the 'truths' of our social world, social institutions, schools, children's homes. For Haug, 'we need to find/develop new ways for girls to go through adolescence' (1995: 3). We also need to find/develop new ways for our boys to go through adolescence. Our young people are our future. Haug maintains that the starting point is the individual, but it is only collectives that are able to break through structures of power. In developing cultures of collective responsibility we need gendered relationships that are based upon intersubjective mutual recognition and acknowledgement of the dialectical tension between mimesis and constructive rationality, between psychic and social processes and structures, between subject and object, between autonomy and dependency, rather than gender polarities and binary oppositions.

Summary

In summary, we know a certain amount about young people's needs and experiences and a limited amount about their involvement in prostitution through media reports and published research located within the sociology of deviance and what has come to be called criminology. What we do need to explore in greater depth than can be found in the literature is: the through-care experience of young people in care; the needs of young people in care contextualized within wider knowledge about their pre-care experiences, their experiences of care and their experiences of leaving care; how their lived experiences, including homelessness and psychic and social alienation, impact upon doing prostitution; the structure, management and organization of care. We can reach a better understanding of the needs of young people and their experiences of the institutions they live in and through from their narratives and by listening to them.

Jill Jesson (1993) pointed out that sexual behaviour and sexuality are topical issues of concern for child-care social workers. Sexuality and sexual behaviour and sexual violence are central to the experiences and needs of young people in care. What exactly are the needs of young people in care related to sexuality, sexual identities and sexual practices? What are young people saying and how might these be related to action or policy change regarding being in care and being in care and doing prostitution?

The relationship between young people, prostitution and residential care has to be explored within the context of: the experiences and problems that bring young people into the care of the local authority, usually problems within the 'family'; the residential care experience itself and the social stigma, margin-alization, 'otherness' relating to being in care; the financial resources allocated, the training and education of social workers and carers − indeed the overall 'management' of 'care'; the benefit system for young people and education, employment and training opportunities. There is little point in blaming social services or the system of residential local authority care for young people's involvement or drift into prostitution. What social services, and we, ought to be doing in policy terms is ensuring that the system of residential care is adequately funded, staffed and resourced to meet the needs of needy children and young people who are sometimes very damaged by their pre-care and through-care life experiences. We need, first of all, to ensure that these young people are really cared for. Young people should be represented in this process. Their voices should be central to any working party or forum on these matters.

Attempting to change state policy in line with feministhumanistic object-ives entails a thorough analysis and critique of state policy. Clauss Offe (1984) describes the state as the 'institutional form of political power', underpinned in capitalist societies by the myth of 'democratic and representative govern-ment'. As I have argued elsewhere (O'Neill 1994), a feminist analysis of prostitution must be concerned to challenge, resist and change the policies and practices of a 'masculinist state' (and the assumptions and ideologies on which they are based) tied to the capital accumulation process, on the one hand, and underpinned by the 'myth of democratic legitimation', on the other. This involves revealing and highlighting the 'between men' culture and seeking, making, new ways to live as women, through for example

Irigaray's notion of sexed rights (1993). This also involves working towards, developing, making, conditions in which and through which our children and young people can develop autonomous individuality and a commitment to collective responsibility.

Mark Sobey's examination of prostitution in one local authority (1994) stressed the need to develop more effective, coordinated responses to child and juvenile prostitution that would include Child Protection Procedures as well as address the involvement of young people, particularly those with learning difficulties.[11] He suggests that:

- outreach workers from child-care establishments should be enabled to work with young people in the community;
- that there is a vital need to develop therapeutic responses for the individuals involved;
- that there should be better links between child protection workers and specialist workers;
- that staff need training around the issues of sexuality, race, gender and disability;
- that strategies should be developed to enable work with other agencies (*multi-agency work is not a panacea but it is most important given the emphasis here upon collective responsibilities*) [my emphasis];
- that there should be active discouragement of secure accommodation as a response to youth prostitution and that other responses should be explored.

Certainly a central need in working with young people involved in prostitution is *not* to criminalize them (see Lowman 1987: 99–116); intervention should be based upon child protection and not criminal procedures.

Research into male prostitution has also drawn links with care. Forty per cent of clients (all male) at the Streetwise Youth Centre in London over the 1992 period had run away from home for reasons such as ill-treatment, sexual abuse or family conflicts, and over half had truanted and left school with no qualifications. A majority had spent substantial periods in local authority care, both residential institutions and foster homes.

Routes into prostitution are varied: a combination of psychic and social alienation, marked by experiences of child sexual abuse and economic need in an economic climate of recession, inadequate benefits, unemployment and increasing debt. Young people drift in through association with friends already working. An option not thought of before presents itself and a decision to try prostitution is made. Young men and young women drift into prostitution through peer association and peer pressure. Coercion from pimps is not uncommon. Prostitution in order to make the money to support one's own or another's drug habit is not uncommon.

Advocacy, and further research based upon young peoples' needs and citizenship rights are vital. Listening to their experiences, their voices, shows that a system of planned interventions based upon care, concern and respect is desperately needed. Planned interventions need to be developed which focus upon: sexuality; sexual identity; racial, sexual and social identity; education; welfare; health needs; personal safety; counselling and therapeutic needs; the whole spectrum of incivilities faced by young children and young people in care, from intimidation, harassment and lack of care to physical, sexual and emotional violence; leaving care and support in the community; continuity of care; relationships with courts, police and remand institutions; and secure accommodation.

The emotional strain of life-history work with marginalized, criminalized and often abused and damaged women and young women has had an impact upon me. The emotional labour that has gone into this work with and for women and young people has been a central learning experience. It has been essential to talk some of the painful experiences through with trusted colleagues working in similar areas. I have experienced difficulties in leaving my own children in the care of others. Imagining that the very men I trust might actually be 'other', might actually be secretly like 'those' men, the men who pay for sex with children and young people, or who rape and abuse and violate young people and children; imagining that the men I see in public spaces (ice rink, roller-skating rink, swimming-baths) who are in the vicinity of my children could be potential abusers – I am more watchful, more careful in monitoring their activities than I was before I began my research. This is a simplistic but understandable response which highlights 'stranger danger' but does nothing to draw attention to the trusted men in their lives. The lives of my children have not been touched by abuse.

The delicate balancing act of providing 'good enough' role models, mutual respect, safety and independence in their social and psychological development, and the love and care that create stable, strong individuals with a strong sense of community concern and responsibility is a most difficult task. Of course, it is one of the most important tasks there is and, in the 'between men' culture, it is particularly important when our children happen to be boys.

The importance of the interrelationship between the development of social knowledge as social critique, inspired by feminist social theory, informed by lived experience told through life-stories that have a 'primary role in the household of humanity' (W. Benjamin 1992: 83–107), centres upon the development of work linking feminist critical theory, interpretive research and practice/praxis. Such links are of vital importance to social transformation and a politics of feeling, through what Jessica Benjamin (1993) defines as 'mutual recognition' and Fals Borda (1983) defines as 'participatory action research' *with* women, young people and policy makers. Conducting ethnographic work with young people in prostitution can help us to understand their experiences and lives through the mimetic faculty. Re-presenting mimetic experience through critical reflection can help to illuminate the necessary mediation of autonomous individuality and collective responsibility involved in feminist praxis.

Part III
Feminist Postmodernisms and Ethnographies of Difference: Between Modernity and Postmodernity

Part III explores the social organization of desire and the aestheticization of the whore in contemporary society, focusing upon our sign worlds of sexuality – on historical and fictive texts as well as on women's narratives of 'self' and men talking about why they visit 'prostitutes'. The aim is to further problematize the categories of 'prostitute' and prostitution.

Our social worlds are made up of structures of gender domination embedded in psychic and social practices, structures and processes. Postmodern interpretive ethnographies, working in participatory ways across disciplines and genres – for example across community arts, photography or performance art – can illuminate and challenge ideological structures and effects through 'feeling forms'. 'Feeling forms' can incite us to feel and engage with the affects, sentiments and experiences of marginalized peoples and motivate us to act, thus giving rise to *a politics of feeling*. In this part, historical and fictive texts are explored to better understand the self-sustaining discourses and images that re-present the 'prostitute' and are part of the re-presentation of women and men more generally in reflexive modernity/ postmodernity. Furthermore, in the shifts and transformations taking place within the context of what is defined as postmodernity, we can see a freeing up of some of these discourses and images,[1] which leads to greater hybridity in the re-presentation of research findings. Hybridity involves the complex intersections of discourses and genres (see Denzin 1997; Trinh 1989, 1991) as exemplified in the re-presentation of ethnographic data in visual, artistic form.

Renewed methodologies provide alternative, dialogic routes to understanding women's lives, meanings and actions by triangulating analysis of fictive texts, ethnographic material and artistic re-presentations of ethnographic material, such as performance art and photography. The concepts of mimesis (drawing upon Walter Benjamin and Adorno) and micrology (Adorno 1966) are pivotal to this critical hermeneutic approach in participation with women and young people. A key outcome of participatory action research is feminist praxis as purposeful knowledge, alongside hybrid texts that can be made available to a wider audience beyond academic communities, thus helping to 'neutralize negative alienation' (Fals Borda 1983: 97) and foster processes of cultural citizenship and inclusion with and for marginalized peoples.

5
Imagining Women: Prostitution, the Aestheticization of the Whore and the Social Organization of Desire

> As Hannah Arendt has emphasised, from the time of our birth we are immersed in 'a web of narratives' of which we are both the author and the object.
>
> Benhabib 1992: 198

In this chapter I will show, through art, literature and women's narratives, that the status and representation of 'prostitutes' are maintained through and by a set of self-sustaining discourses and images which are part of the representation of women and, more generally, men in postmodernity. The chapter is organized around two major themes (and sections) that together address the problematic concept and category of 'the prostitute' in our sign worlds, in socio-cultural texts. First, the representation of prostitutes in cultural texts from tradition to postmodernity, which includes a focus upon the prostitute as body object, or the *Trauerspiel* (tragedy) of the 'prostitute-body'. Within this section I will explore certain historical texts; the regulation of female bodies and female sexuality; the notion of submissive female bodies; the prostitute as body-object and the prostitute as subject-object. In the second section I will focus upon the importance of triangulating cultural/fictive texts and interpretive ethnography through renewed methodologies to explore the social organization of desire and to re-present the complexity of women's lives in postmodern times. 'Embodiment and ethnography in reflexive modern/postmodern times' will explore prostitution as (postmodern) performance and the global sex industry as a postmodern leisure phenomenon.

Gendered bodies/cultural texts: from tradition to postmodernity

Cultural texts as 'feeling forms' represent dominant cultural attitudes, values and feelings towards 'prostitutes' and can be read not only to 'unmask the images, the *sign* of women [as prostitute], to see how the meanings that underlie the codes function' (Hirschman and Stern 1994: 576), but also in order to read transgressive possibilities for resistance and pleasure in certain moments, fragments, spaces. Highlighting transgressive possibilities can serve to resist and challenge sexual and social inequalities.[1]

Manet's *Olympia* raised a storm when it was first exhibited in 1865. Here the female form was not contextualized in the classical tradition, where the sexual element is introduced into the picture in disguised form (Witkin 1995: 100). *Olympia* disrupted conventional discourses on art, style and the treatment of women in a society that accepted and took for granted what Clark calls 'le discours prostitutionnel'. The characterization of the courtesan in *Olympia* 'could not be disentangled from the specification of Woman in general in the 1860s it was some disturbance in the normal relations between prostitution and femininity' (Clark 1980: 261).

The central problem with Manet's *Olympia* was the fact that *Olympia* transgressed the normal relations between prostitution and femininity. There was no framework of meaning at the time to accommodate this transgression. Olympia in her nakedness failed to support the representation

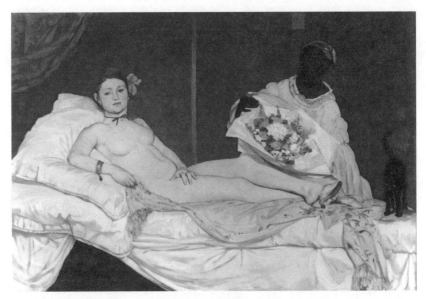

Figure 7   Edouard Manet, *Olympia*, 1864, oil on canvas. Musée d'Orsay, Paris/photo © RMN

of the whore as lower class/underclass, polluted, decadent and decaying, as represented, for example, in Vermeer's *The Procuress*, within 'an atmosphere of lechery, alcohol, and good cheer' (Witkin 1995: 101). *Olympia* violated:

> the tradition of the nude in Western art. . . . In the classical tradition, nudity is intended, according to Clark, to be sexually alluring to the male gaze. . . . The body does not bear the marks of desire upon it but the sexual motive was usually present in such pictures in all extraneous figures – cupids holding up mirrors, fishtails and the like. (Witkin 1995: 100)

Olympia represented an 'odd co-existence of decorum and disgrace . . . neither set of qualities established its dominance over the other – which was the difficulty of the picture in 1865' (Clark 1980: 267). For Witkin, the 'transition of the nude from the kind of generalized (ideologically) "purified" type of depiction to the threateningly particular and sexually undisguised figure of Manet's painting is in line with the whole general tendency towards "naturalism" which was as characteristic of literature as it was of art' (1995: 100).

Art can be read as social history and particular artworks can be read as ciphers of the general experience, as the sedimented 'stuff' of society (Wolff 1981, 1983, 1995).[2] Manet's *Olympia*, via 'mimesis' (Adorno 1984), pointed to a way of perceiving, saying and showing that highlights the double standards in the way women were/are seen and treated, and which also spoke in a genuine way about the relationship between the body, sex and society. Art (cultural texts) as a social product can speak about society, cultural frameworks of meaning and meaning-giving practices, and about experience.

In order to examine prostitution, the social organization of desire and, of course, the aestheticization of the whore, it is useful, in the first instance, to look at cultural texts that symbolically represent the harlot, the whore, the prostitute, through time – from tradition to postmodernity.

Historical texts

Nicki Roberts (1992) states that sacred prostitution was a tradition of sexual ritual that has persisted since the Stone Age and has become a central part of religious worship in the earliest civilizations. Temple prostitutes were both sacred women and prostitutes. The first known representation of the prostitute is a Babylonian statue of a temple prostitute which is mentioned in the *Epic of Gilgamesh*, 1700 BC, one of the earliest recorded poems and an epic poem (Kishtainy 1982; Roberts 1992; *Gilgamesh and Enkidu* 1995). Tablets containing parts of the epic were found by Austen Henry Layard in the first half of the nineteenth century.

The poem tells of a temple harlot who was sent to tame Enkidu, a wild man who is described as 'strong as a star' and was living with the beasts. Enkidu had been created by Aruru, the goddess of creation, as an equal on earth for King Gilgamesh. Enkidu 'ate grass in the hills with the gazelle and lurked with the wild beasts at the water holes; he had joy at the water with herds of wild game' (1995: 4). Enkidu would fill in the trappers' pits and help the beasts to escape. In response the trappers went to the King Gilgamesh and asked for a harlot so that her power could overpower the wild man. 'When next he comes down to drink at the wells she will be there, stripped naked; and when he sees her beckoning he will embrace her, and then the wild beasts will reject him' (1995: 5–6). The harlot 'made herself naked and welcomed his eagerness; as he lay on her murmuring love she taught him the woman's art' (1995: 7). Then, 'when the gazelle saw him, they bolted away; when the wild creatures saw him they fled. . . . Enkidu was grown weak for wisdom was in him, and the thoughts of a man were in his heart' (1995: 7).

Nicki Roberts states that the harlot lavished upon him 'a combination of mother-love, tenderness, comfort, mystical enlightenment and sex' (Roberts 1992: 5). 'The "prostitute compassionate" then led him away "like a mother" to take up a new, harmonized life in the city' (Roberts 1992: 5). She led him to the city and taught him the ways of civilization. However, for Enkidu, the price of civilization was, eventually, disease. Enkidu cursed the harlot from his deathbed. His ambivalence towards her is marked by a great curse:

> I will promise you a destiny to all eternity. My curse shall come on you soon and sudden. You shall be without a roof for your commerce, for you shall not keep house with other girls in the tavern, but do your business in places fouled by the vomit of the drunkard. Your hire will be potter's earth, your thievings will be flung into the hovel, you will sit at the cross-roads in the dust of the potter's quarter, you will make your bed on the dunghill at night, and by day take your stand in the wall's shadow. Brambles and thorns will tear your feet, the drunk and the dry will strike your cheek and your mouth will ache. (*Gilgamesh and Enkidu* 1995: 14)

Shamash the wise god of the city disapproved of the curse for the woman and tells Enkidu that she gave him much to be thankful for. Enkidu then added the following:

> Woman, I promise you another destiny. The mouth which cursed you shall bless you! Kings, princes and nobles shall adore you. On your account a man though twelve miles off will clap his hand to his thigh and his hair will twitch. For you he will undo his belt and open his treasure and you shall have your desire; lapis lazuli, gold and carnelian from the heap in the treasury. A ring for your hand and a robe shall be yours. The priest will lead you into the presence of the gods. On your account a wife, a mother of seven was forsaken. (1995: 48)

On the one hand, the prostitute and prostitution symbolize dirt, decay, corruption. The curse is directed at the organic body of the prostitute: she will sleep on a dunghill, have thorns and brambles pierce her feet, she will suffer physical violence, live and work in poverty. On the other hand, she is blessed and adored. For Khalid Kishtainy (1982) she is an 'instrument of civilisation'. It is woman, the prostitute, who leads humanity out of rural/animal experience and into culture and civilization. To be sure, as far as our understanding of recorded history shows, prostitution has been an accepted part of social organization, and most certainly of social organization based to varying degrees upon private property.[3]

For Henriques (1962) whores achieved a certain level of autonomy which led to education and status in Ancient Greek society: 'In the early days of the church prostitution was already a recognised profession. Commercial activity was taxed by the emperors, and the vectigal yielded a handsome return to the imperial treasury' (1962: 26).

Whores became bad-girls with the growth of Christianity and later of Protestantism, contrasting the ideal of good wife and mother with bad-girl and sinner (Mazo-Karras 1989; Roberts 1992, Kishtainy 1982). Ruth Mazo-Karras writes: 'Sinful men, theologians held, would corrupt respectable women – even their own wives – or turn to sodomy if they did not have the prostitute as a sexual outlet' (quoting Augustine, 'De Ordine' in *Patrologiae Cursus Completus Series Latina*). She continues: 'Remove prostitutes from human affairs and you will destroy everything with lust' (1989: 399). In medieval England, prostitution was one of a limited range of options to women not able to marry for lack of dowries, because of sex ratios, because too few men were in a position to marry, and because of limited opportunities in the labour market due to a rise in population following a period of labour shortage after the Black Death of 1348. The medieval brothel was recognized as a necessary evil, contextualized against 'tolerated and institutionalized' brothels elsewhere in Europe at this time. Thus brothels were licensed or municipally owned. The whore stigma has thus operated for centuries. In medieval society prostitution was necessary because 'of men's natural, if sinful, sex drive' but 'this did not lead to respect for the prostitute herself. The church considered her one of the worst sinners: lust was considered the woman's sin *par excellence* and the prostitute epitomised it' (Mazo-Karras 1989: 400). Furthermore, Mazo-Karras writes that women's sexual immorality, love of ornament and shrewishness were common themes of medieval sermons, and in the iconography of sin, lust is embodied/represented as a woman.

More contemporary historical analysis points to relationships between whores, the state, working-class communities and the regulation of the body, knowledge of the role and position of women in society, and the fact that prostitution has always been 'work' that women can engage in to make a living (Walkowitz 1980; Finnegan 1979).

Jane Rendall focuses upon the Burlington Arcades in the West End of London and explores women's experiences of the city through their roles as shoppers and shopgirls: 'As wives, mothers, virgins and prostitutes, women are the objects of physical and metaphorical exchange among men' (1997: 35). Rendall tells us that the millinery shops in particular were sites where prostitutes (shoppers) could pick up rich clients and use the upstairs quarters; indeed the upstairs quarters, separated from the shops by an outdoor staircase, were used part-time by the shopgirls themselves. Furthermore, given women's limited access to public spaces in the nineteenth century, 'the ways in which women occupied the arcades were conflated with the image of the prostitute' (1997: 36). Thus, women are displayed and consumed as visual and sexual commodities (1997: 36).

The history of prostitution is framed by attempts to repress and make morally reprehensible the women involved in prostitution, while aestheticizing the desires and fantasies symbolically associated with the whore, the prostitute, the fallen woman (Corbin 1990; Stallybrass and White 1986). The history of prostitution is also tied to the history and social organization of sexuality, cathexis and the social organization of desire; gender relations; masculinity and property relations; capitalist exchange relations which increasingly commodify everything, even love (see Fromm 1967; Bertillson 1986; Jackson 1993; Theweleit 1994; Giddens 1992; Connell 1987).

Prostitution is accepted by bourgeois society (it is not illegal), but the prostitute, the whore, is not accepted; she is 'other' perceived as immoral, a danger, a threat to 'normal' femininity and, as a consequence, suffers social exclusion, marginalization and 'whore stigma'. The following two excerpts represent the contradiction revealed from the time of the epic of Gilgamesh: the body-object of the prostitute is, on the one hand, despised; on the other hand, what she *represents* is adored.

> It may be a perverse taste, but I love prostitution, for itself, independently of what is beneath. I've never been able to see one of those women in *décolleté* pass by under the gaslights, in the rain, without feeling palpitations, just as monks' robes with their knotted girdles arouse my spirit in some ascetic and deep corner. There is, in this idea of prostitution, a point of intersection so complex – lust, bitterness, the void of human relations, the frenzy of muscles and the sound of gold – that looking deeply into it makes you dizzy; and you learn so many things! And you are so sad! And you dream so well of love! Ah, writers of elegies, it is not on the ruins that you should go to lean your elbows but on the breasts of these gay women! Yes, something is lacking in a man who has never awoken in a nameless bed, who has not seen asleep on his pillow a head that he will not see again, and who, leaving at sunrise, has not passed bridges with the longing to throw himself in the water, since life seemed to be rising up in belches from the depths of his heart to his head. If it were only for the shameless dress, the temptation of the chimera, the unknown, the *caractère maudit*, the ancient poetry of corruption and venality! . . . I make only one reproach to prostitution: that it is a myth. The kept woman has invaded vice just as the journalist has invaded poetry: we are drowning in halftones. The courtesan does not exist any more than the saint; there are *soupesses* and *lorettes*, who are even more fetid than the *grisette*. (Gustave Flaubert, from Letter to Louise Colet, 1853, cited in John 1994: 64–5)

> Prostitutes are as inevitable in a metropolis as sewers, cesspits and rubbish tips; the civil authority should treat the one as it does the other – its duty is to supervise them, to reduce the dangers inherent in them as far as possible, and to this end to hide them and relegate them to the darkest corners; in short, render their presence as inconspicuous as possible. (Alexandre Parent-Duchâtelet, from *Prostitution in the City of Paris, 1836*, cited in John 1994: 44–8)

One response to the diseased/adored, menace/remedy dichotomy of the 'prostitute' is the formal and/or informal regulation of prostitution.

The regulation of female bodies and female sexuality

The problem of prostitution (usually understood by the state, agencies of the state and in the public imagination as the problem of women) is often dealt with by regulating women working as prostitutes, by regulating and controlling women's sexuality, women's bodies, with particular regard to the sexual health of their bodies (C. Smart 1992). Throughout recorded history we find examples of this: Victorian Lock Hospitals (Walkowitz 1980); the regulation of medieval brothels (Mazo-Karras 1989); dress codes that distinguished prostitutes from 'respectable women' (Roberts 1992; Tseëlon 1995); the militarization of the regulation of women and women's bodies around the US airbases in the Philippines and Korea (Sturdevant and Stoltzfus 1992); the regulation of women in zones of toleration in Germany and the Netherlands (Drobler 1991); the informal regulation of saunas/parlours by the police in England; the suggestion by academics and policy makers for 'zones of tolerance' and the formal regulation of clubs and bars by the police in Spain, Germany and the Netherlands. A universality develops as a consequence of masculine discourse and topography – which is about regulating the bodies of women.[4]

Alain Corbin's analysis (1990) of commercial sex in nineteenth-century France describes how the interrelated discourses of municipal authorities, hygienists, the police and the judiciary combined to organize the regulation of prostitution around three major issues: the need to protect public morality; the need to protect male prosperity; and, finally, the need to protect the nation's health. The prostitute was perceived as an active agent for the transmission of disease. For Corbin, these three major issues are rooted in five key images of the prostitute:

- the prostitute as the *putain* 'whose body smells bad' (Corbin 1990: 210);
- the prostitute as the safety valve which 'enables the social body to excrete the excess of seminal fluid that causes her stench and rots her' (1990: 211);
- the prostitute as decay, symbolically associated with the corpse, with death;
- the prostitute as disease, symbolically associated with syphilis;
- the prostitute as submissive female body 'bound to the instinctive physical needs of upper class males' (1990: 213).

For Corbin, these five key images reinforce the ambiguous status of the female body, the lower-class, submissive body of the prostitute, 'at once menace and remedy, agent of putrefication and drain...at the beck and call of the bourgeois body' (1990: 212–13).

Corbin goes on to illustrate how these discourses led to a series of principles that structured the regulation of prostitution: the principle of tolerance; the principle of containment; the principle of surveillance. Contain and conceal, but keep under continual surveillance: 'The first task of regulation is to bring the prostitute out of the foul darkness and remove her from the clandestine swarming of vice, in order to drive her back into an enclosed space, under the purifying light of power' (1990: 215). With the rise of utilitarianism the image of the brothel as 'a seminal drain' (1990: 215) closely supervised by the police develops out of the image of the brothel symbolic of debauchery, perversion, disease and decay.

The relationship between submissive female bodies and the gratification of male 'needs' does need to be more thoroughly researched. This is an absence in Corbin's otherwise thorough and critical analysis of prostitution. In Corbin's work, the class relationship appears to subsume the gender/sex relationship. Here, the development of a rationalized modernity alongside the regulation of the bodies and dangerous sexualities of working-class/underclass women is a very good example of the operation of instrumental reason and the development of gendered structures of domination.

The prostitute, for Tseëlon, 'represents the spoiled identity that awaits the woman who fails to keep up the mask of virtue, the veil of beauty. Such a Fallen woman then simply lapses back and reaffirms her essential nature – that of ugliness, with a face of a prostitute' (1995: 95). In her analysis of the masque of femininity Tseëlon equates women's love of finery, of personal adornment, as sufficient grounds for her to be regarded as a prostitute within Christian doctrine and teachings (1995: 95). Indeed, popular culture continues to offer motifs that depict the fear and fascination of sexually independent women who are continually represented as potential whores, as 'others' to 'good women'.

Tseëlon asks: what 'is the secret of the power of the prostitute metaphor?' (1995: 96). One existing as the shadow of the other? The wife and the prostitute, the wife and the other woman? Her answer is that man's fear of independent sexuality led to him stigmatizing it as a characteristic of the prostitute 'no matter how high the woman's social rank' (1995: 99):

> the sexually independent woman embodied all of male fears of female sexuality. Demarcation rendered her mythical quality containable, and the institution of female prostitution allowed society to make money off their transgressions. (1995: 97)

Prosper Mérimée's novella *Carmen* provides 'one of the most persistent myths responding to archaic desires and fears about women marked as "other"', because Carmen 'embodies a fascinating sensuality and passion which is disruptive of masculine order, reason and control' (Bronfen 1992: 187). Such women must be either sacrificed – and so cultural norms are reconfirmed – or transformed into 'good-girls', which also serves the purpose of reconfirming cultural norms. Either way, through the death of such a woman or through her transformation into 'good', 'pure', 'submissive' woman, the social order which was momentarily lost is re-established and existing norms are preserved (Bronfen 1992; O'Neill 1998).

Theweleit's two volumes on *Male Phantasies* (1987, 1989) are invaluable to help us understand this phenomenon. Theweleit studied the letters and diaries of the *Freikorps* (private, volunteer armies hired by the Socialist Chancellor Ebert to bring order to post-First-World-War Germany between 1918 and 1923). The *Freikorps* are described as roaming and largely autonomous armies that fought and triumphed over the revolutionary working class. They also formed the core of Hitler's *Sturm-Abteilung* (Theweleit 1987: x). There are, for the *Freikorps* men, three kinds of women: absent women, their wives and fiancées; women appearing in their imagination – white and chaste, the white mother, the white nurse; and those who are 'class enemies', associated with angry mobs, red women, whores. For Theweleit, the relationship between proletarian women and prostitution is embedded within patriarchal men of the left and the right:

> We are confronted with a remarkable phenomenon here, namely, that in their comments about prostitutes and women in general 'reactionary' and 'revolutionary' men are able to find some common ground. . . . The men are bonded together by their deep seated fear and vengeance of women. . . . I don't want to make any categorical distinction between the types of men who are the subjects of this book and all other men. Our subjects are equivalent to the tip of the patriarchal iceberg, but it's what lies beneath the surface that really makes the water cold. (Theweleit 1987: 167–71)

Theweleit's detailed research found that for the men he studied women who don't conform to any of the 'good woman' images are automatically seen as prostitutes, as the vehicle of 'urges'. The women are represented as evil and out to castrate, and they are treated accordingly. Theweleit describes the violence meted out to women defined as 'class enemies' in the following forms: flares sent up women's skirts, singeing the buttocks and calves; repeatedly whipping the buttocks and back, to such an extert she will have to lie on her stomach for three weeks; being beaten into a bloody mass with a whip; trampling women with kicks to the abdomen and buttocks; a bullet in the mouth; being beaten with a rifle; being ripped apart with a hand grenade; being gored by bulls horns; a 'club' thrust in a 'hole' (see 1987: 90–204).

Pahlen says softly, his face a frozen mask: 'you'll have to beat this woman to death. But not with those clubs of yours. Use that little Cossack whip that's hanging from her wrist' (Theweleit 1987: 188). And later, 'as the cavalry riders of the squadron move off', they are treated to the following scene:

The last body they ride past seems to be that of a woman. But it's very hard to tell, since all that is left is a bloody mass, a lump of flesh that appears to have been completely lacerated with whips and is now lying within a circle of trampled, reddish slush. As Pahlen rides past it, he takes out his gold cigarette case, lights one up, and draws the smoke deep into his lungs. Then they break into a trot. (Theweleit 1987: 189)

Breaking through Freudian analysis, Theweleit utilizes Deleuze and Guattari (1983) and Reich (1983) to make sense of the men's narratives/actions at unconscious, pre-conscious and conscious levels. For Theweleit, these men:

> are forced to relinquish their life to a parasitic, linguistic onslaught, which seems to find 'pleasure' in the annihilation of reality. Reality is invaded and 'occupied' in that onslaught. . . . It is above all, the living moment of women that forces it immediately into a defensive-aggressive stance. It either screens itself against their existence (e.g., wives, 'white' mothers, and sisters), or destroys them (e.g., proletarian women, 'rifle women', and erotic sisters and mothers). The emotional force and sexual intensity emanating from women seems unbearable, incapable of being worked over by this language. (1987: 215)

Indeed '"woman" is a code word for the whole complex of nature, for anything at all having to do with "feelings" and the unconscious' (1987: 215). Their actions, perceptions 'divest social products, both people and things, of the life that has entered into them, especially in war. Their mode of production is the transformation of life into death, and dismantling of life' (1987: 216). On one side destruction, on the other 'creativity': 'the monumentalism of fascism would seem to be a safety mechanism against the bewildering multiplicity of living. The more lifeless, regimented, and monumental reality appears to be, the more secure the men feel. The danger is being-alive itself' (1987: 218).

Desiring production turns into murdering production! Theweleit also discusses the contradictions in Brecht's approach to prostitution. In his writings, female prostitutes are not treated in a negative way. However, in his diaries we find Brecht reinforcing images of 'defiled' and 'bad' women. Marianne Zoff was pregnant by Brecht and was being pursued by the industrialist Recht, who wanted to marry her. Marianne opts for Recht. The diary entry is as follows: 'Then I went out and dictated a letter, a note, telling her she was carrying my child and leaving me, though I had asked her to stay with me until the child was born' (30 April 1921).

> Marianne Zoff has taken leave of her senses. It began with her running round with men and ended with the corpse of a child in a doctor's bowl. That whore didn't deserve to have a baby – mine left her because her heart was impure!
> I dragged myself home, feeling as if I had been hit over the head. The vulgarity of it all! I could strangle that whore! It's the filthiest thing I've ever been through, but it's something I know so little about . . . I've never seen such a naked display of the prostitute's bag of tricks, of her romanticism. So that's

how a pregnant whore unloads! . . . Get away from me! Away! Away! Let her be used as a whore now! Throw her to that other man! Leave her for R. (echt!). (Theweleit 1987: 163–4).

For Theweleit, what surfaces here are very powerful emotions from 'previously hidden anti-prostitute syndrome, emotions that completely contradict the man's intellectual insights' (1987: 164).

Theweleit also documents the tendency within society to equate the working-class girl with the prostitute. Lower-class women, (Corbin's 'submissive female bodies') are extremely vulnerable to assaults on their bodies by 'gentlemen'.

Submissive female bodies?

In Maupassant's first published story, *Boule de suif*[5] (Suet dumpling; 1995), a group of travellers are fleeing occupied Rouen and travelling by coach to Dieppe during the outbreak of the Franco-Prussian war in 1870. The story documents lucidly both the 'moral shame' associated with prostitution and the ways in which discourses on 'bad-girls', 'prostitutes', help to maintain and sustain social order and social hierarchies. In the behaviour and sentiments, mores and affects displayed in the interactions between the travellers and the courtesan (Boule de Suif), social order is sustained through hierarchies of social class, gender and morality.

Boule de Suif illustrates the double standards in the ways women of 'easy virtue' were treated by mainstream society in the nineteenth century – resonant still in contemporary times – and the fickleness and cruelty displayed in our interactions with the 'others' against whom we define ourselves. At one and the same time, Maupassant's portrayal of Boule de Suif presents the courtesan as being little different from the 'good women' who are also travelling to Dieppe, indeed as 'better' than they in her generosity, both material and spiritual. Of course, one could also read into this presentation of Boule de Suif an example of the sacrificial woman, offering herself, her body, to purchase 'freedom' within the confines of patriarchal capitalism in which women and women's bodies are commodities. Moreover, through Maupassant's story, we access the psychic and social dilemmas faced by the courtesan and her travelling companions, as well as the author's critical insights into class hierarchies and social order and the role of the church, against all of whom the poor courtesan is pitted.

Ten people travel in a coach to Dieppe: Monsieur and Madame Loiseau, wholesale wine merchants and members of a 'superior social class'; Monsieur Carré-Lamadon and Madame Carré-Lamadon; the Comte and Comtesse Hubert de Bréville, who 'bore one of the oldest and noblest names in Normandy'; and 'two nuns telling their beads and muttering *paternosters* and *aves*'. Opposite the two nuns was Cornudet, 'the democrat, the terror of all respectable people', and a woman:

one of those who are generally known as of easy virtue, was famous for her premature corpulence, which had earned her the nickname of Boule de Suif, or Suet Dumpling ... her freshness was so attractive that she none the less remained desirable and much sought after.... As soon as she was recognized the respectable women began to whisper among themselves, and the words 'prostitute' and 'absolute scandal' were whispered loudly enough to make her raise her eyes. (Maupassant 1995: 10–14).

The story concerns the relaxation of the 'good' citizens, attitudes to Boule de Suif on the journey (when it emerges that no one but she has brought provisions, and in the freezing cold and on the lengthy journey they all welcome a share in the provisions she had packed to save on her expenses) and their subsequent betrayal of their 'good citizen' principles when faced with a German officer's refusal to let the party continue (following a stop at a Hôtel du Commerce after thirteen hours of travelling) unless Boule de Suif will sleep with him. On hearing this there 'was a chorus of reprobation against the despicable soldier, a storm of anger which brought them all together in a common feeling of resistance, as if each had been asked to share in the sacrifice demanded of her' (1995: 37).

This did not last long; the men joined the women in discussing their anger at 'the wretched woman' for keeping them all there and they began to develop a plan to persuade her to agree to the Prussian's demands. The first moves were made over lunch, stories of self-sacrifice, of women turning their bodies into battlefields: 'By the time they had finished, anybody might have thought that woman's only duty on earth was the perpetual sacrifice of her person, a continual surrender of her body to the lustful caprices of military men' (1995: 45).

Finally, the Comte talks to Boule de Suif. He emphasizes the service she would be doing for them and how grateful they would be to her. Boule de Suif sleeps with the Prussian officer. The following morning Boule de Suif appears late. The coach was ready, as was the rest of the party, but she was visibly 'ill at ease and shamefaced'. As she joined her companions they turned away as if they did not see her:

> The Comte took his wife's arm with a dignified air and drew her out of range of that impure contact.... Everybody seemed very busy to give her a wide berth, as if she were carrying some infection in her skirts. (1995: 53).

After three hours of travelling each couple and Cornudet (the democrat) unwrapped the provisions they had prepared for the journey. In the hurry and confusion Boule de Suif had had no time to prepare anything. Angry and indignant, she was ignored by the entire party. 'She felt overwhelmed by the contempt of these respectable boors who had first sacrificed her, and then cast her aside like an unclean object for which they had no further use' (1995: 56). She remembered her big basket full of 'good things which they had guzzled – her two chickens in aspic, her pâtés, her pears, her four bottles of claret.... She made a tremendous effort to control her feelings, bracing herself and swallowing her sobs like a little child' (1995: 56).

Maupassant's tale can be read as demonstrating very clearly that the prostitute is a submissive female body, at once both 'menace' and 'remedy', at the beck and call of the bourgeois body. Her profession is tolerated by the 'good' citizens via social/psychological distancing until it touches them too closely and they appear 'contaminated' by her 'body-object', yet they are relieved and released by her actions. Social order and propriety are regained in the coach as they travel on, the prostitute in their midst ignored as 'other', as despised 'other', as 'nothing' to them all – the good citizens of Rouen. Boule de Suif silently sobs in the darkness, the void and the darkness a metaphor for her psychic and social alienation. However, at one and the same time, Maupassant presents her, throughout the tale, as better than the good women of Rouen. But she must suffer for her role and her actions in releasing them from the hold of the Prussian officer.

Maupassant's mimetic tale represents the loss of order in the flight from occupied Rouen and the subsequent regaining of social order through the actions of Boule de Suif, through the use value of her body-object. However, by giving us insight into psychic and social processes through the feelings/emotions/actions of Boule de Suif and the narrative voice, we get a better understanding of the personal, lived experience as well as a better understanding of the interrelationship between social mores and the wider social order at this time. Through the characterization of Boule de Suif, we also get a sense of resistance to social order, of a humanism much larger than social class hierarchy and the 'order of things', even though ultimately she is reduced to a body-object and suffers both social and psychic alienation. Hers is an independent female sexuality which is both despised and feared. Indeed, one could argue: how could it be otherwise in a tale told by a socialist realist?

The prostitute as body-object, or the *Trauerspiel* (tragedy) of the 'prostitute-body': psychic and social alienation

The 'commodification' of the female body in and through prostitution serves to reinforce the stereotype of the prostitute as sex object in the public imagination. Stereotypes are concerned with ideologies of 'bad', 'fallen', 'victim', 'deserving victim', 'lazy', 'diseased', 'feckless', but are also concerned with specific images of the bodies of prostitutes: the prostitute as *body-object*. Bodies of female prostitutes are stereotypically represented by images of women in miniskirts, fish-net stockings, garish clothing, a red gash of a mouth, lots of make-up, high-heeled shoes or boots, skin-tight clothing – cheap and tacky – often labelled 'tarty'.

Bodies of female 'prostitutes' (body-objects) can be explored through the representation of 'prostitutes' in fictive texts – film and literature.[6] Discourses and representations of the prostitute or prostituted women help to sustain the ways in which meanings associated with the prostitute as 'other' are maintained in the public imagination. Such discourses are deeply embedded in the patriarchal imagination and are enacted through hegemonic heterosexuality.

One example to illustrate this is the image of the black prostitute. For black women, race adds one more dimension to stereotypical images of the bodies (body-objects) of prostitutes. Lola Young, using Franz Fanon's understanding of the ways in which psychic processes serve to foster and maintain white experience of black people around feelings of fear and revulsion, describes how, in the film *Mona Lisa*, fear and loathing of blackness, of foreigners, combine with the controlling and commodification of black bodies in the figure of Simone, the black prostitute: 'The figure of the black prostitute is – like the mammy – a de-sexualized black female inasmuch as she is not an object of desire but there to service or care for white people' (Young 1996: 169). We don't get to find out about Simone's background in the film. For Young, her:

> racial isolation also contributes to her diminution as a real threat to the 'natural' order of white male dominance. The anxiety stimulated in men by women's sexuality is especially acute when considered in terms of black and white sociosexual relations. Blackness in itself connotes 'difference': when the subject is also a woman, the difference is heightened. The danger signified by all sexualized women is displaced onto her 'Otherness': ... The narrative serves to pathologize Simone in four areas: as a black, as a lesbian, as a prostitute, as a woman. These four elements are drawn from the repertoire of fantasies which see the black/female/lesbian as the sign of anomalous sexuality and as a sexual and social threat which needs to be controlled (1996: 170).

For Young, there is an association between animal imagery, sexuality and blackness in the film and this is a recurring feature of eighteenth-century racism. 'Simone, the "tall thin black tart", describes Anderson, her former pimp, as "an animal born in a butcher's shop"' (1996: 171). Racist notions relating black males to animals, particularly gorillas, links 'the animalistic images of the black people engaging in oral rather than "normal" sex, and sexual deviancy and danger is embedded in the text and interwoven with the image of a voracious, cannibalistic black woman' (1996: 171).

Laurie Shrage describes how perceptions of racial purity, moral purity and sexual purity are somehow linked in our contemporary world. Moreover, North American and European males desire 'racialized sexual others as morally impure, and thus sexually available and sensual' (Shrage 1994: 150). The ethnic structure of the 'prostitute' work force is 'conditioned by racial fantasies white people have about themselves and others ... commercialized exchanges of sex may offer some people the opportunity to confront and sample these exoticized sexualities and eroticized races in semi-public sex districts' (1994: 150).

Interestingly, because prostitutes transgress the boundaries between public and private, marriage and market, paid and unpaid work, Anne McLintock feels they were experienced in Victorian England as 'white Negroes'. They inhabited 'anachronistic space, their "racial" atavism anatomically marked by regressive signs . . . exaggerated posteriors, unruly hair and other sundry "primitive" stigmata' (1995: 56). McLintock draws comparisons between domestic workers, female miners and working-class prostitutes in Victorian England. These three groups 'were stationed on the threshold between the white and black races, figured as having fallen farthest from the perfect type of the white male and sharing many atavistic features with "advanced" black men. Prostitutes – as the metropolitan analogue of African promiscuity – were marked as especially atavistic and regressive' (1995: 56).

Through social stigma, marginalization, criminalization and the effects of disempowering sexual relations with paying and non-paying partners who perceive and treat women as body-objects, both black and white women and young people experience psychic alienation. To 'be denied an autonomous choice of self, forbidden cultural expression, and condemned to the immanence of mere bodily being is to be cut off from the sorts of activities that define what it is to be human' (Bartky 1990: 31). This constitutes alienation, 'an estrangement from self, a splintering of human nature into a number of misbegotten parts' (1990: 31); or, using Fanon's term, this constitutes 'psychic alienation'. Black women working as prostitutes experience a further 'splintering'.

However, it is only partly true that the black prostitute is like the mammy, a de-sexualized being giving care and attention. All 'prostitutes' fulfil this role to varying degrees. The black 'prostitute' is in some ways further sexualized through the erotics of 'difference' and through clients' use of fantasies and ideologies around racist myths of black sexuality and sexual practices, which we found in the narratives in chapter 4.

Social stigma, marginalization and criminalization of black 'others' is exemplified in the case of Lana, who is working as a prostitute, and her partner, who is a black woman. Lana told me the police attitude to her was that she was 'some stupid little white girl who gives her money to her black lesbian pimp', whom the police also suspect of 'running' Lana's little sister. Following an incident in their local pub, Lana and her partner were held overnight in custody, yet the man who attacked them was 'free to go'. Lana had refused his attentions. He slapped her face and her partner intervened. Lana's partner and the man fought. The police were called and Lana's partner was charged with assault. Lana and her partner were locked in cells overnight and a doctor was called to look at Lana's arm. The man had brought a table down on top of her and she had put her arm up to protect herself. The doctor declared her arm was OK; it was broken. Lana felt the police treated her partner more harshly and with more contempt than they had herself (a prostitute) because her partner is black, a lesbian and, in their eyes, a pimp.

The marginalization and stigmatization of women working as prostitutes and the focus upon the prostitute as body-object can lead to psychic and social alienation. In our exploration of the fictive/cultural texts (above) the prostitute-body appears to be little more than a metaphor for the commodity body. For Christine Buci-Glucksmann (1994) the conversion of female bodies into articles of mass consumption took place in the mid-nineteenth century, in big-city prostitution – although, undoubtedly, the shifts began in previous centuries, and more markedly in the eighteenth century (Sennett 1992). This 'conversion' took:

> the form of a crisis of looking: new relations between the visible and the invisible, representation of the non-representable, and a series of practices and discourses engendered by it. More than anything else, the female body is the support of this 'archaeology of the look' to which Foucault referred. (Buci-Glucksmann 1994: 99)

The prostitute as subject-object, mass consumption, the male gaze and the 'crisis of looking'

For Walter Benjamin, it is the woman's body, the body of the prostitute, which provides the metaphor for the extremes of death and desire, life and lifelessness, 'petrified unrest'. The female body is a metaphor for the commodity body. The possibilities of serialized prostitution with large numbers of female bodies, understood as lifeless bodies offering themselves for pleasure, facilitates the image of the prostitute as 'second-degree allegory of the "commodity allegory"' (Buci-Glucksmann 1994: 100). In the act of prostitution, there is for Walter Benjamin an unconscious knowledge of man, an empathy with commodities. In the figure of the prostitute, the prostitute-body, beauty is petrified. The commodification of women's bodies is premised upon capitalist exchange relations, and the male gaze.

The male gaze is marked by desire, fear (Theweleit 1987, 1989; Whitehead and Dominelli 1994) and by difference embedded within gendered power relations. The getting and maintaining of power is part of this: for example, power 'over' and power 'to'. The male gaze, male pleasure in looking, is theorized by Laura Mulvay through the concept of scopophilia.

Scopophilia is the basic human need to look at others that causes feelings related to lust and fulfilment. For example, looking at film, separated from the rest of the world and engaged in the narrative, satisfies the urge to look at others and produces scopophilic pleasure. Related to scopophilic desire is 'narcissistic identification' – which cinema also satisfies. This is understood as the need to identify with others – in this case those on film. For Freud, this was related to the ego. This identification is directly related to the mirror-phase Lacan and Freud describe. The child comes to recognize herself or himself in the mirror and believes the child in the mirror to be more powerful, complete and beautiful. For Mulvay this same process occurs for the spectator in the cinema – identifying with the movie characters produces a feeling of enhancement, omnipotence. These two are connected in the cinematic experience. Looking is defined as a male activity and being looked at as a female function in Hollywood film – functioning as erotic objects for the male audience to gain scopophilic pleasure, and also erotic objects for the male characters with whom the male spectator identifies. Camera angles and the production of film enhance this pleasure. Thus, for Mulvay, the conflict between libido (via scopophilia) and ego (via narcissistic identification) are resolved through film by the display of women as erotic objects. In film, the strong, central, controlling male character reinforces narrative structures based upon the pleasure of/for male spectators.

The scopophilic gaze is not unproblematic. Within the psychoanalytic framework, for the male spectator 'woman' signifies sexual difference and also lack of penis, which is related to 'unpleasure'. (Lack of penis symbolizes castration.) Male pleasure in looking can always be potentially destabilized through the anxiety women signify, i.e., 'unpleasure'. This can be remedied by eliminating the threat of castration women signify by taking control of the visual representation of woman and also denying woman's lack of penis by the use of fetish objects that signify penis – high-heels/earrings – turning her into a fetish object herself, fragmenting her into fetishized body parts.

Indeed, Margaret Whitford (1991) tells us that the corporeal morphology of the body informs the symbolic and the social at many levels, and that the male imaginary is constituted by 'ec-stasy', the projection of erection, male narcissism and scopophilia. This is linked to castration: 'whatever the subject cannot dominate, or overlook and perceive from his transcendental elevation, threatens the subject with castration' (Whitford 1991: 151). Castration fantasies 'are linked to the symbolic split which assigns women to the carnal, excluding them from the spiritual and relegating them to a domain of lesser (and despised) being' (1991: 151). Knowledge, discourse, philosophy 'reproduces in one form or another the morphology or imperatives of the male body' (1991: 152).

To illustrate: there are striking resonances between Theweleit's work on the *Freikorps* soldier-males (1987) and Walter's *My Secret Life* (Eberhard and Kronhausen 1967), a narrative account of the amorous adventures of the anonymous Victorian author (Casanova) with servant girls. It is the sexual parts which are more than present for Walter: buttocks, firm breasts, white thighs and quims or splits/quims – quims with little or no hair – pre-pubescent quims. Sadistic practices are present in the narratives of both Walter and the *Freikorps* – violence, power, desire are interconnected. It is the bodies of women which both focus upon, not their faces, not whole bodies but fragments of the bodies. In both it is the same fragments.

What we have to remember, following Jessica Benjamin, is that Oedipal gender polarity is not simply involved with psychic processes at the level of the individual but can also be found in broader social processes and structures, in the binaries of Western culture, such as irrationality and rationality, subject and object, autonomy and dependence (J. Benjamin 1993: 184). Woman is defined as passive to man's active, emotion to his reason, night to his day.

Hélène Cixous goes further:

> but at the same time, man had been given the grotesque and unenviable fate of being reduced to a single idol with clay balls. And terrified of homosexuality, as Freud and his followers remark. Why does man fear *being* a woman? Why this refusal (*Ablehnung*) of femininity? The question that stumps Freud. The 'bare rock' of castration. For Freud, the repressed is not the other sex defeated by the dominant sex, as his friend Fliess (to whom Freud owes the theory of bisexuality) believed: what is repressed is leaning toward one's own sex. (Sellers 1994: 141)

In asking ourselves why, we do need to examine the 'other' to women's many – men and masculinities. (This is developed in chapter 6.) But, first of all, we need to examine women's responses to the interrelationship between the male gaze and the social organization of desire, which appears to rest on the commodification and aestheticization of the female body-object.

Women working as prostitutes are very clear about the ways in which they work to support and flatter the male imaginary. They do not use terms such as 'scopophilia', 'narcissism' or 'morphology', but they 'dress up' and 'role play' the fantasies and exercises in domination or submission that their clients request. The role of theatre and the 'performative theory of gender' (Butler 1994) is thrown into high relief in the gestures, roles, styles, language uttered by the 'prostitute' in her temporal encounters with her clients.

'Being a sex worker is first and foremost an act, and this audience is paying. Changing after the show makes a personal distinction between work and not-work, and is a strategy to avoid labelling and stigma' (A. Murray 1995b: 68). As O'Sullivan states (in Murray 1995b) we need to get beyond the 'tired old stereotypes of sex worker as sad (junkie/victim), bad (immoral nympho, slut) or mad (acting out unresolved childhood abuse), but unfortunately this is not so' (1995b: 68).

Audrey Extavasia and Tessa Dora Addison (1992) manage to transgress the 'tired old stereotype' in their exploration of escort prostitution using Deleuze and Guattari's *A Thousand Plateaus* (1988) and 'The telephone book' by Avital Ronell (Extavasia and Addison 1992). Escort prostitution is very different to street or sauna work in terms of the social organization of sex work and in part the social backgrounds of the women/young women who are involved. The women involved in escort work are sometimes working in mainstream 'middle-class' employment – teachers, nurses, actresses, secretaries: 'We are very particular about the young ladies who work for us. They must work or go to school during the day, or be actively pursuing a career in the arts or modelling' (Extavasia and Addison 1992: 3). Furthermore, the agency screens the clients: 'For the man who asked, "whaddya got tonight?" the answer was a dial tone' (1992: 5).

THE CALL is the interaction of THE MODEL and THE CLIENT within a particular spatial and temporal frame. . . . THE MODEL is a student, an actress, a nurse's aide, a teacher, or a secretary. . . . THE CLIENT is a businessman, a dentist, a banker, a construction worker, or a computer programmer. . . . THE MODEL gets ready for THE CALL, prepares to become a 'fantasy girl,' by imitating media representations of women as objects of DESIRE: she wears garters and hose and high heels; the nails of both fingers and toes are painted. These are signifiers on a fragmented, coded body, signifiers that THE CLIENT will be drawn to (through DESIRE), that will reinforce his FETISHISM and in turn contribute to the construction of his BODY WITHOUT ORGANS (BWO). . . . THE MODEL and THE CLIENT . . . interact together, their bodies intermingling with DESIRE, FETISHISM, representation, the SPACE of the room, the TIME measured by THE MODEL'S watch as well as the TIME elusively marked by THE CLIENT'S memories, fantasies, and anticipation of orgasm. (1992: 1–2)

In relation to fetishization of representations of women we are told by the authors that 'models' are a fantasy for the client and if someone were to sit down and write a description of what a high-class call girl would be like, it would probably be as follows: 'well, she'd have a beautiful hairdo, gorgeous make-up, she'd be very pretty and elegantly dressed, and sophisticated. That's exactly who our clients expect you to be. You just can't walk in there looking like the woman he sees every day at work, like his secretary, or the wife he goes home to, or the girls he passes by on the street' (1992: 4). And the clients are:

> people who want me to wear costumes, people who want me to sit with them while they watch dirty movies and jerk off, people who want to be tied up, people who want to wear diapers and be given a bottle. (1992: 13)

Of course, one's 'gender' is an identity constituted in time and space, and for some people their 'gender identity' is more fluid than for others. To survive, some women, like Moira, who worked on street, have to be strong enough, emotionally, to counter intimidation, harassment, violence and potential violence:

> There is a lot of violence. . . . There has to be no hesitation you have to make out you're in control . . . men like to dominate women . . . up there they think they can dominate you because they pay for you . . . sometimes they get rough and grab you and I say 'eh unless you're willing to pay more hands off'. . . . I've always noticed the girls who are being attacked are the weaker vulnerable looking girls. . . . I always get across to them that I am not a stupid prostitute. (Moira, in O'Neill et al. 1994)

To 'make out' they have to be able to manage the performativity of their work role and separate the 'work role' from their more personal 'real' narratives of self. Extavasia and Addison do not mention 'making out' and violence as an aspect of the escort role and experience, but clearly violence is an endemic aspect of the 'prostitute role'. To 'make out' women have to be good at 'gentling' men, at flattering, counselling and consoling the male ego while at the same time providing his ideal fantasy woman, even though he may make her 'feel sick' (see Cherie's narrative in chapter 3). Women have to become expert in managing to portray smiling warmth and care, or get into domination mode and verbally abuse or physically reprimand their clients, while distancing themselves psychologically and socially from the client.

> CHERIE: As soon as I get home I just go back to being normal... because down there I have to pretend... that... like... I love me job and I like the men in there... pretend that they're special and you like them.... Sometimes I can be dead rude when they just get to me... they all say 'I know you love this job' and I say 'Yeah'... they say 'yeah I can tell' and I say 'yeahh' [laughs].... You just switch of... I think it would be worse if I had a man waiting for me at home... but if I had a man I wouldn't be doing this... even though I don't enjoy it. I would be thinking he's thinking I am enjoying it.... I'm trying to get out of it.

Emotional labour is a central aspect of the working women's relationships with their clients. Emotional energy is directed at minimizing their own feeling worlds at work, and emotional energy is used in and around their interactions with and for clients. Women on street and women working in parlours aim to make clients (men) feel good, mostly by caring for them, which sometimes includes dominating them. Sandra Bartky (1990), writing upon heterosexual relationships, tells us a woman may be:

> ethically and epistemically disempowered by the care she gives, this caregiving affords her the feeling that a mighty power resides within her being. The *feeling* of out-flowing personal power so characteristic of the caregiving woman is quite different from the *having* of any actual power in the world. (1990: 115–16)

At one end of the caregiving continuum Bartky places commercial caregiving, which may include giving care by manipulating, suppressing and falsifying one's feeling life (see Hothschild 1983). At the other end is caregiving with no ulterior motive, given in 'absolute sincerity'. Most of us, she tells us, probably fall somewhere in the middle, but we measure ourselves by the latter form.

The issue here is how do women 'make out' in conditions where they must separate body from self to do the intimate work of fulfilling clients' sexual needs/desires, and, at one and the same time, how do they manage to suppress their own feeling life and manufacture care, concern, consideration, a listening ear, indeed a devoted stance to their clients? The answer, in part, can be found in Butler's performative theory of gender.

Corporeality: the lived body and prostitution as (postmodern) performance

Judith Butler's performative theory of gender (1990) is a useful theoretical approach to take, for it helps to uncover the meanings behind the codes linking the microanalysis involved in conducting interpretive ethnography to broader structures, such as hegemonic heterosexuality. Butler's postmodern analysis enables us to move beyond binaries and grasp the multiple dimensions of gender identities and the 'management' of gendered relations. For Butler, the gendered body is performed, and acts, gestures, enactments purport to perform an 'essence of identity', but this is in fact a fabrication which is 'manufactured and sustained through corporeal signs and other discursive means' (Butler 1990: 336). Drawing upon Foucault and psychoanalysis, the essence of identity, for Butler, is manufactured through public and social discourses which help to maintain and sustain the 'regulation of sexuality within the obligatory frame of reproductive heterosexuality' (1990: 337). In this sense, then, the dress codes operating across the globe which fulfil desires/fantasies/fetishes of male clients/pimps/punters/men more generally are 'appearance as illusion' (1990: 337), ideological effects – a parody of 'sexualized' femininity embedded within discourses of hegemonic heterosexuality premised upon male sexualities/desire/fetishism.

Drawing upon Butler, one could argue that the actual performance of doing sex work highlights the distinction between the gender being performed (sterotypical heterosexual, sexualized woman/whore) and the social organization of desire rooted in hegemonic heterosexuality and fantasies revolving around women/woman in the patriarchal imagination.

The performance of doing sex work is illustrated very clearly in Sara Giddens's performance work, described in chapter 2. The ritualized practice of the prostitute as performer undercuts a simple reading of the prostitute as reinforcing patriarchy/heterosexual hegemonic practices marked by desire and fetishism as the product of 'citation'. In his reading of the video performance, Rolland Munro unmasks the sign 'prostitute' to show how the sign functions to hide our own fetishizing of exchange. Munro focuses upon the interrelationship between image and narrative in the text, the exchange relationship between prostitute and punter, and the way the young woman talks about coming to a point where she stops seeing people for who they are and starts seeing them as potential clients. Munro highlights the chiasm in which we live, where we 'are all at it . . . seeing others as friends one moment and crossing them into a prospective client, a regular, the next'. He defines some of the crossings we make as follows: 'the attractive person at a party (might buy us dinner); the colleague who is our friend (could advance our career)'. This fragmenting of others and then 'enrolling the bits into our interests has us in strict denial: immediately we are refracting our commodifications back into friends/good blokes/lovers – forms that will carry the acceptable face of society'. Indeed 'chameleon-like . . . we cross over, we cross back – using the ferryman of class, gender and personality to forget our own fetishizing of exchange' (Munro 1999).

The ethno-mimetic text requires interpretation, and in the process of interpretation we become aware of the ideology of exchange being played out before us as instrumental reason – the reduction of our social world to 'thing-like' equivalences. 'Little by little, this drive for... "equivalence" which is a feature of instrumental reason comes to pervade all aspects of human life' (Battersby 1998: 128). This also includes the tendency to treat persons as equivalents, which helps to separate the 'good' women from those 'bad' women involved in selling or buying sex. What they do becomes who they are, bad-girls, pariahs, sinners. The prostitute is an index for all women in reflexive modernity/postmodernity.

Munro reminds us that, in contrast, the prostitute sees what she/we are up to. The prostitute turns the artefacts of exchange (high-heels, zips, slit skirts) back from fetish to function, and in one part of the narrative she throws out of her house the friend who sits on her sofa and denies what has paid for it:

> my boyfriend's friend sat watching the telly and said look at them dirty prostitutes... and I said just remember I am a prostitute and this is my settee paid for by prostitution and my TV and my carpet, and everybody looked at me horrified.

Munro tells us that we may deny her as we will, but:

> it is the prostitute who sees life as it comes. Yes! Yes! And it is the same figure who – as the unacceptable face of exchange – helps us deny our own everyday commodification of each other. (1999)

The combination of interpretive ethnography and performance art in *Not all the time... but mostly...* (see chapter 2) transports us 'bodily into the everyday world of prostitutes' in which we can momentarily see 'that it is us who have become the observed' (Munro 1999).

The 'prostitute' is marked out as 'other', as separate from ordinary women, a body-object of fascination and desire, an 'aestheticized' body. Our gendered bodies are heavily symbolized in the social construction of everyday life. Embodiment is a cultural process whereby the body 'becomes a site of culturally ascribed and disputed meanings, experiences, feelings' (Stanley and Wise 1993: 196). Bodies are not simply cultural, linguistic creations but physical, material, experiential realities (1993: 197). As such, we need to theorize the physicality, frailty and fragility of the body alongside the interrelationship between bodies, experience and broader social and psychic structures and processes.

Feminist responses to the contemporary focus on the body stress that we 'are always marked corporeally in specific ways, but not as unchanging or unchangeable fixtures' (Price and Shildrick 1999: 8). There is no universal category of the body, but rather 'multiple bodies, marked not simply by sex, but by an infinite array of differences – race, class, sexuality, age, mobility status... none of which is soley determinate' (1999: 8). Stanley and Wise describe their feminist-fractured foundationalism as appreciative of difference and the interrelationships between body, mind and emotion. They describe a way of understanding relations between self and other(s) not as oppositions but as 'co-operative endeavours for constructing selves... through collective relational systems of action and interaction' (1993: 195).

Similarly, Jessica Benjamin stresses that feminist theory should address structures of domination by exploring the relationships between the powerful and powerless, not by imagining a feminine realm 'corrupted by the culture of phallic symbolisation and paternal idealisation' (1993: 223) but rather through mutual recognition – intersubjective feminist theory. Intersubjective feminist theory has opened up possibilities of mutual recognition between men and women, involving recognition that the personal and the social are interconnected. Gender polarity and binary thinking deprives women of their subjectivity, involves the loss of recognition between women and men as equal subjects and involves the broader societal loss of living in an increasingly objectified and postemotional world. However, there are possibilities for transformation if we address interrelationships between psychic and social processes involved in 'lived relations', in 'lived cultures', through cooperative endeavours such as participatory action research. For Irigaray, the 'phenomenological account of the lived body and the lived world needs to be complemented by the awareness that there is an interaction between the lived experience, the imaginary, and the discursive and social construction of both' (1993: 52). Christine Battersby argues beyond Irigaray (who privileges the feminine that falls outside of the masculine symbolic) and using Adorno and Benjamin: that it is possible to reconstruct a a 'nonmetaphysical metaphysics that is alive to issues of difference' (1998: 147); moreover, she argues that we urgently need models that 'allow us to register both difference and sameness' (1998: 127).

Intersubjective mutual recognition is crucial to participatory action research, to working *with* women as subject-objects. It is pivotal in order to build bridges across the binary divide between sex worker feminists and anti-prostitution feminists in order to dismantle binaries and think dialectically in constellations.

Embodiment and ethnography in reflexive modern/ postmodern times

Women's bodies/body parts sell. But, what of the individual woman as subject-object? Embodiment is the personal, experiential, lived experience of dwelling in and through the organic body. Embodiment (prostitutes as subject-objects) can be explored through ethnographic work, through diaries, autobiographies, letters, life-history work, memory work (Haug 1987, 1992) and certain fictive texts.

As Sandra Bartky argues, female subjectivity is constructed through continuing processes, through personal engagement in practices, discourses, institutions that give significance, meaning to social life. In order to better understand the politics of everyday life:

the ways in which we inscribe and reinscribe our subjection in the fabric of the
ordinary... we need to locate our subordination not only in the hidden recesses
of the psyche but in the duties we are happy to perform and in what we thought
were the innocent pleasures of everyday life. (Bartky 1990: 118–19)

In trying to understand the politics of everyday life we need to acknowledge structures that constrain and enable as part of the interrelationship
between social processes and psychic processes. We also need to be aware of
the 'messiness and untidiness of human relations' (Rojek 1995: 106). One way
of exploring and understanding the messiness and untidiness of human
relations is to listen to women's accounts of their particular biographies. In
this study, the voices of women involved in prostitution are central in order to
develop fuller understanding of their lived experiences within prostitution as
a patriarchal institution and within patriarchal capitalism more generally –
for all women. As I have said, women working as prostitutes, particularly on
street, are a muted group. The dominant image of a prostitute is a seedy,
immoral, lazy, drug/alcohol abuser, a lower-class women, in fish-nets, cheap
erotic clothing and garish lipstick. Many documentaries on prostitution
have reinforced this view, as does the media's portrayal of 'the prostitute'.
The Hollywood film *Pretty Woman*, on the other hand, was the stuff fantasies
are made of: glossy and smooth (not much reality save for the attempted rape
scene), the beautiful working-class/underclass tart with the heart of gold goes
from good-girl, to bad and back again to good, thus maintaining social order
and hegemonic heterosexuality, and lives happily ever after with rich business
man Richard Gere.

The whore stigma (and also the whore fantasy) is of course transferable to
all women, but particularly those who transgress the rules and norms that
'control' women morally and socially. Sexual inequalities are deeply embedded
into the fabric of our society, or cultural products and processes, and are
exemplified in our sign worlds – TV, film, advertising (Rojek 1995). Looking
and dressing like bad-girls, for some of the women I spoke to in Frankfurt at
the 1st European Prostitutes Conference (Drobler 1991), can help to challenge
the power of patriarchy, particularly in relation to whores: 'if lots of women
look like whores how can whores be identified?'

However, looking and dressing like bad-girls (for example, Madonna) can
merely serve to reproduce fetish iconography, which, if it is about anything at
all, is about patriarchal power or, for cine-psychoanalysts, it is about appeas-
ing the patriarchal unconscious: visual pleasure is largely organized to flatter
or console the patriarchal ego and unconscious (Mulvay 1975; Gledhill 1988;
Van Zoonan 1994). Like the cards advertising sexual services in telephone
boxes, it also shows the adventurism or limits to our sign worlds of sexuality
(see Rojek 1995: 129–74).

How seriously we take these 'sign worlds' may depend upon where we
locate ourselves theoretically, or upon our ability, intentionally or otherwise,
to move between reality and fiction. What we do need to explore is the

opening up of spaces of resistance, through participatory action research, for previously marginalized groups in the late modern/postmodern world to speak, write and show a multiplicity of standpoints. This is the importance of postmodern ethnographies: the reflexive ability to move between the 'real' and the narratives which are generated by people seeking to place, or locate, or situate their life trajectory.

The relationship between the fictive and the real is unclear and contradictory in contemporary culture, but both are two parts of the same whole. We must not lose sight of the realities of class, race, and gender inequalities in the postmodern societies we live in and through. The crisis in ethnography documented in chapter 2 means that we can no longer presume 'uncontested' realist accounts of people's lives. Ethnographic texts are no longer accepted as 'real' accounts. Self-reflexivity, coupled with deconstruction of conventional discourses, questions the status of ethnographic texts, the role of the ethnographer and the role of the 'subject'.

The tension between the fictive and the 'real', the 'real' and the constructed is always present in the ethnographic stories generated through ethnographic research. Participatory action research re-presented through ethno-mimetic texts can reveal the tension between the 'fictive' and the 'real'. The texts can also reveal through a hybrid combination of stories/narratives and artistic re-presentations what may remain hidden or unsaid in print-based outcomes of ethnographic research. They can help us to access the meanings, affects, actions, practices of individuals to develop 'sensuous knowing', which casts light on the 'real' and counters postemotionalism and compassion fatigue. For example, seeing/experiencing a woman working as a prostitute as a subject-object not just a body-object.

Chris Rojek points out that 'for some observers postmodern culture is dominated by a sign-economy in which fixed referentials have been liquidated. . . . Authenticity has disappeared' (1995: 9). The disappearance of meaning suggests that 'the sign economy is now "the locus of the real"' (1995: 10). The discussion in this text so far is not premised upon the disappearance of meaning, but rather takes a constellational approach which accepts that our cultures are indeed dominated by sign economies which can be described in part as being the locus of the real. However, this is only part of the story. At one and the same time, our lived cultures are based in the material and ideological realities of poverty, class, race, gender inequalities, which can counter the magnitude and importance of sign economies in our lives. Accessing lived cultures through interpretive ethnographic research is an important dimension to uncovering this tension, challenging binary thinking and instrumental reason.

Prostitution for many women is about work/labour. It is also a leisure pursuit for men who can afford to pay. The bottom line for entry into prostitution is economic need. Prostitution and prostitutes are symbolized through the dichotomy of whore stigma and whore fantasy in the patriarchal imagination and in our sign worlds of sexuality, in our organizations and institutions of social order and social welfare. They are also, as we have seen, an index for all women. The figure/image of the prostitute can remind us of the commodified nature of our lived relations/lived cultures, the female body as a metaphor for the commodity body, re-presenting an empathy with commodities.

Prostitution has always been a leisure pursuit for certain men able to afford it. Shannon Bell's book (1994) appears to promote prostitution as a postmodern 'leisure phenomenon' through prostitute performance and workshops.[7] Bell describes how Annie Sprinkle (performance artist/slut/goddess) is using art-space and workshops to educate the general population about prostitution. Sprinkle hosts a salon at her home for women to learn to recognize themselves as both goddess and slut. Women may also learn how it is to be a man for the day by creating a male persona in 'Drag King for a Day Salon'. She also offers workshops in 'Sacred Sex' and 'Spiritual Healing' (Bell 1994: 188).

Bell's work challenges binaries and reinforces sex work as a postmodern leisure phenomenon. For example, in Bell's book prostitution could be 'read' as a strand of 'new age' 'spiritualism', which includes playing around with gender roles and identities – for those women who can afford it. Annie Sprinkle's work certainly appears to blur the distinction between the fictive and the real, but the common denominator between Sprinkle's and Bell's work is the relationship between sex, leisure, lifestyle, transgressing hegemonic heterosexuality and finding pleasure for a particular group/class of women who can pay for it.

The global sex industry as a postmodern 'leisure' phenomenon

Prostitution as a global phenomenon is certainly an element of the leisure industry. Men will travel typically to the Philippines and to Thailand to buy access to the body-objects of women and children (see Bishop and Robinson 1997; O'Connell-Davidson 1998; Kempadoo and Doezema 1999). Some of the narratives from women and from men indicate that paying a prostitute, paying for access to the prostitute as body-object, is about purchasing 'escape', escape from 'mundane' sex with partners/wives/girlfriends; it is about purchasing 'fantasy'.

Prostitution and sex tourism are global phenomena and they help to constitute the political economy of prostitution. Prostitution is historically and culturally rooted in the social organization of desire, male fantasies and possibilities to embody these fantasies.

> Sexual practice is one of the sites of masculinity's – and femininity's – daily construction, but that construction is international. Tourists, colonial officials, international technocrats and businessmen, and soldiers have long been the internationalizers of sexualized masculinity. (Enloe 1992: 24–5)

Bishop and Robinson (1997) state that like all industries the sex industry fosters the myth of worker–client reciprocity. Swiss tour operators describe

Thai women as 'slim, sunburnt and sweet...masters of making love by nature'. One Dutch agency describes the women thus: 'little slaves who give real warmth'. The GI acronym for Thai women is LBFMs 'little brown fucking machines' (1992: 10). Lilian Robinson states: 'there is something in the bar girl's experience that is recognizable to a heterosexual First World woman like me. We are linked by men's ability to turn their own desire into a thing, as well as by an international system of labour and consumption' (Bishop and Robinson 1997: 10).

Thanh Dam Truong (1990) insists that sex tourism is not just related to poor employment alternatives for women but also to the internal structure of the tourism industry and the vested financial interests of the various players. Sex tourism, like any other multinational industry, makes huge profits from underpaid local labour forces and must be explored within the context of the globalization (Bishop and Robinson 1997: 9).

In current times of de-traditionalization and globalization the international sex industry has an estimated turnover of US$20 billion a year (*The Economist* 1998: 23). International tourism and business travel have made prostitution in poor countries a central aspect of the local/national economy. The Internet, technologization and improved quality of home video equipment mean that pornography and prostitution are more widely available as products and services. Additionally, more people have joined the ranks of those who own and control these products and services: 'Most leading porn stars have their own web sites, some of them interactive' (1998: 24). The biggest innovation to affect the global sex industry and help speed up processes of globalization is the Internet and the World Wide Web. The *World Sex Guide* gives detailed and anonymous reviews of brothels, escort agencies and nightclubs in cities across the world. 'If a $50 "private show" in a striptease bar proves to be nothing more than a bored wiggle behind a curtain, a dissatisfied customer has the chance to warn future ones to take their money elsewhere' (*The Economist* 1998: 25). Additionally, the Internet cuts the cost of sending paper-based advertising in the form of brochures and videos to advertise escort agencies. Moreover, 'prostitutes can tempt their customers much more effectively in cyberspace' (1998: 25) than by paying for advertising space in small ads, telephone cards and contact magazines.

The ownership and control of the global sex industry remains in the hands of a few international sex industry tycoons: 'California's pronography industry already wields considerable political clout....One of the Arab world's best known pimps founded a bank. The current top Russian pimp in the Middle East is building a hotel' (1998: 25). The sex industry is big business and prostitution, pornography, striptease, sex aids are brought together through Internet sex. Globalization is an extension of rationalization. For whether it concerns a brothel in London, Paris or Bangkok, the Internet helps to regulate, survey and control the international sex trade. It also opens up spaces where the bodies of women can be displayed, viewed, offered up as whole bodies or in parts. We can pay to see live sex, watch a woman pee, or book time with an eprostitute. As a discursive space it is also an arena for the reproduction of instrumental reason, the social organization of desire and scopophilic pleasure, the pleasure in looking.

Summary

Certainly, for Meštrović, Walter Benjamin and Trinh the imaginary is central to Utopian political thinking, but in current times we are witnessing the petrification of the imagination indicative of postemotionalism. To counter petrification both Benjamin and Trinh stress the need to transgress and revolutionize our image worlds. The possibilities for our sign worlds of sexuality are both creative and destructive. Opening up new and more democratic ways of 'being' and 'becoming' are dependent upon imagination, imaginaries and hope for the future.

The links between the self-sustaining discourses and images which are part of the re-presentation of women and, more generally, men in reflexive modernity/postmodernity, and the social organization of desire, are deeply rooted in our psychic worlds. The corporeal morphology of the body informs the symbolic and the social at many levels. Whitford tells us that to live one's own morphology as 'woman', to be for oneself in the current social order, in social spaces, is to 'forge' a 'tenuous identity against or in the margins of the symbolic' (Whitford 1991: 153).

The interrelationships between gender identity, violence and power are important relationships to explore in understanding gender relations at both symbolic and social levels. Social processes and psychic processes are interconnected at both social and symbolic levels. If we agree with Bauman on the need for a re-moralization of social space, we have to be very clear about the masculine parameters of our social spaces and examine possibilities to forge social spaces which re-new, re-write, re-structure social spaces for us all, based upon the principles of mutual recognition, democratization, while understanding and changing the centrality of violence within gendered relations. Moreover, we need to account for both feeling/sensuous knowing (mimesis) and reason (constructive rationality) in challenging and changing sexual and social inequalities.

By revealing the images and representations of the prostitute in art, film and literature – between fiction and reality – by accessing the sedimented truths of the social world in fictive texts, we can reveal the contradictions of female oppression through the specific experiences of the 'prostitute'. However, in order to get a better understanding we also need to explore the 'prostitute' as subject-object. We can do this by listening to women working as prostitutes, by understanding that for many women prostitution is a 'resistance' as well as a 'response' to their experiences within patriarchal capitalism, marked by unemployment, poverty and difficult, destructive relationships with some men and/or their families. We can do this by conducting ethnographic research founded upon 'partial identification', *'Erlebnis'*, 'care' and 'concern' – a politics of feeling. Through participatory action research and ethno-mimesis the 'act of knowing can be felt as a communion, not conquest' (J. Benjamin 1993: 192). Ethnographic work understood within the contexts of de-traditionalization and multiple perspectives can begin to challenge instrumental reason by prioritizing experiences, feelings, of living in postmodern, postemotional worlds in dialectical, dialogical ways.

Triangulating information gained from exploring historical and fictive texts with the life-story narratives of women working as prostitutes can enable us to get a much clearer understanding of prostitution as an institution within late-modern/postmodern times. The approach taken in this book is that a politics of feeling should be at the centre of our responses to sexual, social and cultural inequalities: not the 'feeling' that is a perversion of sentimentality but rather the feeling rooted in critical interpretation, interpretive ethnographies, intersubjective recognition – in feminist praxis and ethno-mimesis represented in the form of the constellation (Adorno 1984).

Violence is also a central aspect of our sign worlds of sexuality, as witnessed in the narratives from women, the traces of men's fear of women's sexuality in the fictive texts and the narratives from men drawn upon in this chapter. The issue of male violence against the body-objects/subject-objects of women will be developed further in chapter 6. In the following narrative, Moira illuminates the ideology of the prostitute as 'deserving victim' and projects this back to the man fitting her window with amazing clarity:

> There is a lot of violence...this man who came to fit my window...I don't know how we got on the subject...but he said 'well prostitutes that comes with the job doesn't it'...so I said 'why should it come with the job?'...'why should they be abused?' 'Because they are getting paid for it', he said.... 'They are getting paid to do a service'. I said, 'like you come and fit my window if I kick you in the nuts on the way out is that part of the service?'...'No because I only put glass in', so I said 'well I only sell my body but it doesn't mean to say someone can do what they want to me and rape me and abuse me'.

What is clear is that male violence against women working as prostitutes is endemic. Male violence is wrapped up in the development of masculinities. Furthermore, violence creates change in the world, but the most likely change is to a more violent world (Arendt 1970: 87). However, the implications involve broader social structures and processes:

> It is difficult to grasp the fact that the center of male domination lies not in direct expressions of personal violence (rampant though they are) but in the societal rationality which may or may not be defended by men. (Benjamin 1993: 216)

For Jessica Benjamin, male violence is not the actual basis of male power but rather (following Weber) it works through the hegemony of impersonal organization. This involves the formal rules involved in the interaction of autonomous individuals; instrumental knowledge founded in the subject's (male's) view of the object world; and the accumulation of profit. Societal rationalization neutralizes gender difference but intensifies the dichotomies rooted in it. The anchoring of the structures of domination in the psyche gives rise to their inevitability. The psychic processes involved in male domination and 'fear' of the object (women) are dealt with in chapter 6.

6

The City, Masculinity and the Social Organization of Desire: Pimps and Punters

Little attention is given to male involvement in prostitution (see McIntosh 1978) and the literature on prostitution focuses too unidirectionally upon the women involved. Jeff Hearn (1993) develops a thesis founded upon the question: 'Is theory gendered?'. Hearn's thesis is that the category of men in theorizing through 'absence, avoidance, ambivalence and alterity' becomes a taken-for-granted presence and becomes central to the production and repro- duction of the category 'men', helping to reproduce dominant malestream ideologies and social practices. Men are the One to woman's Other (de Beauvoir 1961). For Hearn: 'More careful work needs to be done on the interrelation of men's agency, subjectivity, and practice, and their relationship to men's structural power, both in reproducing that power, and reproducing and abolishing it' (1993: 24).

Andrew Samuels (1994) uses a combination of depth-psychology with social/cultural analysis to examine interrelationships between inner and outer worlds and social change. Here careful work *is* done on the interrelation- ship between men's agency, subjectivity and practice, focusing upon men's issues, the male body, as well as on the market economy, environmentalism, anti-Semitism and nationalism. In a chapter entitled 'Reflecting on men' Samuels explores relationships between men, social change and men's move- ments.

If men are on the move at some level, then, given that they control the sources of economic power, including the production of ideology and repres- entations of sexual difference, the factoring in of male political power to the idea of male change could be decisive. In other words, we could be confronted with a social movement as significant as feminism, but with possession of all the resources from which feminism has been excluded (Samuels 1994: 181).

This chapter hopes, in part, to approach this problem by focusing upon an absence – the men involved in prostitution and the wider sex industry – while acknowledging the difficulties encountered and articulated by Samuels regarding resource and power differentials between research on/with men and feminist research and practice. The wider sex industry includes the management, organization and enactment of pornography, stripping, sex shops, bars and clubs (see Bell 1984). There is a focus upon historical and cultural texts, and specifically on the narratives from women and men involved in prostitution as prostitutes and clients.

Masculinit(y)ies seem to be a taken-for-granted given in the gendered social organization of prostitution. Men are the purchasers of sex, the individuals who operate as pimps, who own and control the sex industry, and also the officials who are involved in the policing of 'prostitutes' through the criminal justice system and the broader system of bureaucratic rationalization. Men are the subjects to women's objects. Invariably, given the relationship between rationalization and the structures of domination, attention is directed at the 'bad-girls' involved in prostitution, as 'victims', business women, pariahs, sluts and slags.

In focusing upon men's involvement in the social organization of prostitution from tradition to postmodernity, we can develop greater knowledge and understanding of masculinities and gender relations by exploring a micrology of masculinities within a broader socio-historical context. This includes the relationship between male psyche, masculinity, social construction and organization of desire, uneven power dynamics, and prostitution as a cultural practice through time and space. In order to theorize the gendered social organization of prostitution we need to understand the interrelationships between men, masculinities and violence against women; and use such understanding to help develop social changes/ transformations regarding current sexual and social inequalities. Analysing and understanding prostitution by addressing masculinities and male sexual and social practices can have resonances for understanding gender relations more widely in late-modern/postmodern times. This analysis may help us to identify possibilities for intersubjective mutual recognition.

Prostitution is, with few exceptions (gigolos/male prostitutes/hustlers),[1] a market for men; women are paid for the sexual services they perform on (with/for) men. Mary McIntosh has argued that issues of sexuality and sexual needs are sociological rather than biological and further that the 'ideology of male sexual needs both supports and is supported by the structures of male dominance, male privilege and monogamy' (1978: 3). Clients state that their involvement with prostitutes is sex without commitment, thrill, compensation for a sterile marriage and sexual relief. As we have discovered in listening to women's voices, women experience relationships with some clients that are long-term friendships; other clients are abusive and violent, some are 'just business' and sometimes aspects of all three are present. Women who manage to 'make out' in prostitution talk about 'doing body work' and 'separating' emotions from the physical embodied experience. Relationships with pimps are often business relationships, but can also be about 'love', 'dependency' and 'protection'.

It is important to acknowledge that meaning and being are wrapped up in the materiality of life. Trying to better understand the personal experience and the interrelationship between the personal/feelings worlds and the wider social, structural worlds can help us to better understand masculinities within the context of prostitution. Examining a micrology of masculinit(y)ies (by focusing upon pimps and punters) within a broader socio-historical context necessitates a look at the environmental context in and through which 'prostitution' takes place – the modern city.

Currently, social policy research is examining conditions in Britain's deprived urban areas. Economic need is the bottom line for entrance into prostitution. Key indicators of deprivation are taken to be: unemployment, education, housing, poverty, death rates and crime. Cuts in government funding have been compensated for in some areas by success in bidding for funds under the single regeneration budget. Brian Robson (1994) states that resources are crucial when targeted to places in distress, and his research showed a positive relationship between urban expenditure and relative improvement. However, 'those areas suffering the worst problems have shown little relative benefit from urban policy. Thus, for example, Manchester, Newcastle and Liverpool all showed greater relative decline than did other districts within their conurbations' (1994: 2). Robson highlights partnership approaches to urban regeneration, linking local authorities, businesses, quangos, the voluntary sector and local communities. Furthermore, that:

> cities continue to act simultaneously both as the creative driving forces of our economy as well as centres of economic immiseration. Only when urban policy resolves the conundrum of exploiting the former and addressing the latter will it best meet the needs of our cities and the country as a whole. (1994: 4)

Certainly, Borden et al. (1996: 12) state that people's identity in terms of their age, gender, class and culture is partially constructed in relation to the spaces and buildings they occupy (see also Hubbard 1999 for an overview of how the lifestyles, experiences and identities of female sex workers are shaped by their urban geographies).

The intention here is to develop a better understanding of one aspect of city life – the gendered social organization of street prostitution. In much of my research the focus is upon working with the stereotypical subjects of research through PAR. This, I feel, has to be the way forward when addressing the multi-layered problems of urban decay and decline in our cities with a view to developing multi-agency initiatives that focus upon participation, inclusion and regeneration in response to some of the problems. This chapter is organized into three major sections: a socio-historical context focusing upon consumption and the city; pimps and punters; and male violence against women working as prostitutes.

Socio-historical context: consumption, the city and later modernity/postmodernity

Traditionally conducted within the public sphere, prostitution is most pro-lific within major cities and seaports for historical reasons and due to the economics of the market or industry, and it is inevitably tied to politics.[2] The effects of Victorian morality and of the social purity movement, together with the social organization of gender relations (heterosexuality as the norm; hegemonic heterosexuality), have in Britain created a legacy enshrined in law through Wolfenden and subsequent sexual and street offences legislation (see Walkowitz 1980; McLeod 1982; Phoenix 1999; O'Neill 1996) which punishes the prostitute but is relatively ineffective at sanctioning the client or pimp, and, furthermore, claims concern for the prostitute's welfare.

McRobbie states that whether or not modernity and postmodernity

> are opposing or interrelated concepts, they have each insisted on the integrated experience of everyday life including the urban environment, architecture, consumer culture, and the 'passage' of the individual at whatever precise historical moment in time through these forms, whether he or she, for example is the *flaneur* of urban modernity, or the insulated *walkman* of postmodernity. (1993: 149)

The perspective taken in this text is one that accepts the concepts used to articulate and describe postmodernity but maintains that interconnected with de-traditionalization, plurality, diversification and risk are unifying struc-tures, practices and processes that we would define as 'modern' or constitutive of 'modernity'. The figurational sociology of Elias is a useful approach to draw upon in order to explain this point. For theorists who use Elias's work, such as Kuzmics (1994, 1997), Wouters (1986) and De Swaan (1981), the civilizing process is still 'becoming'; the overlaps in time and space in affects and inner experience show the interrelated aspects of social experience through time and space. Civilization is a 'theoretical concept which links a psychological model to a macro-sociological one with the purpose of explaining the subordination or integration of affects in more differentiated and stable social structures, whereby rather massive constraints by others turn to rather invisible ones and partly (and increasingly) operate by self restraints' (Kuzmics 1994).

The interrelation of psychic processes and social processes is what interests me here. The women and men I am involved with through the research are not articulating their lived experience in ways that solely describe and define experiences as 'postmodern', but rather as reflexive modern/postmodern. The relationships between psychic processes and social processes speak of 'making out' in harsh conditions related to sexual inequalities, poverty, violence, racial tension and discrimination, experienced at the level of both the personal individual (including experiences of living in and through and then beyond the care system) and at the local/national levels. A central aspect to their experience of living in the city is the overwhelming deluge of advertising rooted in consumerism and the desire to consume. The excitement and frisson of being in the city is a sensual experience dominated by noise and images. The senses are bombarded with smells, pictures, sounds, messages, and the dominating message is 'consume'.

Pasi Falk (1995) argues that the general principle of consumer society is the supplement-generator model, creating simultaneously surfeit and deficit, superfluity and lack, desire and lack. The logics of consumption are made up of imitation, separation/distinction (lack) and introjective self-fulfilment (desire). Introjective and distinctive moments are reciprocal. This, for Falk, is the dynamic conflict of modern individual self-construction, which corresponds to the social dynamics of imitation and distinction and is finally linked to the dynamics of the supplement-generator model. Falk thus avoids falling into a simple analysis of consuming as filling up the empty self: 'Our imaginary worlds nourished by the culture industry' (1995: 116). And consumption is deeply 'rooted in the existential conditions of individual self-construction involving an historically specific mode of the reproduction of lack – and desire' (1995: 144).

For Walter Benjamin, consumerism was centred around the city. The city was the enchanted forest of children's fairy tales (McRobbie 1993); but, as McRobbie states, the image of Benjamin's 'flaneur' is a gendered image. Jenny Ryan through her readings of Deutsche (1991), Massey (1991), and Morris (1992) points to the 'trivialization of issues of (gender) difference in political terms ... matched by a failure to grasp the different subjectivities within which modernity and urban experience has been structured' (1994: 38). Women are absent in the literature, not present in the development of the arguments/discourses, and feminist analysis is not accorded a place. For Ryan, it is important to problematize the urban experience through examining conditions of difference and the interrelationships between class, gender and other social relations. Central to her project is the concept of 'social spatialization', drawing upon the work of Rob Shields:

> Shields ... argues for the analytical integration of the study of spatial practices, discourses and representations of space. He cites, as an emergent property of the dynamics of both of these, the new cultural struggles over, and in space through which discourses and practices are restructured. (Ryan 1994: 40)

Jenny Ryan explores the ways in which assumptions and judgements about spaces and places become commonly defined due to the ways in which they are rooted in 'discourses and practices deeply structured in prevailing relations of power' (1994: 40). Such power relations, rooted for Ryan in patriarchy, must be seen in terms of gender and class to understand modernity and the city. To this I would add the dimension of race: the specific experiences and inequalities and ideologies which intersect with racial issues, with racism. 'Social spatialization' is a useful theoretical concept to get to grips with the historical development of street prostitution, the specific areas marked out through time and through negotiation as 'red-light areas', and the power relationships that are played out between prostitutes, pimps, punters as well as residents and the police.

The major site of my initial research in 1990 was a city in the Midlands. The 'red-light area' stretches for one square mile across a multi-racial neighbourhood (with a transient population of council house tenants, students and flat dwellers; high unemployment, deprivation and crime rate) and a more middle-class area, with a high proportion of houseowners and flat dwellers in employment as well as a number of student dwellings. The women working are mostly white, and aged between 14 and 54. The clients are mostly white and in their 20s to 50s, mostly employed and married with children. The pimps are mostly black, and some of the men became involved in 'pimping' women through their familial networks. 'Working' women is an addition to income support. Some of the relationships are not just based on the women's earning potential but are described as 'love' relationships. Some of the women, through life-story work, talk about 'surviving in both cultures', black and white. The interrelations between working women and pimps are complex and, as O'Connell-Davidson states, it is simply not useful to define pimping as a single set of activities but rather to talk about patterns of pimping (1998: 46–60).

The racial dimension is absent in the literature on prostitution.[3] Clearly defined power relationships operate. Women do not tend to work autonomously on street. They are hustled under the guise of 'protection'. Pimps take their cut from the earnings of women; some say when she does and does not work. Street etiquette is largely observed, women tend to stand in their own areas of the street, and there is a general rate that is charged by all the women. Women tend to look out for each other, swapping information on dodgy punters, and they are usually fastidious in their use of condoms. But, the interrelation with drug cultures does have an effect: 'I would always protect myself. A lot of girls say they do but don't because that is what most men want and some girls go unprotected so that the client will come back' (Louise 1997: 13). Some men will offer more money for sex without a condom. Some of the women say 'who better to educate the punter but the prostitute'. 'Prostitutes' are recipients of the male gaze – they invite the look through body language, through dress and through their representation of dominant stereotypes of male desire in public spaces, street spaces.

Sites of street prostitution are clearly defined areas of our major cities and seaports, developing through a process of negotiation between *history*, women, environmental contexts and punters. Modern-day punters need access to drive around the area; women need areas or locales where they can take punters (if not back to their flat/house) to do business and which will enable them to be back on the beat quickly and also safely – women tend to know where they each 'take' clients. Typically, these are the poorer areas of the city, where more transient populations are housed and where the women encounter less hassle from residents/vigilantes (see Hubbard 1999 for an excellent discussion on how the location of prostitution reflects the differential ability of social groups to 'purify' social space).

Pimps are sometimes nearby or in local clubs or cafes/bars – hanging out with friends while the women work nearby – in order to collect the earnings or 'protect' the woman. 'Protection' is not usually about protecting her from the violence of clients but from being pimped by other guys. The 'protection' offered is merely that of being 'owned', 'run' or 'looked after' by one man. For some women, the 'pimp' and/or the boyfriend will sometimes stand nearby watching and taking car number plates if necessary, thus offering an element of 'protection' in exchange for part of the income. Often these young men will take coffee and condoms from outreach workers and join in the conversations between women and outreach workers while waiting around for their 'girl-friends' or 'partners' to earn enough for their drug requirements. However, the downside to this is that these men then know exactly how much a woman earns, and if they are particularly punitive they may take most if not all the woman's income (see also O'Connell-Davidson 1998: 49).

Crucial to Ryan's analysis and understanding of modernity and the city is the concept of patriarchy: 'Whilst the city was the birthplace of a new set of values constituted within modernity and capitalism it was also the arena for the reformulation of a pre-capitalist patriarchal culture' (1994: 49). This served to site middle-class and working-class women differently and, for Ryan, can be explored by focusing upon the processes whereby women were regulated. The sexual and social regulation of women is crucial to understand gendered social and cultural processes and practices through time and space/place. Even a cursory glance at the literature on prostitution shows that it is women who are the focus of attention; it is their sexuality which is marked out/defined; it is women who are categorized in a fixed way, 'common prostitute', while their client or pimp is defined in a temporal way; it is women who are stereotyped and castigated, who commit crimes against morality and who suffer what Pheterson has called 'whore stigma'. It is mostly women who suffer through the criminal justice process – carrying huge fines, going to prison for fine default and sometimes losing children to local authority care (O'Neill 1995; O'Neill, Goode and Hopkins 1995). It is very difficult to get a successful prosecution against a pimp. Kerb-crawlers are either bound over to keep the peace for a year or fined £100 plus costs of about £25. The women I have interviewed were carrying fines ranging from £50 to £2,000. There is then a need to examine the socio-historical involvement of men in prostitution within the urban context of the city.

Understanding street prostitution and the experiences of women by focus-ing upon pimps and punters must include an understanding of the urban social spaces in which these activities takes place. A more detailed analysis relating psychic and social/cultural processes and practices can be developed in the interest of sexual and social transformations. In policy terms we need to engage with the interrelated psychic and social processes by looking at masculinity and gendered relations in order to better understand prostitution and develop interventionary practice and policies.

Practice and policy should not just respond at an environmental level – traffic calming, road closures, regulating dwellings to prevent women from working.[4] An important focus of concern is consumption, desire and masculinity, alongside issues of poverty, class, race and gender (Presdee 1997). An important place to begin is to analyse/understand the interrelationship between pimps, punters and women working as prostitutes vis-à-vis hegemonic masculinit(y)ies. This may help us to better understand prostitution as a cultural practice/process as well as a culture of resistance (see Hubbard 1999) for both pimps and prostitutes (operating on street or from massage parlours) whose lived relations are embedded in working-class/underclass milieux.

One way forward in understanding and explaining pimping, and the racial dimension to pimping, is to explore this phenomenon as a culture of resistance within spaces, environments, marked by urban decay, deprivation, high rates of unemployment (particularly for men of colour) and the fact that historically, traditionally, prostitution is a 'fact' of life in such urban, inner-city, geographical spaces. For example, at the turn of the nineteenth century in the city of Nottingham many of the pimps were Irish migrants.[5]

In exploring the socio-historical context to men's involvement in prostitution the intention is to try and get at some of the complexity of the lived relations of the men and women involved in prostitution, and to see how these lived relations have changed and/or stayed the same through time, by exploring men's accounts of their involvement in prostitution as clients, by exploring the literature on the pimp and by exploring women's accounts of men as pimps and punters.

The political economy of street prostitution

Socio-economic structures mediate cultural practices. But this is not to be understood in a unidirectional/deterministic way. For example, in the process of addressing, understanding and analysing prostitution as a cultural practice it is vital to untangle the moral/ideological approaches to prostitution from the material, economic and social contexts for prostitution (O'Neill 1992). The personal, experiential and gendered experiences intertwined with the macro-sociological structures need to be unravelled and explored to gain a better, fuller, account of continuity and change through time or the conditions of reflexive modernity/postmodernity.[6]

What are the continuities and changes in the gendered social organization of prostitution? What are the personal experiences and feelings of the men involved as pimps or as punters? What might analysis of such social knowledge mean for better understanding the dynamics of gender, race and class in the city and the development of policy-oriented practice? Outlining and exploring the gendered social organization of prostitution necessitates theorizing men and masculinities in relation to women more clearly and in more focused ways, illuminating the sources of power and oppression that are indicative of sexual and social inequalities and structures of domination.[7] This theorizing must explore the interrelation between the experiences, needs and desires of individuals and the wider social, historical contexts through which they live out their lives. This theorizing explores the interrelation of psychic processes and social processes and structures and highlights the processes of consumption, desire and violence against women.

The interrelation of social and psychic processes

The mediating influence that psychic/social processes have upon cultural practices (such as prostitution) is an important line of analysis to understand social change and also to help make sense of the gendered social organization of prostitution. The emotional/psychological and feeling dimensions to our lived experiences are central to understanding the social contexts in which and through which we live. Wouters (1986) and De Swaan (1981) provide important clues to the nature of changing social processes and the interrelation of social and psychic processes. Wouters talks about formalization and informalization processes. The 1960s and 1970s corresponded to a process of informalization (and simultaneously an intensification and relaxation of self-restraints). In the 1980s a process of formalization came into effect. Law, order, discipline and moral values shifted to centre stage:

> Informalization processes do not develop in a straight line. Waves of informalization have been followed by new waves of formalization, but in a long-term perspective from the end of the last century onwards a spiral movement can be discerned in which informalizing tendencies had the upper hand. Since then, social life in general has become less strictly regulated, more multifarious. In following currents of formalization, apparently not all the informalization from the previous period was undone, and certain informal modes of conduct and life-styles, or certain aspects of them, were formalized. . . . The long-term process of informalization is part of the civilizing process. (Wouters 1996: 5)

Wouters talks further about the interrelationship between people who are dependent upon each other and where there exists an unequal power balance. Until the 1960s he notes a tradition of 'harmonious inequality' between husband and wife and a lifespan biography ending in marriage, having children and growing old together as 'the natural order'. The build-up of pressure in the 1960s (counter-culture movement) resisting and challenging this 'traditional' order brought with it 'a phase of emancipation and resistance' (1996: 7):

> For many people, it became more and more difficult to picture any kind of unequal relation as being harmonious. . . . It was no longer true that anyone

born a woman was a victim of bad luck; now she was much more a victim of injustice, and specifically a victim of injustice on the part of men who held women in a subordinate position, not on the basis of personal qualities or merits, but of socially inherited superiority. (Wouters 1996: 7–8)

The 1980s brought a return to formalizing tendencies and a new stage of stabilization and resignation. One could suggest that informalizing tendencies are indicative of the 1990s in the wake of world recession, an increase in AIDS, the greater development of neo-Nazi movements and increases in tensions through war and conflict, along with an increase in global risk, insecurity and diversification.

Abram De Swaan (1981) writes about the changes in emotional and relational management in contemporary society, tracing the patterns of social change that correspond to the difficulties people have in relating to each other, in caring for one another, problems in living, and the concomitant psychic problems that emerge. Not content with sociological accounts which collapse 'judgement and description of social developments' De Swaan presents history as more complex and more ambiguous and prefers analyses that focus upon one small segment of life to develop a fuller account. For De Swaan, there has been a relaxing of societal mores, and he interprets these in the context of a shift in 'the predominant modes of relational and emotional management within a bureaucratising society' (1981: 361). It is worth quoting him at length here:

> The early development of capitalism resulted in a strong limitation on the presence in public of urban bourgeois women, whereas bourgeois men could continue to move wherever they wished and, possibly, could allow themselves greater liberty than before towards women in public and with public women, since their own daughters had disappeared from the streets. In the past hundred years, however, women have begun to move more freely in public and, possibly, bourgeois men have lost some of their privileges in approaching women in public.... Insofar as these equalizing developments have occurred, they represent an aspect of increasing mutual dependency of ever greater numbers of people upon one another, as more and more of their strivings are being taken care of within larger organizations of production, reproduction and government.... Rape, roughness, scorn, and degradation, so common and acceptable for employers to inflict upon factory girls, or customers upon prostitutes only a few generations ago, have become more disasteful to the contemporary public, even as the indignation of the women's movement against the remnants of these manners increases. Self-aggrandizement and violence have become less acceptable and are increasingly subject to social compulsion, social compulsion to self-compulsion and self-control, in that order.... In this process, many intimate relations have become less predictable for they no longer depend as much as before on the commands of social canons and personal conscience, but are shaped in a process of negotiation between relatively equal and autonomous parties.... Relations between people are increasingly managed through negotiation rather than through command. (De Swaan 1981: 368)

De Swann describes how the transition from management through command to management through negotiation is the result of various societal developments. For example: the increasing and generalizing dependence of people upon one another and the resulting increase in equality between them; the consecutive tides of emancipatory movements, campaigns for universal suffrage, organized workers' struggles, movements for women's liberation, and the many ethnic, racial and religious liberation movements – with each movement learning from a preceding one, and with inequalities, considered natural until then, being abolished; and, finally, the emergence and development of large organizations.

The transition to management through negotiation is onerous and hazardous. Where no command can be heard within or without, people may adopt fears and compulsions to help them refrain from doing what they are now allowed to do by others but what they find too difficult, too dangerous and too lonesome (De Swann 1981: 368–77).

In his conclusion De Swaan stresses that modes of emotional and relational management mediate between individuals and the larger social 'entities' they make up. Furthermore, by ignoring the 'double-character' (helping and controlling) mediating institutions, such as professions and service bureaucracies, we are in danger of seeing them as 'monoliths', stressing the controlling aspect and overlooking or not seeing the effect and affect of modes of interaction within small circles in intimate relations.

This is an important line of analysis for acknowledging possibilities for multi-agency responses via praxis in the interrelation between academic knowledge and social action/policy. For example, the consensus approach to prostitution in the initial site of my research, which operated between 1991 and 1994, developed from collaboration between mediating institutions – social services, probation, magistrates, the police anti-vice team and women working as prostitutes represented by a voluntary grass-roots agency. This collaboration was pioneering in that it was woman-centred and developed from independent research. It was not 'led' by a professional or statutory organization/institution. The woman-centred approach was pivotal to the terms and conditions under which the group operated, and it opened up new possibilities for the double character (helping and controlling) of the mediating institutions to operate a more reflexive response based upon women's needs.

De Swaan's study is illuminating and useful in pursuing themes of the micrology of daily life through time and how psychic processes interrelate with social processes in everyday lived relations. Management through negotiation rather than management by command is an interesting dimension to the process of social change and has implications for the state and for agencies of social control and welfare. Economic and social realities, the materiality of lived relations, have a great bearing on psychic processes. The following all have a bearing on emotional and relational management: economic need; the daily struggle to feed and clothe one's family; the emotional labour that goes into parenting and providing basic necessities for the satisfaction of basic needs; experiences of racism – intimidation, harassment, violence; experiences of violence and threat of violence; where one is positioned in the social class/underclass structure; the emotional and material resources one has access to.

Increasing equality is a relative concept depending upon where one is positioned in relation to access to power in our society. Asymmetries of power in our society have gender, racial and age as well as commodity dimensions. The history of social change is a morally informed process; it is also a history framed by gross inequalities between the sexes, and has been socially constructed in ways that have tended to write women out. Instrumental reason, rationalization, the disenchantment of the social world and the relegation of feeling to the private world, and binary oppositions valuing rationality, autonomy and order, and all that constitutes the male as subject, are embedded in our psychic worlds and reproduced through our actions and interactions, albeit unintentionally.

There are two aspects to De Swaan's and Wouters's work which can be taken forward to help explore masculinity and the gendered social organization of prostitution within the context of this chapter: the concept of periods of formalization and informalization and the notion of a shift from management by command to management by negotiation. Both Wouters's and De Swaan's work can help illuminate the historical processes and the psychic processes within an understanding of society as 'less strictly regulated and more multifarious', where management through negotiation rather than command is paramount.[8]

Thus, in contemporary society there has indeed been a loosening up of social, economic and moral structures, the process of de-traditionalization ('less strictly regulated and more multifarious') that Giddens writes about in *The Transformation of Intimacy* (1992), which focuses upon sexuality, love and relationships. Alongside these changes, De Swaan also notes the development of a certain restraint on males in the 'expression of their needs', related to embourgeoisement and the developing 'sexual revolution'. This 'restraint' must also be considered alongside the shifts from command to negotiation in the management and organization of contemporary society and the responses of some men to feminism (see Hearn 1990).

There are, however, many modes of behaviour, attitude and practice that have remained relatively unchanged through time: the taken-for-granted 'acceptance' of male infidelity/promiscuity – he's a 'lad' but his female counterpart is a 'whore'; the taken-for-granted 'acceptance' that men (mostly) will 'organize', 'run', 'pimp' women working as prostitutes; the social stigma relating to the women who work, particularly on street, which Pheterson (1986) calls 'whore stigma'; and male violence against women. Violence, abuse and assaults on women, be they physical or emotional assaults – about power over women or about a distorted desire/need for 'care' and 'respect' – may not be seen in public (unless we include assaults on prostitutes in public places) as often as they were a generation ago but are still around in the private sphere. For Pheterson (1986) the whore stigma legitimates violence against all women.

Giddens problematizes the psychic structures whereby men's anxiety about sexuality can remain hidden from view so long as the various social conditions which keep it hidden are in place, for example the subordination of women (1992: 118). But more than this: 'men are laggards in the transitions now occurring – and in a certain sense have been ever since the late eighteenth century. . . . Today is the first period in which men are finding themselves *to be* men, that is, as possessing a problematic "masculinity"' (1992: 59).

Men visiting prostitutes, as we shall see in a moment, often use prostitution as an alternative to adultery, as sexual relief, as thrill, but always as their right. Prostitution is closely related to pornography and the wider sex industry. Prostitution is also related to the control and debasement of women through various acts and taunts and violence. Prostitution, for many of the women working as prostitutes and for the men who pay for sex with prostitutes, has much in common with the exchanges that go on between regular partners when love ceases but economic dependence exists and 'favours' or 'promises' are given and taken. Rationalization is linked with Marx's idea that domination is located in the principle of commodity exchange (J. Benjamin 1993: 186). Exchange value for use value – what is in fact unequal exchange and socially constructed, the exchange of money for sex – becomes an acceptable and taken-for-granted 'equal exchange'.

Interestingly, the contemporary stereotype of the average punter as middle-class, employed and married with a couple of children may not be too far removed from the truth, although in fairness clients are 'from all walks of life'. The stereotype may be related to the economics of income: the middle classes and aspiring working classes have a history rooted in questioning what De Swaan calls 'commands' and have, through their action and choices and decision making ('upward pressure'/intended and unintended), been in part instrumental in freeing up some of these commands by authority/tradition. The working classes have traditionally been tied much more closely to commands of this kind, but as the post-war years have shown, with the development of cultures of resistance (see Weeks 1986) many commands and traditions have been resisted, challenged and changed. My own life experiences of the changes wrought within working-class Irish/Catholic communities are indicative of a freeing up of commands by authority/tradition of both religious and secular/state origin and of the development of resistance during the course of one generation.

The greater economic power of men, the reification of the use value vis-à-vis the exchange value of the female body, the feminization of poverty, power and domination expressed through violence and manipulation are all examples of continuities within gender relations through time. 'Upward pressure', changes in the continuous structuring of socio-economic structures (via the interplay between individual and society), de-traditionalization marked by freeing up of 'commands' and an increase in management by negotiation are examples of changes through time.

A recent paper by Helmut Kuzmics throws more light upon the relationship between psychic and social processes and the socio-historical context to lived experiences in contemporary society. Kuzmics analyses civilizing processes via his work on Weber and Elias and the social control of violence in and between whole societies (1994: 198–201). He states: 'Civilizing processes are, according to Elias, long term structural changes of personality and society, changes, that is, of social and psychological structures' (1993: 198). '"Material" processes are directly linked to psychic structures' (1993: 213). The 'apparatus of self-control' (1993: 233) and corresponding 'affective households' are regulated by fears and constraints shaped by social relationships of competition or by hierarchical imbalances of power. Rationality is double-edged: restraint characterized by strong fears vis-à-vis punishment or reward; a distancing of one's self from one's own affects. Civilization, as an ongoing process of civilizing processes is understood as the growth of more tightly woven self-constraints through the growth of interdependence (1993: 210–11).

The issue of violence is important here. Kuzmics locates the threat of violence within the social relationship and the balance of power between the strong and the weak: 'The greater the distance the less consideration will be given by the stronger: the weaker will be handed over to the strong. But if the relations between persons of equal rank become more numerous, one will restrain oneself, but it is also justified to demand this from other persons' (1993: 213).

Thinking about the issue of male violence within the mishmash of competing forces at play in everyday lived experiences, or within the individual/society relationship, we have a double-edged problem. Materially, women clearly, as a group, suffer inequalities of income and life chances. Feminist epistemologies, feminists and feminist activists have demanded social changes to address sexual and social inequalities. These demands are centrally involved in civilizing processes. Feminist praxis evokes changes for the benefit of women as subjects and citizens. The distance between the social standing of men and women has closed to some degree over the past thirty to forty years. However, the issue of male violence against women is a far-reaching problem that raises all sorts of issues about sexuality and the social organization of desire, the process of socialization, agencies of social control, patriarchy, the state and the constitution of gender relationships with regard to power, labour and cathexis (Connell 1987) in our society – indeed with regard to the civilizing process itself.

Taking an interpretive approach to explore, illuminate and better understand masculinities within the gendered social organization of prostitution through time necessitates a focus upon the men as well as on the women involved. What are their feelings, emotions and reasons for involvement in the sex-for-sale industry? Research on clients conducted by McKegany and Barnard (1996) highlight five key reasons their respondents (143 men) gave for purchasing sex from prostitutes: the opportunity to pay for specific services; the opportunity to have sex with many different women; the opportunity to have sex with women with specific physical characteristics; the fact that the encounter was limited to the sex act; and the thrill involved. These reasons are also found in Rosie Campbell's research (1997: 49), in her discussion of Faugier and Cranfield's research and in the following section.

Pimps and punters

This section contrasts the text of James Boswell – an eighteenth-century man of letters (friend and biographer of Dr Johnson) – and three men interviewed in April 1993 (by a leading women's monthly journal) about their visits to prostitutes. This is followed by the contemporary voices of women who are working as prostitutes talking about men as pimps and punters. The intention is to illuminate similarities and differences in the contrasting narratives through time, to explore possible overlaps in sentiments and affects since the time of the Enlightenment, modernity and the origins of the industrial revolution that came to fruition in the nineteenth century.

In the eighteenth century Hogarth produced the six pictures of the *Harlot's Progress*, riddled with disease and dying. Cleland's *Fanny Hill* provided readers with a vivid depiction of sexual life in London through the eyes of the heroine, complete with marriage as a happy ending. The form and organization of prostitution changed in the eighteenth century with the onset of the industrial revolution and the growth of cities. Henriques notes that there were 50,000 prostitutes in London in the eighteenth century and 20,000 in Paris (1962: vol. 2, 143). Certainly, London in the mid-eighteenth century was populated by 750,000 'souls' (Sennett 1992: 50) and was the largest city in the Western world, followed closely by Paris. The bourgeois class had begun to flourish, cities grew, what Sennett calls 'networks of sociability' developed: places where strangers might meet, coffee houses, urban parks, cafés and theatres and opera houses, where tickets were on sale rather than 'aristocratic patrons distributing places' (1992: 17). The focus of this renewed public life was the city.

How have things changed in the affects and sentiments expressed by social actors in the past two hundred years? To explore this, I will focus upon the experiences, sentiments and affects of James Boswell in his *London Journal* 1762–1763 (1950) which details his 'sexual wanderings' (Seymour-Smith 1969: 115).[9] The style (form) of the two sections documenting both Boswell's and contemporary clients' involvement in prostitution are understandably very different. The sentiments expressed, cognitive rationalizations and action/practices (content), however, are very similar.

James Boswell

On 11 December 1762 he had breakfasted with James MacPherson, then at the height of his fame as the 'translator' of Fingal. Boswell took comfort from 'the Scottish forger's philosophy of love' (Seymour Smith 1969: 116). In short, he told Boswell that London was the best place in the world to cure 'tormenting love':

> 'In the country', said he, 'we see a beautiful woman; we conceive an idea that it would be heaven to be in her arms. We think that impossible almost for us to attain. We sigh. We are dejected. Whereas here we behold as fine women as ever were created. Are we fond of one of them? For a guinea we get the full enjoyment of her, and when that is over we find that it is not so amazing a matter as we fancied. Indeed, after a moderate share of the pleasures of London, a man has a much better chance to make a rational unprejudiced marriage'. (Seymour-Smith 1969: 116)

Boswell was thinking and looking for a woman in order to 'enjoy delightful sex'. But, not just any woman. For although 'there cannot be higher felicity on earth enjoyed by man than the participation of genuine reciprocal amorous affection with an amiable woman . . . the surgeons' fees in this city come very high'. Further, he could not 'think of stooping so far as to make a most intimate companion of a grovelling-minded, ill-bred, worthless creature, nor can my delicacy be pleased with the gross voluptuousness of the stews' (Seymour-Smith 1969: 118). Boswell was looking for someone 'worthy' of him, 'a safer lay than he would have been likely to get in St James's Park' (1969: 118).

He made several calls on a 'handsome actress . . . by the name of Louisa'. Seymour-Smith notes that there 'is no doubt that this young man wanted not only sex but also romantic elegance' (1969: 119).

> We chatted pretty easily. We talked of love as a thing that could not be controlled by reason, as a fine passion. I could not clearly discern how she meant to behave to me. She told me that a gentleman had come to her and offered her £50, but that her brother knocked at the door and the man ran out of the house without saying a word. I said I wished he had left his money. We joked much about the £50. I said I expected some night to be surprised with such an offer from some decent elderly gentlewoman. (Seymour-Smith 1969: 119–20)

And the next day:

> Madam, you are at present a single woman. 'Yes Sir'. And your affections are not engaged? 'They are not Sir'. But this is leading me into a strange confession. I assure you, Madam, my affections are engaged. 'Are they Sir?' Yes, Madam, they are engaged to you. (She looked soft and beautiful.) I hope we

shall be better acquainted and like one another better. . . . What I like beyond
everything is an agreeable female companion, where I can be at home and have
tea and general conversation. I was quite happy to be here. 'Sir, you are welcome
here as often as you please. Every evening, if you please'. Madam I am infinitely
obliged to you. (1969: 120)

And the next day – Saturday:

> I talked on love very freely. 'Madam', said I, 'I can never think of having a
> connection with women that I don't love'. 'That, Sir', said she, 'is only having a
> satisfaction in common with the brutes. But when there is a union of minds,
> that is indeed estimable. But don't think Sir, that I am a platonist. I am not
> indeed'. (This hint gave me courage.) . . . (I thought it honest and proper to let
> her know that she must not depend on me for giving her much money.)
> 'Madam', said I, 'don't think too highly of me. Nor give me the respect
> which men of great fortune get by custom. I am here upon a very moderate
> allowance. I am upon honour to make it serve me, and I am obliged to live with
> great economy'. She received this very well. (1969: 120–1).

Seymour-Smith notes: 'it is by now clear that Boswell, like so many men
before and after him, was trying to have it both ways, and at the same time
preserve his money' (1969: 121).

On the following Monday he visited Louisa after breakfast and found her in
poor humour. Louisa owes two guineas for a debt; a friend has turned down
her request for a loan. Boswell tells her she must tell him when she is in
distress and he will tell her what he can do.

Seymour-Smith notes: 'Louisa was ultimately not real to him as a human
being: on to her he determinedly, if always with delicacy, projected a fantasy-
image, of what was to him the romanticized beloved he wanted to enjoy'
(1969: 122).

The saga goes on. Louisa borrows the money and by the following Sunday
Louisa had not exactly said yes to his advances, but had not said no either;
although Boswell was moving closer to his aim. The following Saturday she
'surrendered' (metaphorically) and told him to call at three the next day while
her landlady was at church. However, the landlady returned and they 'were
stopped most suddenly and cruelly from the fruition of each other'. Boswell
organizes the hiring of a room in an inn for the night under the pretext they
are man and wife. Seymour-Smith writes: 'Boswell could not take Louisa into
an "indecent" house, of which there are hundreds, and in any case he did not,
"romantically want to"' (1969: 124). One week later, Wednesday 12 January,
'he at last had – and enjoyed – her' (1969: 125).

> Five times was I fairly lost in supreme rapture. . . . But, couldn't help roving in
> fancy to the embraces of some other ladies which my lively imagination
> strongly pictured. I don't know if this was altogether fair. . . . I really conducted
> this affair with a manliness and prudence that pleased me very much. The
> whole expense was just eighteen shillings. (1969: 125)

Boswell begins to think of Lady Mirabel or Lady Mary Coke:

BOSWELL: You must know, Madam, I run up and down this town just like a wild colt.

LADY MIRABEL: Why, Sir, then, don't you stray into my stable, amongst others?

BOSWELL: Madam, I shall certainly have that pleasure. (1969: 125)

The following Saturday Louisa refused him, the next day she permitted him 'the rites of love . . . yet I felt my passion for Louisa much gone. I felt a degree of coldness for her and I observed an affectation about her which disgusted me' (1969: 125). On the Monday 'he had her again, but found his real enthusiasm was over' (1969: 126). He then called for Lady Mirabel. 'She seemed like a good deal. I was lively, and I looked like the game. As it was my first visit, I was very quiet. However, it was agreed that I should visit her often' (1969: 126).

Boswell discovers he has 'the clap' but cannot understand why as he has been with no woman recently but Louisa. He visits her to confront her; she owns that she knows nothing and has been in perfect health, for six months having 'to do with no man but yourself'. He leaves promising to tell no one of the affair. Later he sends a letter for he felt that 'the treacherous Louisa deserved to suffer for her depravity':

Madam: My surgeon will soon demand upon me of five guineas for curing the disease which you have given me. I must therefore remind you of the little sum which you had of me some time ago. You cannot have forgot upon what footing I let you have it. I neither paid it for prostitution nor gave it in charity. It was fairly borrowed, and you promised to return it. I give you notice that I expect to have it before Saturday sennight.

I have been very bad, but I scorn to upbraid you. I think it below me. If you are rendered callous by a long course of disguised wickedness, I should think the consideration of your deceit and baseness, your corruption both of body and mind, would be a very severe punishment. Call not that a misfortune which is a consequence of your own unworthiness. I desire no mean evasions. I want no letters. Send the money sealed up. I have nothing more to say to you. (1969: 128)

The two guineas are returned in a carefully sealed envelope 'without a single written word'.

Contemporary clients

Simon is a builder from East London, married to Tracy and quoted in *Living* (April 1993):

It was a typical lads' weekend away . . . a few beers and a good time. I suppose it started as a bit of a lark, really. We got into a taxi after the pubs closed and asked the driver to take us to the red light area. The place was crawling with prostitutes.

So I went for it. She took me down an alleyway, through a door and up to a small bedroom. I ripped my clothes off, she undressed, and that was that.

It was a bit like losing my virginity for the second time. I can't remember much about it, but I do remember thinking this is so easy. Sex with no hassles, no commitments, no build ups. I didn't need to ask her if she was in the mood. I just did it pure and simple. She ripped me off, though. I paid £50. Now I won't pay more than £30 unless I really like the girl. I once even had it for £10, though. Unbelievable.

I am genuine about my marriage. My wife's a diamond girl, we've always been the best of friends and had a great sex life. But she knows I've always been a bit of a Jack the Lad, the kind who used to love chatting girls up on a Saturday night, flirting with two or three before I made my choice. That's how I was brought up and I see nothing wrong with it. I just like a bit of a change, a bit of variety. With these girls you pay them, then it's up to you – whatever I want I can ask for. And they know what they are doing. They're professionals, trained and practised in the art of turning a man on.

I've calmed down a bit of late. When I came back from the Plymouth trip I was trying all sorts – picking up girls at King's Cross, saunas in Soho, massage parlours. I suppose AIDS does scare me. But I don't need to insist on condoms, they do that for me.

I've deliberately avoided anyone regular. That would be too much like having a long-term commitment. It's strange, really, I don't feel like I'm being unfaithful because I have no one favourite. I am just in it for the sex and happy to keep it that way.

I'm lucky that my wife doesn't suspect. She knows I work long hours, sometimes doing building jobs on the side after work, and that I spend a lot of time out with the lads. There would be hell to pay if she found out, but I do take precautions. I never do it in the car in case I leave some evidence and I always carry a clean set of clothes, just in case.

All in all, I just don't see what the fuss is about. It's seen as normal in many other countries, like Holland and Germany. Why can't it be like that here?

Barry, is a civil servant from Cardiff married to Angela:

I suppose you could say I've always been a bit shy over sex. I have always been a bit overweight. I was the podgy one at school, the last one to get a girlfriend, the one who always had the mickey taken out of them.

Of course I felt bitter about it. I was dreadfully under-confident until I met my wife when I was 27 and while that has helped, it's hardly proved to be the ideal sexual solution. For a start she seemed to regard sex as something for a special occasion. Normally we'll get into bed on a Friday night, she'll look at her watch, and say 'Right, you've got ten minutes and then it's time we're off to sleep'.

Under those circumstances there was no way I could open up to her and ask for what I really wanted. Take oral sex – the closest we got to discussing that was when she read out a letter in a magazine from a wife whose husband wanted oral sex. 'Thank goodness you're not like that', she said and closed the magazine. That was it. End of discussion.

So I went looking for it. . . . Sex was only a part of it. There was also a buzz of excitement, the thrill of travelling to new territory, opening new horizons. Picking up the girl was simplicity itself. There must have been ten, maybe twenty, to choose from, all standing on street corners at regular intervals. I just pulled in the car, wound down the window, asked her how much and she got in.

And that was it. I couldn't believe it was so easy. And it may sound strange but I didn't even notice her looks.

We headed back to her place, a room in a house, cosy enough. Yes, I suppose she was acting a role but she was surprisingly gentle with me. She put on some soft music, sat by me and asked me what I wanted. I think, in all honesty, that was the first time anyone had sat down and asked we what I wanted to do in bed. . . .

I hoped that it would help my marriage, but I can't really say it has. . . . And it has become progressively more difficult to cover up. . . . But my big fear is getting caught. The police have recently launched a crackdown. I'm not so worried about my marriage, I could survive that breaking up, but I think it would affect my future job prospects.

Using phone contact numbers would be safer, but it almost becomes a ritual now. The drive, the choice of women, perhaps that's part of the thrill. But I try not to analyse it too much and just enjoy it while it lasts.

David is a sales executive from Brighton, married and father of a four-year-old daughter.

To be honest I've always thought of prostitution as a rather sordid scene – hookers with oversexed bodies, selling themselves for cash.

In fact, I still don't consider myself as a prostitute's client, although if I was honest I'd have to admit that, yes, I do regularly get sexual relief by hiring a masseuse.

Just after Emily was born, Debbie seemed to lose interest in sex. From a fairly regular three or four times a week, we slipped down to once a week, once a month. . . . As I say, we were just too tired to think about anything, let alone the gradual deterioration of our sex lives. . . . I realised that we had a problem which I felt I couldn't solve with Debbie alone. I needed some outside help.

I tried to convince myself that the call to the massage service was an accident. . . . The strange thing was that I tried to convince myself that it really was what it said it was – a bonafide massage service. . . .

After the frustrations of the last couple of years, it was almost a relief to cast away the sexual stalemate of my marriage and have some good, honest sexual relief from someone who clearly knew exactly what they were doing. . . .

The problem with using these massage services is that there is something addictive about the kind of relief they offer. It was a couple of months before I rang again. . . . Since then I've been going about once a month – she's changed the number twice so that the police don't catch up with her – and I tend to use it as an escape, a complete sexual break that really is like a breath of fresh air. There's nothing particularly sordid about it – we don't even have full sex – and its almost as if I'm going out of my way not to get too attached.

That's how I rationalise it – by saying it's not as bad as having an affair. I don't feel any commitment to Belinda – in truth, I know very little about her, we don't talk much, and that's not what I'm there for. . . .

> What if Debbie found out? She'd be heartbroken, distraught, she'd probably go to pieces. That's why I'm careful to cover my tracks.... AIDS would worry me if I was having full sex. Perhaps that's why I've just kept it to safer forms of sex. Hopefully that's the way it will stay.

Male ownership and right of access to women's bodies does not seem to have been affected greatly by the passing of almost 200 years, nor have the ways in which female 'prostitutes' or 'bad-girls' are described by the very men who use them. Louisa was at fault and culpable for Boswell's dose of the clap, and the words used to describe her are 'baseness', 'deceit', 'wickedness', 'corruption of body and mind'. Simon described the 'place' as 'crawling with prostitutes'.

In Boswell's account we learn little about Louisa; she is a relative absence save for our reading of her through Boswell's desire and the fulfilment of the desire, at which point he is quick to move on to the next female to whom he is attracted and who shows him attention. Also, in the accounts by Simon and Barry the women they pay for sex are absent, and through the narratives there is a clear impression of the women's 'thing-like' status. The men all move on, not wanting to create commitment or emotional attachment to the women (objects) they pay for sex. There is a very strong sense of the predatory dimension of some men's encounters with women here which is directly related to 'machismo' – the need to demonstrate masculinity/virility linked to the biological reductionist, instrumental view of male sexual desire having to be satisfied once aroused. Boswell cloaks it in the niceties of 'romance', but it looks very much as though he is rationalizing it at an intellectual level, which includes the fact that he wanted to 'lay' someone in keeping with his own social class and who would not be likely to pass on a sexual disease. Giddens writes: 'Men have tended to be "specialists in love" only in respect of the techniques of seduction or conquest' (1992: 60). A respondent interviewed in London Weekend Television's documentary *Vice Trade* (1998) tells the camera 'a man is born and he dies; in between he tries to have as much sex as possible'.

Contemporary punters do not cloak this predatory aspect at all; they rationalize their actions according to their 'need', while maintaining a sense of commitment to wives and partners which is actually indicative of their control over the relationship. The wife/partner/good-girl would be 'heartbroken' if she knew. Men it seems are 'just in it for the sex'. Two respondents interviewed in *Vice Trade* (1998) about their visits to a classy brothel in Amsterdam appeared shocked at the suggestion that the sex they had just paid for could be similar to sex with a girlfriend. One said: 'You love your girlfriend...well...you would if you had one.' Indeed the sentiments expressed by MacPherson in 1762 could easily have been expressed by Barry or Simon in 1993:

> For a guinea we get the full enjoyment of her, and when that is over we find that it is not so amazing a matter as we fancied. Indeed, after a moderate share

of the pleasures of London, a man has a much better chance to make a rational unprejudiced marriage. (Seymour-Smith 1969: 116)

There is a much more obvious class dimension at play in the account by Boswell. The son of a judge and the biographer of Dr Johnson, Boswell wanted someone 'worthy' of him, a 'safer lay', particularly regarding the potential for disease. He was not looking for straight sex but wanted to court the woman, in this instance, the courtesan Louisa. Contrasting the narratives by women working as prostitutes about the men who pay for sex and those of the pimps they pay for 'protection' adds a further dimension to an interpretive approach that combines narratives and fictive/cultural texts:

MOIRA: Some clients are into weird things. Unprotected sex without a durex. Anal sex without a durex. They don't even want to pay more without a durex. Some bribe younger girls with extra fivers and tenners. The best are the older, married clients. An everyday client is better. Some clients will buy you things, give extra money, pay for holidays. Not all clients are weirdos. There is the client who loves his wife, has been married for 35 years and just wants to relive his youth. Some don't even want sex, but friendship. They will buy the shopping, pay for gifts and lots besides. A man can always find money for sex.

JENNY: You get a cross-section of men. What they have in common is that they demand from hookers the jobs they expect all women to do for them. We, like housewives, are psychiatrists, sympathizers and listeners, doing emotional work as well as sexual work. (*Company Magazine* 1990)

The women quoted in chapter 3 talked about the socialization process: how boys learn to become men in our society; the way they (the women) could be described as the clients of pimps; the emotional work they often perform alongside sex work; the extent of male violence against women; and the ways in which the operation of the law (sexual and street offence legislation) supported by the whore stigma fails to protect women from male violence.

In practice (politically and socially), there have been great changes in law, in education, in the major socializing agencies and in the development of equal opportunities legislation – all fought for by feminists through the women's movement. The attitudes expressed here by men towards women and access to women's bodies are unspeakable now in many circles – but they clearly exist, as most women are aware.

Prostitution as a cultural practice has undergone some changes in its organization and structures, changes have taken place in the negotiations between men and women around love, sexuality and relationships, and, as Giddens shows, there have been transformations of intimacy. But women are still, as Margareta Bertillson states: 'the chief means of symbolic exchange in the modern world' (1986: 33).

Certainly, the realities of management by command (by authority/tradition via the state/church/regularized conduct) indicative of the eighteenth and nineteenth century have shifted somewhat, and management by negotiation is largely indicative of contemporary society. Initial research from France on the evolution of prostitution from tradition to modernity shows us that there is a reduction in the numbers of visible female prostitutes on street, an increase in male prostitution, an increase in transsexual prostitution, increasing self-regulation and organization of prostitution by women themselves, and new forms of machine sexuality, coinciding with the AIDS era (WelzerLang 1993).

The above is a result of: a shift in the social relations of gender, a freeing up of the binary opposition of masculinity and femininity, framed within the heterosocial construction of sexuality and desire; AIDS; an increase in world poverty, particularly the feminization of poverty; the development of the global sex trade (organized and managed by men and the porn industry); the growth of prostitutes' rights movements; the link with feminism; the rise of grass-roots organizations supported by 'experts – professionals' (see Jennes 1990, 1993); and increasing sexual tourism. These all influence the social organization of prostitution on a global as well as on a local and nation/state scale.

An increase in the aestheticization of the whore in contemporary culture, from 'Whore' to 'Pretty Woman', is not only a variation on the 'fairytale',[10] but also exemplar of the cultural practice of prostitution as sexual practice related to male desire and female enactment and embodiment. The sale of marital sex aids, dressing up and role-play as part of the sexual encounter (good-girls dressing as bad) are clearly reflective of the dynamics of the intersexual play between partners. Dressing up 'bad' turns men on (or so it seems – an example of the adage 'wives in the kitchen, whores in the bedroom'?). However, in acts of violence against women men are also likely to verbally assault women with the label slut, whore, slag, bitch.

Prostitution is a complex phenomenon and needs to be explored in relation to pornography and violence to better understand and prevent violence against women and to educate against the taken-for-granted ownership and use value of women's bodies.

JENNY: Prostitute women are vulnerable to being attacked. I always worry about what I am going to be walking into. The physical dangers are compounded by our illegal status. We can't fall back on the law because they'll tell us it is our own fault, that we asked for it. So, if you're in a dodgy situation, as I have been several times, you cannot call hotel security, a caretaker or anyone to help you – even if you manage to shout. You are isolated and vulnerable and the men know that. (*Company Magazine* 1993: 77)

LOUISE: I only had one violent punter... punters pull up and something tells me yes go with them or no don't go with him.... This time I knew something funny about this bloke but I was desperate to get some money... he raped me and beat me up afterwards and left me stranded in this field. . . . I was all dressed up ready for this wedding. . . . I had to go to a pub . . . running up the street trying to pull up my tights . . . I have seen him afterwards. . . . I can still remember his number plate. . . . I saw him two weeks afterwards . . . and I was frightened not for me but for other girls who went with him . . . he only wanted the younger girls. . . . I put a brick through his windscreen . . . he is rough. . . . I think he hated women . . . he called me all these horrible names.

Violence against women working as prostitutes is endemic (Hoigard and Finstad 1992; Root 1986; O'Neill 1994, 1995; Radford and Russell 1992; Barnardo's 1998; Kelly et al. 1995; WHISPER[11]); not from all clients, but all the women I have spoken to have experienced violence in some form from clients and/or pimps.

Male violence against women is a part of all women's experience, whether it is as a result of violence directed against our physical bodies; emotional violence and abuse; threats of violence in our encounters with men we know and men we do not know; and varying levels of harassment and bullying represented in action/practice, through the organization and operation of rationalized institutions and agencies, such as the media, workplaces, daily news, criminal justice process and practice.[12] Male violence against female prostitutes is a crucial issue to address with regard to masculinities, the social organization of prostitution and gendered relations in conditions of reflexive modernity/postmodernity.

Male violence against women working as prostitutes

Exploring the relationship and interrelationship between psychic and social processes related to male violence against women working on street can have resonances for male violence against all women and may lead to the development of policy-oriented practice.

Pimps may initially offer support and love. Hooking a new girl is often done gradually – drinks, flattery, attention, promises of care, window-shopping and promises about their life together – until she is hooked, and then comes the reality of street life, often sharing the man with other women and, for many women, a spiralling process of physical and emotional violence.

One of the worst examples documented is that of Colin Gayle. Simon Garfield reports that:

The pimp doesn't protect the girl. The pimp is there to get the money. If she gets beaten by a punter and the pimp is on the scene, then obviously he'll intervene because the pimp is damaging the goods. Colin Gayle didn't mind damaging his string of London prostitutes. But the relationship between a pimp and his girls is a complicated one. For the police, the problem was to get them all in front of a jury. (Garfield 1990: 3)

Pauline Green and Kim Nunn were two of Gayle's 'girls'. Pauline Green was kicked down steps, kicked in the legs and kidneys and punched, her knees hit repeatedly with a hammer. Kim Nunn was hit with a long, white metal tube around the knees and kicked repeatedly for not showing enough respect and for missing some dust while cleaning a cupboard. He beat Carol Rossiter with a brick so badly that she couldn't see through bruised eyes, and he threatened Sharon Blake with death by 'putting her into an acid bath and scattering her bones on a motorway'.

Gayle seems obsessed with the need that his girls show him and his friends respect. His idea of respect is decidedly bizarre and is about exercising as much power and control over 'his girls' as he could muster. Respect means subservience/submission. There are many resonances here of women's experiences of domestic violence. A major problem for the agencies of social control and welfare, such as the policing and subsequent criminal justice system, is that pimps are notoriously difficult to 'get at'. Women are usually too terrified to give evidence, under threat from the perpetrator and/or his friends. On arrest, the men involved refuse to talk and often they are simply released due to lack of evidence. Gayle received fourteen years' imprisonment. The team of police officers who tracked him down and developed the case were lucky enough to have four witnesses (many others withdrew their evidence): Pauline Green, Kim Nunn, Carol Rossiter and Gillian Kemper. Kemper muddled her evidence and Gayle was acquitted on all charges relating to her.

The Black Posse Trial, which took place in Wolverhampton in 1984, is an example of the problems inherent in 'getting at' pimps. Five pimps from Wolverhampton were charged with offences similar to Gayle's. They were sentenced to seven years. Eighteen months had been served in custody and they were out after a further eighteen months. The message to the women as witnesses is clear – what is the point of giving evidence?[13]

The gendered social organization of prostitution is founded upon patriarchal relationships and hegemonic heterosexuality. Pimps hold physical, emotional and material power over women working as prostitutes. Power over women is exercised in the interrelated spheres of work, sexuality, love and violence and underpinned by the ideology of exchange and the use value of women and women's bodies. This relationship is premised upon the earning potential of the woman related to coercion, bullying and, ultimately, fear – psychological fear as well as fear of physical violence.

Strong emotional attachment expressed as love is common in prostitute/pimp relationships. The demand for the use of women's bodies for sexual relief, for fantasy, for thrill, or simply for physical contact with another human being is a demand founded upon patriarchal relationships embedded in psychic structures of domination. A key aspect of this is the economic power of men and the relative poverty and economic need experienced by some women.

Fear, bullying, coercion and violence are also central aspects of the client/prostitute relationship. The relationship of both pimp and punter to the 'prostitute' is based for many upon her use value. Hearn (1993) and others (Harding 1989; Coole 1993; Benhabib 1992; Benjamin 1993) have outlined the masculinist construction and reproduction of social theory. It is important to build upon this work by uncovering the ideological (the ways in which meaning is used to sustain domination) via social theory which is feminist (women-centred) and which focuses upon men, masculinity, power and violence in lived relations in order to underpin and serve as the backdrop for the development of policy-oriented practice that resists, challenges and changes the dynamics of power and domination that are often taken for granted in society.

Exploring the ideology of exchange in prostitute/client and prostitute/ pimp relationships (historically rooted in the God-given right of men to control and own women's bodies and women's work as well as their sexualities) and also in many heterosexual relations based upon commodity fetishism, economic reductionism and instrumental reason may lead us to develop practice based upon more egalitarian models. Challenging attitudes, prejudice and instrumental value systems is of course very difficult. However, feminism and socialism have taught us to speak out in our many voices about injustice, inequality and repression, and to envision new models and new modes of living. Through feminist praxis (purposeful knowledge), through action, writing and speaking, through action research and through our sign worlds of sexuality, we can move towards real and practical changes.

Exploring the materiality of gender relations, the vast economic, sexual and social inequalities that women experience daily, leads us back to the ideological and to the interrelationship between experience and structures of domination. As second-class citizens, as dependants on men in the eyes of the government and major institutions, such as banks, welfare benefit and social services, women do not have nearly enough access to material resources within the social organization of society. Lack of adequate childcare services, welfare benefits, social benefits and employment maintains and reinforces the feminization of poverty. The interrelation of material inequality and the ideology of exchange (women's bodies can be bought, sold, abused, used and 'if she doesn't want it she only has to keep her legs shut') serve to reify sexual and social inequalities and the owning and controlling of all women's bodies.

Furthermore, lack of access to emotional resources can have a detrimental effect on self-esteem, confidence and self-worth, maintaining a woman in a lifestyle she has neither chosen nor wants. Many of the young women I have spoken to drift into prostitution, often from the residential care system, often through the need to 'go along' with new friends or a peer group which offer (what is perceived as) much-needed emotional support to these young women. Once they have 'done three or four punters' they begin to 'get used' to prostitution. Working from the street and in the street subculture invariably brings the problem of being pimped and the problems of male violence, as well as problems of psychic and social alienation.

Focusing upon pimps and punters to develop awareness about masculinity through the gendered organization of prostitution has raised the following issues:

- women's involvement in prostitution is related directly to the emotional, economic and social oppression of women;
- women who are pimped are being controlled by men at emotional, physical and labour/work levels;
- the controlling aspect of 'masculinity' is interrelated with the predatory and machismo dimension, which also includes 'fear' of the 'feminine';
- issues related to cathexis and desire (such as thrill, fantasy, sexual relief) need to be explored further, focusing upon masculinity and the exchange of money for sex;
- issues of male power and use of women and women's bodies must be located within a wider understanding of the patriarchal organization of society as hegemonic heterosexuality, women's relative absence from the major agencies and institutions of our society, the feminization of poverty and the misogynist base of much of our advertising imagery.

Indeed, as Rosie Campbell (1997) states, in order to make sense of men's involvement in commercial sex we must locate the meanings they give within understandings of dominant cultural constructions of male sexuality. Many of Campbell's telephone interviewees referred to purchasing sex as 'just business . . . just sex'.

Summary

Exploring issues of masculinity can shift attention away from the ideology of sex workers as 'helpless, feckless' or 'victims' and on to the men who organize, control and use women working as prostitutes for money and for sexual and/ or sadistic pleasure through consumption and consuming desire. Shifting attention on to the men involved and exploring their involvement at a deeper level that interrelates psychic and social dimensions may lead to both better understanding *and* interventionary strategies that do not simply criminalize the whore morally and materially or offer piecemeal solutions to sanctioning pimps and punters.

The picture is complex, for at one and the same time the international prostitutes' rights movements are alerting us to the realities of life for many women caught in poverty, situations of war and famine, and arguing across the board that prostitution is work and women should be given the same rights and liberties as other workers. Moreover, the movements are arguing that all laws which criminalize prostitution should be dropped, and that laws which protect women from violence, abuse and coercion should be enforced.

We need to stop approaching subjects like prostitution by focusing upon the women as wrongdoers, as transgressors of 'normal femininity', as law-breakers, whether this be against moral, criminal or civil law. In order to develop a clearer understanding and analysis of the gendered organization of prostitution we must turn our attention to the men involved in prostitution and the wider sex industry. To do this we need to explore more fully the historical, social, economic and environmental relationships between men, masculinity and prostitution (including pornography) and machismo, male sexuality and male violence against women. It is hoped that this chapter has encouraged the problematizing of 'masculinity' in relation to pimps and punters by making pimps and punters more than just an absence (Hearn 1993), and by contextualizing this within an understanding of the modern city, consumption and Elias's concept of the 'civilizing process' – thus developing a more interpretive approach to understanding male involvement and the gendered social organization of prostitution in the city in conditions of reflexive modernity/postmodernity.

This chapter has endeavoured to develop a better understanding of masculinities and gender relations by exploring a micrology of masculinity within a broader socio-historical and cultural context. The interrelation of psychic and social dimensions is crucial to all this. In order for this work to develop three key dimensions need to be explored further:

- a fuller analysis of masculinities, particularly the concept of hegemonic masculinities relating to labour, power, cathexis and violence and the interrelationships of psychic and social processes in the shifts from modernity to reflexive modernity/postmodernity;
- a more thorough analysis of the social organization of desire, particularly relating to consumption and consuming desire in current times (an analysis that could be contextualized in Giddens's approach to the transformations of intimacy in later modernity);
- finally, a more through analysis of continuity and change in gendered relations through time and space, particularly relating to environmental contexts – to social spatialization (currently being developed by Hubbard 1999).

These three key dimensions need to centre upon the personal and experiential as well as on the materiality of lived relations, of 'lived cultures', with regard to pimps and punters. This can be achieved through the development of ethnographic work premised upon the mediation of mimesis and constructive rationality – ethno-mimesis.

Sennett's critique of the emphasis upon life-histories, upon inner worlds to the exclusion of the wider social world, the social environments in which we live, is very pertinent. The relationship or tension between self and society need to be such that we are 'other directed' – out there directed – we must not retreat further and further into 'the recesses of the self' indicative of the sentimentalized and self-indulgent society O'Hear describes. Benhabib and Bauman make similar points. We should 'be' autonomous individuals *and* responsible members of collectives. For Sennett, we have centuries of collect-ive learning to base this upon: 'The thesis of this book . . . is that these blatant signs of an unbalanced personal life and empty public life have been a long time in the making. They are the result of changes that began with the ancien régime and the formation of a new capitalist, secular, urban culture' (Sennett 1992: 16).

Certainly, Erich Fromm's critique of the greatness and the limitations in Freud's thought is centred upon a key problematic in Freud's work – if only the development of work on the self, on the individual, had developed into a critique of the wider social world, of wider society. The current social order is marked by increasing narcissism and flight from reality, as well as by increasing postemotionalism. We need to try and gain a balance between autonomous individuality and collective responsibility. We need to develop gendered relations based upon intersubjective mutual recognition, upon the mediation of mimesis (as sensuous knowing) and upon constructive ration-ality (interpretation, commentary and criticism). Collaborative work, multi-agency work and collective action premised upon PAR are representative of intersubjective mutual recognition and purposeful knowledge. As sociolo-gists, feminists and researchers, we should be directing our interpretive skills and energies in this direction.

Conclusion: Towards a Politics of Feeling

The simplest vehicle of truth, the story is also said to be 'a phase of communication', 'the natural form for revealing life'. Its fascination may be explained by its power to give a vividly felt insight into the life of other people and to revive or keep alive the forgotten, dead-ended, turned-into-stone parts of ourselves.

Trinh 1989: 123

Storytelling: her words set into motion the forces that lie dormant in things and beings.

Trinh 1989: 147

A politics of feeling: between theory, lived experience and praxis

Rooted in the development of critical feminist standpoint(s) methodology, critical feminist praxis can provide a thorough account of prostitution in conditions of later modernity/postmodernity and look towards, envision, transformations in sexual, social and cultural inequalities. To repeat a point made earlier in this book: feminism is a practice, a politics as well as 'a strong intellectual movement' (A. Gray 1997: 90). Within this text, *a politics of feeling* describes how emotionality/feeling is embedded in the materiality of social life and how, through interpretive ethnography, we can access feeling worlds to provide a fuller understanding of lived cultures and the interrelation of psychic and social processes and structures in all our lives. *Ethno-mimesis* provides a theoretical organizing construct which describes a research process as 'feeling form'. Immersion, identification in the lived cultures of individuals and groups and subsequent commentary and criticism may lead to feminist praxis. Ethno-mimesis also describes a research outcome. For example, participatory research may lead to the production of ethno-mimetic texts which evolve from the hybridity and intertextuality involved in re-presenting social research through performance art, as illustrated in chapter 2 (in focusing upon the work of Sara Giddens). Ethno-mimetic texts re-tell the narratives of women's life-histories in visual, poetic or print-based form and may reach a wider audience than the usual audience for social research.[1] Academic involvement in the public sphere, situated between critical feminist theory and renewed methodologies for social research, can be transformative and can facilitate purposeful knowledge.

The fragments of stories documented throughout this text are fragments of the politics of everyday life; they speak and show the embeddedness of feeling, meaning, being and becoming in the lived, embodied experiences of the women, men and young people working as prostitutes. There are resonances for all women in the stories which unfold here. Prostitutes are indices for all women in reflexive modernity/postmodernity.

Any attempt to understand prostitution in current times must be very clear about the socio-economic and historical contexts to prostitution. These contexts include:

- the activities of the state, including the development, operation and interpretation of the criminal and civil law (see Phoenix 1999 for a useful account of the law);
- the globalization of prostitution;
- the activities of those institutions and agencies (statutory and voluntary) working with and for women and young people working in prostitution;
- inequalities of income, education, welfare and health, employment and training opportunities;
- the realities of sexual, cultural and social inequalities and oppression through time (especially in the UK since the nineteenth century with the rise of industrialism and the growth of towns and cities);
- the increasing feminization of poverty, male violence, gender relations – masculinities and the social organization of desire;
- above all, any attempt to understand the complex issues involved must avoid maintaining and reproducing the ideology of prostitution. By the ideological, I mean that which serves to conceal unequal and oppressive sexual and social relations and practices. Sectional interests presented as universal interests, the denial of contradictions and the naturalization of that which has been socially constructed are all examples of ideological effects (Giddens 1991a, 1991b).

As a society we cannot move forward in an any enlightened way until we start calling things by their name, until we start seeing things as they are. Seeing things as they are and cutting through ideology and ideological effects involves connecting lived experience, feeling, meaning with theory and practice. This inevitably involves accessing the multiple experiences and realities of the women and young people involved in prostitution, including those who pay for sex and those who pimp and manage 'sex work'. It involves bringing agencies working with and for sex workers together with sex workers to plan, to organize service provision and to engage in critical discourse.

Multi-agency work with women working as prostitutes (for example women-centred multi-agency forums) can act in a way similar to the Habermasian concept of the 'counter-public sphere' (see Felski, 1989: 154–82) – a relatively autonomous sphere where agencies, individuals and groups sharing commonalties of experience and interests (if not ends) can engage in discourse and development and move towards the possibility of transformative consequences. Currently, Hilary Kinnell coordinates a UK-based network of sex work projects. Regional forums also exist where those involved in running projects in the regions can meet to discuss various issues that come up for workers and women. These organizations are premised upon health needs, but could be extended to include the development of multi-agency regional forums that are women-centred (not led by a statutory agency, which is currently the norm in some cities), which in turn could feed into women-centred bi-annual national forums.[2]

The study presented here is founded upon a desire to understand and change sexual and social inequalities through critical feminist theory and feminist practice. In the course of the initial study (in 1990) I was committed to listening to women involved in doing prostitution, and I saw the absolute centrality for creating intellectual and practical spaces for women's voices. I felt that theoretical work should develop from the reality of everyday life, from our lived experiences. In talking to women, getting to know them better and listening to life-histories full of hope, pain, struggle and humour, I saw the resonances for all women in the experiences of prostitute(d) women as 'other'. This 'otherness' is generated through whore stigma. These resonances are to do with relationships with men as clients and partners; the attempt to maintain control in situations where they were relatively powerless; the extent of violence against them along the entire continuum described by Liz Kelly (1988) (which was seen in high relief in my interviews with young people in the care of a local authority); and the fear of the feminine or their own feminine side that is so deeply marked in some men within patriarchal society.

For some women, limited access to material and/or emotional resources led to their involvement and entrenchment in the subculture of prostitution. In asking 'why?', we need to take into account the following: the commodification of women's bodies, sexualities and use value in society; the relationship between pornography, advertising imagery and women's view of themselves; the ways in which, as girls, we grow up watching ourselves being watched and internalize the male gaze (Berger 1978; Mulvay 1975; Theweleit 1987, 1989, 1994; Benjamin 1993); hegemonic heterosexuality; indeed, the many ways in which we all consciously and unconsciously help to reproduce patriarchy.

The 'whore stigma' (Pheterson 1986, 1989, 1990) is transferable to all women, but particularly to those who transgress the rules and norms that 'control' women morally and socially. The relationship between ideology and materiality; the lived experience of the body as subject/object, as embodied and disembodied; the experiences of male violence – are part of all women's experiences to lesser or greater degrees. The 'prostitute' is simply the 'end stop' in discourses on 'good' and 'honest' women. Discourses around prostitution are part of self-sustaining discourses and images which feed into and are part of the representation of women and men in general. These discourses and images, symbolic and material, feed into the actual material and ideological treatment and status of women through instrumental reason.

For Jessica Benjamin (1993) intersubjective analysis that tries to untangle the bonds of domination is the way forward for personal and social transformation. 'Mutual recognition' of equal subjects is central to individual and social change. The principle of rationality is the hallmark of modernity and reduces the world to objects of exchange, calculation and control. Male rationality sets the stage for domination that appears to be gender neutral but 'its logic dovetails with the Oedipal denial of women's subjectivity, which reduces the other to object' (Benjamin 1993: 185). Psychic repudiation of femininity includes the negation of dependency and mutual recognition. This is homologous with the private/public split and the social banishment of nurturance and intersubjective relatedness to the private domestic realms of women and children. The public/private split is further linked to the autonomy of the father and dependency of the mother. As rationalization intensifies (Wouters's formalizing tendencies – see chapter 6) in society, so does erotic domination, the subject (male) fears becoming like the object (woman) he controls.

The crisis of masculinit(y)ies (Samuels 1994; Hearn 1990, 1992, 1993; Brittan 1989; Giddens 1992; Connell 1995) are directly related to feminist challenges to the privileging of reason, rationality and modernity. Feminist critiques of the Enlightenment as progress and the masculinist basis of our institutions embedded in hegemonic heterosexuality have had a large role to play in the development of postmodernity and postmodernism. But so too have feminist critical theorists across the major disciplines as well as outside the academy (for example, Nicholson 1994; Trinh 1989, 1991; Wolff 1995; Price and Shildrick 1999; Battersby 1998). Intensification of the processes of postmodernity and postmodernism – emphasizing de-traditionalization, plurality, multiple perspectives, a loosening up of previous structures and practices – can, I would argue, help to create spaces where intersubjective mutual recognition can unfold.

Engaging with the realities of women's lives through feminist research grounded in the multiple standpoints of women within the context of social order, insecurity and social change, at an everyday as well as on a more global level, may enable us to understand the lived relations of women working in the sex industry. Renewed methodologies for social research can counter postemotionalism and engage with the standpoints of (in this case) women working in prostitution through PAR. PAR can help us to develop better understanding of the complexities of lived experiences and facilitate spaces for collective action. Doing participatory action research is, for me, about a politics of feeling – both in the research process, through a feminist standpoints approach and in the outcomes of the research – as feminist praxis.

Our social worlds are made up of structures of gender domination embedded in psychic and social practices, structures and processes. Postmodern interpretive ethnographies, working in participatory ways across disciplines and genres – for example, across community arts, photography or performance art and ethnographic research – can illuminate and challenge ideological structures and effects through 'feeling forms'. 'Feeling forms' (for example as illustrated in chapter 2) are developed or constructed in the tension or mediation between mimesis and constructive rationality. 'Feeling forms' could incite us to feel and engage with the affects, sentiments and experiences of marginalized peoples and may motivate us to act, thus giving rise to *a politics of feeling*.

How can the voices of women articulating needs, experiences and meanings, 'told' through ethnographic research, be addressed by women-centred research? My answer here is by collective responses through action research, through participatory action research, through working with and for women working as prostitutes. As I have argued throughout this text, in order to develop a better understanding of prostitution and the sex industry we need to examine the interrelationships between the micrology of women's lives and the meta-conditions of wider society, including historical analyses. This includes an examination of masculinities and the social organization of desire. This, in turn, can facilitate the development of work, including policy-oriented practice by women who identify as feminists working in the sex industry and women who identify as academic feminists, activist feminists or simply feminists. Involving ourselves in action research – working together – and developing analyses that acknowledges the sameness, the difference and the need for collective responses is a useful and productive place to start.

Understanding prostitution and developing feminist praxis: deconstructing binary dichotomies

In summarizing the two major storylines (problematizing categories of prostitutes and prostitution; and problematizing feminist research) it is absolutely clear that we need to develop better understanding of prostitution and feminisms by acknowledging the paradoxes, the contradictions and the similarities and differences between and amongst women by problematizing prostitution and feminism. In chapter 1 I explored the need to bridge the divide between radical feminist analyses (which, in seeking to address the painful sexual inequalities and injustices, silences some of the women working in prostitution) and sex-positive feminists, who are linked to libertarian versions of sexual politics (and who, in turn, help to silence the voices of women whose stories do not represent their version of prostitution and the sex-for-sale market). At present we are simply reinforcing binary thinking. We need to deconstruct the binaries and privilege constellational thinking. We can start by recognizing each other's perspective, recognizing 'the other', acknowledging the paradoxes and contradictions, the similarities and differences and the possibilities for consensus. As outlined in *Part II*, this must be centred around the voices, the stories of women working as prostitutes across the entire continuum of the sex, or love-for-sale, industry. This also includes deconstructing the relationships between researcher and researched through participatory forms of feminist research – working *with* not simply on or for. Moreover, through ethno-mimesis we are involved in deconstructing binaries of what constitutes research data, for example using interview material *and* material from cultural/fictive texts – art, film, literature.

In *Part III* I explored the symbolic imaginings and re-presentations of the prostitute and prostitution in art and literature alongside ethnographic work with women and young people, and argued that this can help to provide a better understanding of 'prostitutes' and prostitution. Cultural/fictive texts tell stories of historical conditions, the way 'prostitutes' were and are perceived, and they can show us the 'real' behind appearances. Cultural texts are formed from the 'stuff' of society, they contain sedimented aspects of our social worlds. Moreover, through collaboration across disciplines and genres, we can produce socio-cultural analyses of prostitution in current times.

The second storyline problematized doing ethnographic research in late modern/postmodern times. Reflexive modern/postmodern society is marked by postemotionalism and loss of authenticity, as well as by de-traditionalization, an increase in risks and hazards, the loss of 'the real' and the increasing influence of simulacra. In chapter 2 we explored the shifts and transformations in ethnographic research since the 1980s, marked by the crisis in looking, and the end of the authority of the researcher. There is no longer a privileging of the researcher's viewpoint, but a privileging of multiple realities and the loss of universalizing tendencies, the loss of a single version of the world. Instead, ethnographers provide spaces for multiple voices to be heard, multiple versions of the standpoints of people. Some ethnographers generate knowledge that engages with feelings, emotions, that access the 'lived cultures' of previously silenced, marginalized peoples (Denzin 1997). Through a version of critical standpoint feminisms, through participatory action research, I argue that we can work *with* the stereotypical subjects of research to produce ethnographic texts (visual, aural, print-based) that cross disciplines and privilege the voices of those on the borders. Such work is potentially transformative by re-telling and re-presenting stories of domination and resistance and, to paraphrase Bauman, goes a long way to help citizens to recover the voices they lost or stopped trying to make audible (1995: 284). Conducting participatory action research produces 'knowledge for' as feminist praxis.

In this text, feminist praxis is embedded within a cultural politics of difference.

A cultural politics of difference can be illustrated for example by drawing upon Pakulski's concept of social-cultural citizenship. Social citizenship involves struggles for participation and inclusion, which inevitably has cultural dimensions. These cultural dimensions include the right to presence and visibility versus marginalization; the right to dignifying representation versus stigmatization; and the right to identity and maintenance of lifestyle versus assimilation (Pakulski 1997). These struggles are currently being fought regionally, nationally and internationally, from a bottom-up or grass-roots position, by organizations and agencies and by prostitutes' rights organizations, for instance the English Collective of Prostitutes and Scotpep in the UK. The inequalities and ideological effects of social divisions that mark 'prostitutes' out as 'other', as the end stop in discourses on good or honest women, are illuminated through ethno-mimetic texts, through interpretive research, through a politics of feeling.

A politics of feeling is constituted by the mediation or tension between feeling and reason in the research process and is articulated through interpretive analysis, through socio-cultural analysis. Acknowledging our feeling worlds is an important step in order to gain a better understanding of the realities we might want to transform. As a process and an outcome, ethno-mimesis is also rooted in mutual recognition and the tension or mediation between individual autonomy and mutual recognition. For example, the fragments of the life-story narratives documented in chapters 3 and 4 tell us so much about the life-worlds and 'lived cultures' of the women and young people I interviewed and worked with. But they also have enormous resonances in and for all of our lives, as women and as men. They provide clear pictures of the structures of domination at psychic and social levels. They show the relation of the particular to the general. Micrology of women's lives can and does show the workings of broader structures of power, signification and instrumental reason. Through the power of these stories we can engage with the feeling worlds of the women and young people involved, thus countering postemotionalism and the loss of authenticity that marks our experiences of the world through TV simulacra, the media and the fragmented and fractured communities we live in and through.

Ethnography and ethno-mimetic texts can show the importance of our feeling worlds through sensuous knowing, in print-based texts as well as through dance, art, live art, performing art. The work of Trinh and Sara Giddens are used here as exemplars. Participatory action research and the production of ethno-mimetic texts *with* marginalized peoples are one step on the road to mutual recognition and to getting the balance right between autonomous individuality and collective responsibility.[3]

As a feminist I look forward to a time when we can experience greater individual autonomy *and* collective responsibility. In the meantime we need to ensure that women working as prostitutes are not criminalized, stigmatized or treated as social junk, and that the children involved in prostitution are supported by welfare and social services that intervene through harm minimization practices and policies, *not* through practices and policies that criminalize these young people further. Until we have a thorough understanding of the issue of prostitution from the multiple standpoints of those involved we cannot begin to understand the complexities of prostitution and the lives of those involved. Responses to prostitution should occur with the help of the women involved, the ordinary women who are sold, who choose, who are forced, who drift into prostitution in the context of hegemonic heterosexuality and patriarchal capitalism in postmodern times. Renewed methodologies for social research that incorporate the voices of citizens through scholarly/civic research as participatory research can raise our awareness and understanding of the complexity of lived experience and wider social processes and structures. Moreover, they may also produce critical reflexive texts that may inspire and motivate social change.

This text is located at the intersection of feminist critical theory, sociocultural research (ethnographic participatory research) and alternative forms of re-presentation/interpretation. It is hoped that the hybrid account and analysis of prostitution and feminism(s) which emerges here is of positive value and use to those interested in the complexities of prostitution as a phenomenon in current times. This work is rooted in the influence of the Frankfurt School, especially Adorno and Benjamin; the development of critical feminist theory; and a commitment to purposeful knowledge – rooted in Marx's dictum that philosophers should not be content to simply understand the world but should seek to change it. The interrelationship between theory and practice is a driving force, and specifically the interrelationship between academic knowledge and social power involved in the dynamics of participatory action research. The interplay between critical thought and feminist praxis is one source of resistance to and transformation of the disempowering and reductive psychic and social processes indicative of current times.

Notes

INTRODUCTION: SOCIO-CULTURAL CONTEXTS – RENEWED
METHODOLOGIES FOR SOCIAL RESEARCH

1 The research methodology PAR was launched at the Cartagena World Symposium in 1977. Orlando Fals Borda (1985) describes PAR as an intellectual and practical creation of the peoples of the Third World; their preoccupation with poverty, exploitation and oppression served to unite them into seeking creative alternatives and social transformation. PAR emerged from 'theories of dependence (Cardosa, Furtado) and exploitation (González, Casanova), the counter-theory of subversion (Camilo Torres) and the theology of liberation (Gutiérrez), dialogical techniques (Fréire) and the reinterpretation of the theses on scientists' commitment and neutrality taken from Marx and Gramsci, among others' (1985: 2). PAR is a methodology which encompasses research, political action and critical theory. Analyses and practice are seen as sources of knowledge embedded within grass-roots knowledge and praxis. PAR is a tool for mobilizing people's power through four levels of communication: collective research; critical recovery of history; valuing and applying folk culture; producing and diffusing new knowledge. Disseminating new knowledge complies with Gramsci's notion of transforming 'common sense' into 'good sense' or critical knowledge, which is the sum of experiential and theoretical knowledge. PAR is a dialectical, dialogical response to possibilities for social transformation in collaboration with marginalized peoples.

2 This holds true of the ethnographic work with refugees and asylum seekers that the author is currently engaged in. This PAR project seeks to present the 'voices' of refugees living in the UK in order to raise awareness and challenge media stereotypes. The life story accounts have been re-presented in artistic forms by the people themselves (co-researchers) with the help of artists/photographers. The research is being conducted ethically and sensitively and is taking advice from agencies and groups working with refugees and asylum seekers at grass-roots level. The first exhibition of work opened at the Bonnington Gallery, Nottingham Trent University, 4 October – 13 November 1999.

3 Ethno-mimesis stands in direct contrast to O'Hear's (1998) criticism of society's overindulgence in 'feeling' to the detriment of reason in his critique of the

'sentimentalization of society'. O'Hear is concerned that our society's obsession with sentiment and displays of superficial emotionalism belie a self-indulgent society where feeling is elevated above reason and personal gratification above commitment. O'Hear's paper is one of a collection of essays which offer critiques of the sentimentalization of society. What is missing from O'Hear's paper is a vision of the dialectical interrelationships between feeling and reason, between feeling, thinking and doing. The critiques contained in the collection need to be contextualized within historical, sociological analyses which throw light on the socio-economic and political transformations over time and relational changes in the affects, sentiments and mores of those who people 'society', whose actions and beliefs are both the medium and the outcome of their social worlds. O'Hear does not focus upon the resistances and challenges to self-indulgence, sentimentalization, and the parody of commitment he found in his analysis of the state of modern society.

4 See Adorno and Horkheimer (1979), and especially the essay 'The culture industry: enlightenment as mass deception', pp. 120–67.

5 The author is currently working with Bosnian and Afghan refugees and photographers/artists to help the 'refugees' re-present their life-history work in artistic forms.

6 Recognizing this central tension or mediation between mimesis (as sensuous knowing) and constructive rationality (instrumental reason) necessitates *critical interpretation* in any examination of the social world, or in any examination of art forms, for example in the performance illustrated in chapter 2. Critical interpretation enables us to see (and hopefully feel) that experience related to feeling necessarily turns dialectical, given the tension between objective social structures and lived experience; materiality and feeling/emotion. In acknowledging this we can move towards a social theory which holds mimesis (feeling) in dialectical tension with constructive rationality (instrumental reason) without mimesis's/feeling's/emotion's retreat in an attempt to make sense of and 'speak' or 'show' women's lived experiences in the development of a feminist analysis, or better understanding, of prostitution.

Considering and exploring the relationship between mimesis and constructive rationality through critical thinking will help to: articulate and develop the foundations for the exploration of 'micrology' of women's lives; unfold the general from the particular; show and understand the mediation of subject and object – individual and society; and show the importance of theorizing emotion 'feeling' within the context of women's experiences of the social world. The work of Gudrun Axeli Knapp (1999) and Regina Becker-Schmidt (1999) highlight the important mediation between subject and object and the absence of reconciliation between the two. Feminist analysis must develop an interdisciplinary integration of different theoretical perspectives that acknowledge the restricted ideal of universal knowledge and grand theory but must also analyse large-scale societal constellations.

PART I FEMINIST KNOWLEDGE AND SOCIAL RESEARCH: UNDERSTANDING PROSTITUTION

1 See Trinh T. Minh-Ha 'Grandmother's story' in *Women, Native, Other* (1989). This involvement is not based upon writing what Trinh calls 'a pet negro system'

– reducing the 'other' to versions of ourselves. It is based upon respect for differences and an openness to learn from women's stories, the interweaving of sensuousness, history writing, fact and fiction. See also Sassower (1993) *Knowledge Without Expertise*, chapters 5 and 6; Fals Borda (1985) *Knowledge and People's Power*.

CHAPTER 1   FEMINISM(S) AND PROSTITUTION

1 As a response to Alexander: I am not *afraid* of being called a 'whore', but I am angry at the meanings and violence behind the term which are directed at me when men use it aginst me and against other women.
2 See the reader from the 1st European Prostitutes Conference (Drobler 1991). The conference focused upon prostitution as work and concluded with a statement to be included in the European Charter of the rights of employees.
3 See O'Connell-Davidson (1998), Kempadoo and Doezema (1999), O'Neill and Barberet (2000). The latter is the result of a comparative analysis of the social organization of prostitution in Spain and England, funded by the British Council. Our chapter unfortunately opens with an editorial error: our examination of prostitution in semi-rural Staffordshire is described as taking place in Stoke-on-Trent. We examined urban prostitution in Stoke-on-Trent. The editor will make the correction if the book is re-printed.
4 POW! evolved out of a one-year research project conducted by Professor Pam Gillies at the Department of Epidemiology and Public Health, Nottingham University. Women involved in researching (via snowballing techniques) the relationship between prostitution, drugs and HIV developed their own voluntary agency based upon principles of peer education. POW! workers have developed the organization to address issues relating to: health, welfare and legal needs, drug-related needs, vocational guidance, education, training and counselling; the need for places of safety; and work with young people from local authority care. The philosophy of the organization is based upon principles of peer-led education and empowerment.

Launched in 1990, WHIP was started by volunteers from the following agencies: Leicestershire AIDS Support Services (LASS), Drug Advice and Lesbian and Gay Line. Founded upon the need to respond to problems experienced by working women concerning HIV prevention, education support, violence, and welfare needs. Soliciting for Change was coordinated by a youth worker who developed outreach work with women working as prostitutes on streets in the Caldmore area of Birmingham. With the backing of the local church and professionals associated through the steering committee, Soliciting for Change organized a local conference and later a national conference to look at reforming the laws around prostitution. The national conference was held at Nottingham on 25–6 September 1993 and was a keypoint in the development of a national platform for the human rights and civil liberties of women working as prostitutes.

Scotpep is a peer-led education project that was founded in Edinburgh in the spring of 1989. They are committed to harm reduction in relation to the sex industry and drug use. The project operates on a self-help model using the knowledge and expertise of prostitutes, drug users and others, with the intention of raising awareness of those still working and those entering the sex industry.

5 See Diduck and Wilson (1997) for a fuller discussion of these issues. The authors draw upon comparative studies and judicial decisions through time and across nations, e.g. Canada and Australia.

6 Ravenscroft (1997) informs us that until the Sexual Offences [Amendment] Act 1985 indecent assault on a man had warranted ten years imprisonment, and on a woman two years. This was the legacy of the interpretation and the horror with which homosexuality was viewed. Since SOA 1985, the maximum penalty for both forms of indecent assault is now ten years.

7 Communication from the coordinator of the national network affiliated to EURO-PAP, March 1999.

8 The British government are currently undertaking a review of sex offence legislation. It will be interesting to see if the results of the review address the current piecemeal and discriminatory legislation on prostitution and related activities. The Home Office have been very clear that decriminalization is not on the agenda or an option. The author provided a critical review of the available literature on offences of sexual exploitation to inform the work of the review team.

CHAPTER 2   FEMINIST KNOWLEDGE AND SOCIAL RESEARCH: ETHNO-MIMESIS AS PERFORMATIVE PRAXIS

1 Safer Cities was a national programme, administered by the Crime Prevention Unit of the Home Office, which operated in twenty cities during 1990–3. The aims of the Safer Cities Programme were to: reduce crime, lessen fear of crime and create safer cities with the emphasis upon community development. For further information see Nick Tilley's paper *Opportunity Knocks! – Crime Prevention and the Safer Cities Story*, presented at the Social Policy Association Annual Conference, Nottingham University, 9–11 July 1991. Nick Tilley is Professor of Sociology, Department of Applied Social Studies, Nottingham Trent University.

2 The street-level centre was developed within the context of research led by Pam Gillies, then Professor of Epidemiology and Public Health, Nottingham University.

3 This work could not have been progressed without the research assistance of Michaela Woods. Her help was invaluable.

4 Karen Hughes was at the time also working towards opening a street-level centre. Her commitment to her work and her relationships with women were an inspiration.

5 Thanks to Richard Harvey Brown who kindly sent me Fals Borda's *Knowledge and People's Power* (1985).

6 See Giddens (1992), chapters 3–5, for an excellent discussion on the development of love relationships since the eighteenth/nineteenth centuries – from tradition to modernity/later modernity – particularly with regard to the role played by men and the interrelationship between women's expectations/development and men's expectations/development.

7 I use Adorno's account of coming to know the work of art (1984, 1997) in defining my involvement with women and subsequent reflexive critical interpretation. See the introductory section for more detail.

8 For a more thorough discussion of these issues see Sandy Lawrinson (1995) and Dawn Whittaker (1995).

9 See Liz Stanley's ch. 8, 'Afterword', in Stanley and Wise (1993) for a very useful set of discussions about ethics and the relationship between ethics and feminist epistemology.

10 Denzin (1997) informs us that ethnography has passed through five historical moments: the traditional (1900 to World War 2); modernist (World War 2 to the mid-1970s); blurred genres (1970–86); the crisis in representation (1986 to the present); and the present. The sixth moment charts the future (1997: xxi).

11 See O'Neill (1999). The concept of mediation was crucial to Adorno's theories. Mediation is a pivotal concept in *Aesthetic Theory* (1984). The relationship of art to society is one of mediation. The sedimented aspects of reality, of the subjective/ collective arise/unfold in certain works of art. Truth resides in the form and is activated and released via interpretive philosophy. Art is a product of society; it is formed through the objective demands of the material – the historically given techniques and means of production – and the subjective experiences and playful-ness of the artist. Art is a feeling form. So art is a product of society *but* at the same time an independent force in society. This is linked to the central dialectic of mimesis and constructive rationality:

Mimesis	*Constructive rationality*
Subjective freedom of artist	Objective demands of the material
Mimetic sensual	Rational constructive
Sensuous appearance	Disinterestedness
Hegelian theme	Kantian theme

For Adorno, art could not be understood until its social essence was understood. Society is mediated through aesthetic form as content expressed through antag-onisms and conflicts, between the mimetic sensuous and rational constructive poles in the dialectic of art.

12 For an interesting analysis of dialectics of mimesis in Adorno and Freud, see Matt Connell's PhD thesis, 'The psychoanalytic dimension of Adorno's critical theory', Nottingham Trent University, 1997.

13 See O'Neill (1999).

14 Sara (choreographer) was given certain transcripts (which had been rigorously anonymized) and asked to develop a re-presentation of the data in the form of live art with Patricia (live artist) and Darren (sound artist). This group set about interpreting the data based upon key themes, images, rhythms, moments, and parts of the many stories contained within the transcripts that were meaningful and resonant to them. The text images and sounds used in the video were finalized and agreed through discussions between us all. Both the video and live perform-ances include fragments of the interview transcripts (the developed version of the performance includes small fragments of text which are spoken live). One outcome of this work is that it provides a visual re-telling and speaks to people about women's lives, sexuality, prostitution in non-conceptual ways through dance/ movement and the fusing of text, sound, video and dance, making available to a wider and different audience the ethnographic data in visual (feeling) form mediated by Sara, Patricia and the technical forms of production (video).

15 See Ruth Holliday's current work (1999) which focuses upon the comfort of identity, drawing upon video diaries as a method to access the visual dimensions

and playfulness of the communicative role of identity. This work raises important messages about queer identities but also about throwing off and taking on identities as an inherently reflexive process.

16 In a critical appraisal of this work Rolland Munro (1999) writes: 'The stunned silence that greeted the first showing of this multi-media dance performance, at the British Sociology Association's conference on "The Body", was reminiscent of the long pause that met the curtain on *Waiting for Godot* – the audience coming to terms with performance instead of theory was like having to watch a play without anything having ever happened. Except for the uncomfortable fact of one's own arrival, somewhere else.'

17 See O'Neill, Goode and Hopkins (1995); O'Neill (1999); Green, Mulroy and O'Neill (1997).

PART II   INTERPRETIVE ETHNOGRAPHIES: LIFE-HISTORY WORK

1 In taking an ethnographic approach, developing trusting relationships with women and young people working on and off street and feeling confident and accepted is vital to the generation of further knowledge and feminist praxis with the women involved. It is also important in developing an understanding of the comprehensiveness of the progress of the research. Close relationships which have continuity are important because the researcher finds differing vantage points from which to view the validity, multiplicity, relevance to the participants, and to the progress of the research.

2 For useful material on interviewing see N. Gilbert, *Researching Social Life*, London: Sage (1993), and Seale (1999). Both are excellent texts accessible to a wide range of readers.

CHAPTER 3   WOMEN'S VOICES, WOMEN'S LIVES

1 See Brewis and Linstead (1998); Phoenix (1999); Phil Hubbard (1997) for discussions on space and place and time involved in analysing prostitution. See also Ruth Holliday (1999) on the communicative role of identity and the comfort of identity, drawing upon her video diary research, and Judith Butler's work on performativity and identity. Holliday's work does not focus on prostitution, but on sexual identity.

2 'Into Europe', *Nursing Times*, 24 October 1990.

CHAPTER 4   ADOLESCENT PROSTITUTION: RUNAWAYS, HOMELESSNESS AND LIVING IN LOCAL AUTHORITY CARE

1 Personal communication with a researcher/programme maker working for Channel 4 documentary on leaving care and doing prostitution, autumn 1995.

2 See also a publication by the European Network for HIV/STD Prevention in Prostitution (EUROPAP/TAMPEP 1998). This publication is an invaluable tool for agencies working with young people and older women involved in prostitution.

3 Barbara Gibson worked for Streetwise Youth in London as a health consultant. The NSPCC is The National Society for the Prevention of Cruelty to Children.

4 I interviewed Jessica (not her real name) while I was managing and conducting the fieldwork for a project examining routes into prostitution from local authority care.

5 These examples are taken from ethnographic work conducted between 1990 and 1994. TWOCing is 'taking without owners consent' – joyriding.

6 See Lupton and Gillespie (1994) and Hester, Radford and Kelly (1995) for further discussion relating to issues around male rape and violence against women, and violence against men and boys.

7 The latest text to address some of these issues is Hester, Radford and Kelly (1995).

8 See O'Neill (1995).

9 For an example, see Green, Mulroy and O'Neill (1997).

10 In his observations within the confines of prisoner of war camps Bettelheim remarks that: 'Psychoanalytic theory stresses the importance of the inner life to the neglect of the total man as he deals with his human and social environment' (1991: 21). Certainly Bettelheim's experiences in the camps taught him that he 'had gone much too far in believing that only changes in man could create changes in society. I had to accept that the environment could, as it were, turn personality upside down, and not just the small child, but in the mature adult too', (1991: 15). Psychoanalysis failed Bettelheim at the time he needed it most. Unable to suggest ways of coping with the conditions he was surviving, it did help him to understand the problems he was dealing with, helped him to understand what was happening to some individuals. He began to see that 'soon how a man acts can alter what he is. Those who stood up well in the camps became better men, those who acted badly soon became bad men' (1991: 16).

11 See Michelle McCarthy's paper in Hester, Radford and Kelly (1995).

PART III   FEMINIST POSTMODERNISMS AND ETHNOGRAPHIES OF DIFFERENCE: BETWEEN MODERNITY AND POSTMODERNITY

1 The postmodern turn is marked by the linguistic turn in socio-cultural research; the focus upon the duality of action and structure, the shift away from privileging either consciousness/agency or structure; the shift away from a focus on knowing the world through empirical research towards an examination of cultural texts and the symbolic re-presentation of social practices, forms, processes and structures.

CHAPTER 5   IMAGINING WOMEN: PROSTITUTION, THE AESTHETICIZATION OF THE WHORE AND THE SOCIAL ORGANIZATION OF DESIRE

1 See, for example, Gledhill (1997), Geraghty (1991) and Modleski (1982) for feminist textual analyses of the re-presentation of women in soap opera, film and literature which explore possibilities for transgression, resistance and pleasure in women's readings of film, soap opera and romantic fiction.

2 For example, see Janet Wolff's essay on Gwen John in *Resident Alien* (1995) to better understand the way John's art can be read as ciphers of the general experience of women from her particular social class; but also as the sedimented 'stuff' of society at that particular time.

3 See Mary Murray (1995) for an analysis of the development of patriarchy as a system of private property relations.

4 For critical exploration of the notion of masculine discourses and topography see Bell and Valentine, *Mapping Desire* (London: Routledge, 1995). This collection explores the fluidity and intersections of sexualities, sexual identities and space.

5 Kishtainy describes Maupassant as showing 'the most profound appreciation of the relationship between the prostitute and society' (1982: 85).

6 Elizabeth Hirschman and Barbara Stern (1994) examine cultural attitudes towards the commodification of women as prostitutes in three Hollywood films. For the authors, films are vehicles of popular culture, carrying and communicating consumption ideology. Film has great impact as an agent for consumer behaviour as well as 'encoding and enforcing society's views of "woman's place"'. The authors conduct a thorough and interesting examination of *The Blue Angel*, *Pretty Baby* and *Pretty Woman*.

7 Shannon Bell's *Reading, Writing, and Rewriting the Prostitute Body* (1994) focuses upon prostitute performance work to construct positive prostitute identities – the prostitute as philosopher, teacher, healer, artist, goddess. Using Foucault and Derrida, Bell focuses upon six performance texts by Annie Sprinkle, Veronica Vera, Gwendolun, Janet Feidel and Scarlott Harlot to destabilize the boundaries between sacred and profane, good and bad, sluts and goddesses, therapists and prostitutes. Her project is a postmodern genealogy, a postmodern feminist philosophy rooted very firmly in discourses of the prostitutes' rights movement in North America and committed to re-presenting prostitutes in a positive light. The approach taken is very particular and relates to a minority of sex workers, i.e., at the 'escort' end of the career trajectory.

CHAPTER 6   THE CITY, MASCULINITY AND THE SOCIAL ORGANIZATION OF DESIRE: PIMPS AND PUNTERS

1 See Peter Aggleton's excellent edited collection of international essays on *Men Who Sell Sex* (London: UCL Press, 1999).

2 Richard Sennett describes the public domain in part as 'dead public space' indicative of 'an unbalanced personal life and empty public life' (1992: 16) resulting from changes that began with the 'fall of the *ancien régime* and the formation of a new capitalist, secular, urban culture' (1992: 16). He charts the history of the words 'public' and 'private'. '"Public" thus came to mean a life passed outside the life of family and close friends; in the public region diverse, complex social groups were to be brought into ineluctable contact. The focus of this public life was the capital city' (1992: 17).

3 Due, in part, to the difficulties of getting access to 'pimps' and also to the sensitivity required of such work. The problem as I see it is that one's work could so easily be used against the spirit in which it was conducted, thus furthering racial tensions rather than articulating the racial, class and gender dimensions to our understanding of prostitution, reflexive modernity and the city. For example, a recent TV documentary exploring gang rape focused specifically upon this phenomenon as though it were only perpetrated by young black men. This simply served to reinforce racist assumptions and binary thinking around essential differences between black/white youth and to demonize all young black males. Paul Gilroy commented: 'They were simplifying and sensationalizing the issue. If you want to look at boys leading hopeless, meaningless, loveless lives in the inner cities, let's deal with that. But race is not an explanation' *The Observer*, Sunday, 22 November 1999. Similarly, in examining the problem of pimps and pimping we cannot look to race as an explanation.

4 See Roger Matthews's work (1986) on social incivilities and the sociology of crime and deviance developed through extensive scholarship rooted in Marxist inspired socialism. The recommendations he makes as part of the de-criminaliza-tion–legalization debate with regard to 'radical regulationism' are not 'women-centred' but are about regulating prostitution. Whilst I am sympathetic to Matthews's theoretical approach, his responses only serve to shift the 'problem' of prostitution into a different social space within current social structures and processes. In the current patriarchal social order we need to look towards women-centred responses to prostitution and related issues that seek to transform the structures and processes of domination.

5 Personal communication with Inspector David Dawson.

6 Elias' work on the process of civilization (1978, 1982) would provide a very useful model to counter some of the more overly macro trends in the work of Giddens (1984, 1991a) and Beck-Gernsheim (1995).

7 See Hearn (1990); Brittan (1989); Cohen (1990); Seidler (1991); Morgan (1992); and Samuels (1994), Connell (1995) for accounts of men, masculinity and sexual politics.

8 Certainly until the later 1980s the relationship between women working as prostitutes and wider society was marked by a tension between the shame of whore status and transgressing the rules of normal femininity and morality. Since the later 1980s, fuelled by feminist responses to prostitution, the rise of the prostitutes' rights movement and the globalization of the sex industry, there has developed a more relaxed attitude to the norms of femininity, morality and the economic basis of many women's choice of entry into prostitution. On the other hand, my experience shows me that at street level the relationship between prostitutes and pimps is still based on relations of command and power over women, and violence is meted out if commands are not met.

9 See Boswell's biography, *The Life of Samuel Johnson*, ed. J. Canning (London: The Softback Preview, 1996), for a more thorough and lively account of life, senti-ments, manners in the mid-eighteenth century.

10 See Jack Zipes, *Spells of Enchantment: The Wondrous Fairy Tales of Western Culture* (New York and Harmondsworth: Penguin, 1991). A transgressive version of the 'fairytale' is represented in 'Fairytale' by Nina Cassion in *Call Yourself Alive: The Love Poems of Nina Cassion* (London: Forest Books, 1988). Thanks to Rachel for loaning me the book.

> Why is it that the ugliest of the ugly,
> the most hideous of the hideous – wants to be called Prince Charming?
> But, answered the Princess, what befits a disguise?
> What if inside the scabby toad there lies bewitched
> the wonderful Prince himself?
> That's a risk I dare not take.
> And the Princess kissed his warts
> and took him to bed,
> And the scabby toad croaked –
> Satisfied.

11 Women Hurt In Systems of Prostitution Engaged in Revolt, PO Box 8719, Minneapolis, MN 55408, USA.

12 In *The Guardian*, Wednesday, 11 August 1993, Edward Pilkington covers Judge
Michael Addison's appalling attitude to the 'date rape' of a woman. The judge
sentenced the perpetrator to three and a half years in prison adding: 'This is not in
my view the more serious type of rape – that is the rape of a total stranger'

Further misogynistic attitudes outlined in the piece include: Judge Ian Star-
forth Hill's comment of an eight-year-old as being 'not entirely an angel herself' –
the perpetrator received two years' probation increased on appeal to four months
in jail; and Judge John Prosser who freed a rapist and ordered him to pay his
victim £500 for a good holiday. On appeal this was increased to two years' youth
custody. Judge Arthur Myerson praised a rapist for showing 'concern and consideration by wearing a contraceptive'. Judge David Wild told a rape jury: 'If she
doesn't want it she only has to keep her legs shut.'

13 I was involved as witness to an assault on a woman 'prostitute' on street while I
was accompanying a health worker on outreach duty. Neither the victim of the
assault nor her friend gave evidence. The health worker and myself attended court
on four separate occasions. Finally we did not have to give evidence, the assailant
pleaded guilty in the light of the strong evidence against him (two good-girls/
professional women! with more social status than that pertaining to the prostitutes abused by such men) and was given a suspended sentence. We were shaken
by the decision. My car had been vandalized the evening before the first three
court appearances; the description of the men witnessed by various neighbours was
always the same. After a 'dressing down' from the judge for 'intimidating a
witness' my car was left untouched the evening before the fourth appearance
(see O'Neill 1995).

CONCLUSION: TOWARDS A POLITICS OF FEELING

1 For example, the author's current research with refugees and asylum seekers is
exhibited in visual/photographic form at a gallery in Nottingham. This work
challenges stereotypes and media images of 'refugees'. It focuses upon the artists'
and co-researchers' lives before the war in Bosnia and through the war years,
separated from families, living in concentration camps and, finally, building
communities in the Midlands.

2 We must avoid at all costs the reproduction of the binary positions that Desirée
(O'Connell-Davidson 1998) experienced at the conference she attended in London.
I have had much feedback about the conference from women working in prostitution and individual project workers as well as from representatives of statutory
organizations working with women. The bottom line was that women working in
prostitution were silenced. There was no space for them to discuss the issues that
were of concern to them – including abuse and oppression. Prostitution was for
them equated with male violence in too simple and divisive a way.

3 See the work of Augusto Boal (1979) and Orlando Fals Borda (1983).

References

Adorno, T. W. (1966) *Negative Dialectics*, trans. E. B. Ashton, London: Routledge and Kegan Paul.
—— (1973) *Negative Dialectics*, London: Routledge and Kegan Paul.
—— (1978) *Minima Moralia: Reflections from a Damaged Life*, trans. E. F. N. Jephcott, London and New York: Verso.
—— (1984) *Aesthetic Theory*, trans. C. Lenrhardt, London: Routledge and Kegan Paul.
—— (1997) *Aesthetic Theory*, trans. Robert Hullot Kentor, Minneapolis: University of Minnesota Press.
—— and Horkheimer, M. (1979) *The Dialectic of Enlightenment*, London: Verso.
Alasuutari, P., Gray, A. and Hermes, J. (1998) 'Editorial', *European Journal of Cultural Studies* 1 (1), 5–11.
Alexander, P. (1997) 'Feminism, sex workers, and human rights', in J. Nagle (ed.), *Whores and Other Feminists*, New York and London: Routledge, 83–97.
—— and Delacoste, F. (1988) *SEX WORK: Writings by Women in the Sex Industry*, London: Virago.
Arendt, H. (1970) *On Violence*, New York: Harcourt Brace and Co.
Ashworth, A. (1988) 'The road to sentencing reform', in *Prison Reform No. 5*, London: Prison Reform Trust.
Atkinson, P. (1992) *Understanding Ethnographic Texts*, Los Angeles: Sage.
—— and Coffey, A. (1995) 'Realism and its discontents: on the crisis of cultural representation in ethnographic texts', in B. Adam and S. Allen (eds), *Theorizing Culture: An Interdisciplinary Critique after Postmodernism*, London: UCL Press, 41–57.
Barnardo's (1998) *Whose Daughter Next? Children Abused Through Prostitution*, Ilford: Barnardo's.
Barrett, D. (ed.) (1997) *Child Prostitution in Britain: Current Dilemmas, Practical Responses*, London: The Children's Society.
Barry, K. (1988) 'Female sexual slavery: the problems, policies and cause for feminist action', in E. Boneparth and E. Stoper (eds), *Women, Power and Policy: Towards the Year 2000*, Oxford: Pergamon Press, 283–96.
Bartky, S. L. (1990) *Femininity and Domination Studies in the Phenomenology of Oppression*, London: Routledge.

Barton, S. E., Taylor-Robinson, D. and Harris, J. R. W. (1987) 'Female prostitutes and sexually transmitted diseases', *British Journal of Hospital Medicine* 7, 34–45.

Battersby, C. (1998) *The Phenomenal Woman*, Cambridge: Polity Press.

Bauman, Z. (1992) *Intimations of Postmodernity*, London: Routledge.

——(1995) *Life In Fragments: Essays in Postmodern Morality*, Oxford: Blackwell.

Beck, U. (1992) *Risk Society: Towards a New Modernity*, London: Sage.

——and Beck-Gernsheim, E. (1995) *The Normal Chaos of Love*, Cambridge: Polity Press.

Becker, H. S., McCall, M. M., Morris, L. V. and Meshejian, P. (1989) 'Theatres and communities: three scenes', *Social Problems* 36 (2), 93–8.

Becker-Schmidt, R. (1999) 'Critical theory as a critique in society: Theodor W. Adorno's significance for a feminist sociology', in M. O'Neill (ed.), *Adorno, Culture and Feminism*, London: Sage, 104–18.

Bell, L. (ed.) (1984) *Good Girls, Bad Girls: Sex Trade Workers and Feminists Face to Face*, Toronto: Women's Press.

Bell, S. (1994) *Reading, Writing and Rewriting the Prostitute Body*, Bloomington and Indianapolis: Indiana University Press.

Benhabib, S. (1991) 'Feminism and postmodernism: an uneasy alliance', *Praxis International* 11 (2), 137–49

——(1992) *Situating The Self*, Cambridge: Polity Press.

Benjamin, H. and Masters, R. E. L. (eds) (1965) *Prostitution and Morality*, London: Souvenir Press.

Benjamin, J. (1991) 'Master and slave', in J. O'Neill (ed.), *J. Hegel's Dialectic of Desire and Recognition*, London: Routledge.

——(1993) *The Bonds of Love: Psychoanalysis, Feminism, and the Problem of Domination*, London: Virago Press.

Benjamin, W. (1978) *Reflections*, New York: Harcourt Brace Jovanovich, Inc.

——(1992) *Illuminations*, London, Fontana Press.

Benson, C. and Matthews, R. (1995) *National Vice Squad Survey*, Enfield: Middlesex University, Centre for Criminology.

Berger, J. (1978) *Ways of Seeing*, Harmondsworth: Penguin.

Berridge, D. (1985) *Children's Homes*, Oxford: Blackwell.

Bertillson, M. (1986) 'Love's labour lost? A sociological view', *Theory, Culture and Society* 3 (2), 19–35.

Bettelheim, B. (1991) *The Informed Heart: A Study of the Psychological Consequences of Living under Extreme Fear and Terror*, Harmondsworth: Penguin.

Biehal, N., Clayden, J., Stein, M. and Wade, J. (1992) *Prepared for Living: A Survey of Young People Leaving the Care of Three Local Authorities*, London: National Children's Bureau.

Bindman, J. and Doezema, J. (1997) *Redefining Prostitution as Sex Work on the International Agenda*, London: Anti-Slavery International.

Bishop, R. and Robinson, L. (1997) *Nightmarket: Sexual Cultures and the Thai Economic Miracle*, New York and London: Routledge.

Bland, L. (1992) 'The case of the Yorkshire Ripper: mad, bad, beast, or male?', in Radford, J. and Russell, D. (eds), *Femicide: The Politics of Woman Killing*, Milton Keynes: Open University Press, 233–52.

Boal, A. (1979) *Theatre of the Oppressed*, London: Pluto.

Bonnerjea, L. (1990) *Leaving Care in London*, London: London Boroughs Children Regional Planning Committee.

Borden, I., Kerr, J., Pivaro, A. and Rendall, J. (eds) (1996) *Strangely Familiar: Narratives of Architecture in the City*, London and New York; Routledge.

Boutellier, J. (1991) 'Prostitution, criminal law and morality in the Netherlands', *Crime, Law and Social Change* 15, 201–11.

Box, S. (1983) *Power, Crime and Mystification*, London: Tavistock.

Boyle, S. (1994) *Working Girls and Their Men*, London: Smith Gryphon.

Brace, L. and O'Connel-Davidson, J. (1996) 'Desperate debtors and counterfeit love: the Hobbesian world of the sex tourist', *Contemporary Politics* 2 (3), 55–78.

Brah, A. (1996) *Cartographies of Diaspora: Contesting Identities*, London: Routledge.

Brewis, J. and Linstead, S. (1998) 'Time after time: the temporal organization of red collar work', *Time and Society* 7 (2), 223–48.

Brittan, A. (1989) *Masculinity and Power*, Oxford: Blackwell.

Bronfen, E. (1992) *Over Her Dead Body: Death, Femininity and the Aesthetic*, Manchester: Manchester University Press.

Brooks, A. (1997) *Postfeminisms: Feminism, Cultural Theory and Cultural Forms*, London: Routledge.

Bryant, C. D. and Palmer, C. E. (1975) 'Massage parlours and "hand whores": some sociological observations', *Journal of Sex Research* 11, 227–41.

Buci-Glucksmann, C. (1994) *Baroque Reason: The Aesthetics of Modernity*, London: Sage.

Buikema, R. (1992) *Women's Studies and Culture*, London: Zed Books.

Bullough, V. and Bullough, B. (1987) *Women and Prostitution: A Social History*, New York: Prometheus Books.

Butler, A. M. (1985) *Daughters of Joy, Sisters of Misery: Prostitutes in the American West*, Champaign, IL: University of Illinois Press.

Butler, J. (1990) *Gender Troubles: Feminism and the Subversion of Identity*, New York and London: Routledge.

——(1994) *Bodies that Matter: On the Discursive Limits of Sex*, New York and London: Routledge.

Campbell, B. (1990) 'Working together for women', *The Guardian*, 6 December.

Campbell, R. (1997) 'It's just business, it's just sex: male clients of female prostitutes in Merseyside', *The Journal of Contemporary Health* 5, 47–51.

——Coleman, S. and Torkington, P. (1996) *Street Prostitution in Inner City Liverpool*, Liverpool: Hope University, Deanery of Hope in the Community.

Carlen, P. (1988) *Women, Crime and Poverty*, Milton Keynes: Open University Press.

——(1998) *Sledgehammer: Women's Imprisonment at the Millennium*, London: Macmillan.

Cavadino, P. (1997) 'Pre-sentence reports: the effects of legislation and national standards', *British Journal of Criminology*, 37 (4).

Cawthorne, J. (1999) '"If only I'd loaded the dishwasher": a gender analysis of prostitution, agency and social exclusion in contemporary Britain', MA thesis, School of Development Studies, University of East Anglia.

Chapkis, W. (1997) *Live Sex Acts: Women Performing Erotic Labour*, London: Cassell.

Clark, T. J. (1980) 'Preliminaries to a possible treatment of Olympia in 1865', *Screen* 2 (1), 18–41.

Clinard, M. B. (1968) *Sociology of Deviant Behaviour*, New York: Holt, Reinhart and Winston.

Clough, P. (1994) *Feminist Thought: Desire, Power and Academic Discourse*, Cambridge, MA: Blackwell.

Cohen, D. (1990) *Being a Man*, London: Routledge.

Company Magazine (1990) *Executive by Day, Prostitute by Night*, November, 42–3.

Connell, R. W. (1987) *Gender and Power*, Cambridge: Polity Press.

——(1995) *Masculinities*, Cambridge: Polity Press.

Conquergood, D. (1992) 'Ethnography, rhetoric and performance', *Quarterly Journal of Speech* 78, 80–97.

Coole, D. (1993) *Women in Political Theory*, Harvester: Wheatsheaf.

Corbin, A. (1987) 'Commercial sexuality in nineteenth-century France: a system of images and regulations', in C. Gallagher and T. Laquer (eds), *The Making of the Modern Body: Sexuality and Society in the Nineteenth Century*, Berkeley, CA: University of California Press.

——(1990) *Women For Hire: Prostitution and Sexuality in France after 1850*, Cambridge, MA: Harvard University Press.

Council of Europe (1993) *Sexual Exploitation, Pornography and Prostitution of, Trafficking in, Children and Young Adults*, Strasbourg: Council of Europe.

Davis, K. (1937) 'The Sociology of Prostitution', *American Sociological Review* 5 (2), 749–55.

Davis, N. (1971) 'The prostitute: developing a deviant identity', in J. H. Henslin (ed.) *Studies in the Sociology of Sex*, New York: Appleton Century Crafts, 297–322.

Day, S. and Ward, H. (1990) 'The Praed Street project: a cohort of prostitute women in London', in M. Plant (ed.) *AIDS, Drugs and Prostitution*, London: Routledge, 61–75.

De Beauviour, S. (1961) *The Second Sex*, Harmondsworth: Penguin.

Delacoste, F. and Alexander, P. (eds) (1988) *Sex Work: Writings by Women in the Sex Industry*, London: Virago Press.

Deleuze, G. and Guattari, F. (1983) *Anti-Oedipus: Capitalism and Schizophrenia*, Minneapolis: University of Minnesota Press.

——(1988) *A Thousand Plateaus: Capitalism and Schizophrenia*, London: Athlone.

Denzin, N. (1997) *Interpretive Ethnography: Ethnographic Practices for the 21st Century*, London: Sage.

De Swaan, A. (1981) 'The politics of agoraphobia: on changes in emotional and relational management, *Theory and Society* 10(3).

Deutsche, R. (1991) 'Boy's town', *Society and Space* 9, 5–30.

Devlin, A. (1988) *Invisible Women*, Winchester: Waterside Press.

Dibblin, J. (1991) *Wherever I Lay My Hat: Young Women and Homelessness*, London: Shelter.

Diduck, A. and Wilson, W. (1997) 'Prostitutes and persons', *The Journal of Law and Society* 24 (4), 504–25.

Dingwall, G. (1997) 'Exploring the definition of prostitution', *The Journal of Criminal Law* 61 (4), 435–8.

Drobler, C. (1991) *Women at Work: Reader for the 1st European Prostitutes Conference, Frankfurt, 16–18 October 1991*, Frankfurt: H. W. G.

Dudash, T. (1997) 'Peepshow feminism', in J. Nagle (ed.) *Whores and Other Feminists*, New York and London: Routledge, 98–118.

Dworkin, A. (1981) *Pornography: Men Possessing Women*, London: The Women's Press.

Earls, C. M. and David, H. (1989) 'A psychosocial study of male prostitution', *Archives of Sexual Behaviour* 18, 401–19.

Eberhard, Dr and Kronhausen, P. (1967) *Walter, the English Casanova: A Presentation of 'My Secret Life' – The Unique Memoris of England's Most Uninhibited Lover*, vol. 2, London: Polybooks Ltd.

Edwards, S. (1984) *Women on Trial*, Manchester: Manchester University Press.
——(ed.) (1987) *Gender, Sex and the Law*, London: Croom Helm.
——(1988a) 'Policing street prostitution: the street offences squad in London', *Police Journal* 61 (3), 209–19.
——(1988b) *Prostitution, Policing, Employment and the Welfare of Young Women*, Report prepared for the Nuffield Foundation.
——(1993) 'Selling the body, keeping the soul: sexuality, power and the theories and realities of prostitution', in S. Scott and D. Morgan (eds) *Body Matters*, London and Washington: Falmer Press, 89–104.
——(1997) 'The legal regulation of prostitution: a human rights issue', in G. Scambler and A. Scambler (eds) *Rethinking Prostitution: Purchasing Sex in Britain in the 1990s*, London: Routledge, 57–82.
——(1998) 'Abused and exploited: young girls in prostitution', in Barnardo's, *Whose Daughter Next? Children Abused Through Prostitution*, Ilford: Barnardo's.
Elias, N. (1978) *The Civilizing Process, vol. 1: The History of Manners*, Oxford: Blackwell.
——(1982) *The Civilizing Process, vol. 2: State Formation and Civilization*, Oxford: Blackwell.
Ellis, A. (1959) 'Why married men visit prostitutes', *Sexology* 25, 344–9.
English Collective of Prostitutes (1997) 'Campaigning for legal change', in G. Scambler and A. Scambler (eds) *Rethinking Prostitution: Purchasing Sex in Britain in the 1990s*, London: Routledge, 83–102.
Enloe, C. (1992) *Let the Good Times Roll: Prostitution and the US Military in Asia*, New York: Free Press.
Ennew, J. (1986) *The Sexual Exploitation of Children*, Cambridge: Polity Press.
Ericsson, L. O. (1980) 'Charges against prostitution: an attempt at a philosophical assessment', *Ethics* 90 (3), 335–66.
EUROPAP/TAMPEP (1998) *Hustling for Health: Developing Services for Sex Workers in Europe*, London and Amsterdam: Imperial College School of Medicine, St Mary's and TAMPEP International Foundation.
Evans, D. T. (1993) *Sexual Citizenship: The Material Construction of Sexualities*, London: Routledge.
Extavasia, A. and Addison, T. D. (1992) 'Fucking (with theory) for money: toward an interrogation of escort prostitution', *Postmodern Culture* 2 (3), http.//jefferson. village.virginia.edu/pmc/issue592/add-ext.592.
Falk, P. (1995) *The Consuming Body*, London: Sage.
Fals Borda, O. (1985) *Knowledge and People's Power: Lessons with Peasants in Nicaragua, Mexico and Colombia*, New York: New Horizons Press.
Fanon, F. (1986) *Black Skin, White Masks*, London: Pluto Press.
Featherstone, M., Hepworth, M. and Turner, B. (eds) (1991) *The Body: Social Process and Cultural Theory*, London: Sage.
——and Turner, B. (1995) 'Body and society: an introduction', *Body and Society* 1 (1), 1–12.
Felski, R. (1989) *Beyond Feminist Aesthetics*, London: Hutchinson Radius.
Finnegan, F. (1979) *Poverty and Prostitution: A Study of Victorian Prostitutes in York*, Cambridge: Cambridge University Press.
Fisher, M. (1986) *In and Out of Care*, London: Batsford Press.
Foltz, T. G. (1980) 'The process of becoming a prostitute: a comparison between lower class and middle class girls', in D. H. Kelly (ed.), *Criminal Behaviour: Readings in Criminology*, New York: St Martins Press.

Fonow and Cook (eds) (1991) *Beyond Methodology: Feminist Scholarship as Lived Research*, Bloomington, IN: Indiana University Press.

French, D. (1990) *Working: My Life as a Prostitute*, London: Victor Gollancz Ltd.

Fromm, E. (1967) *The Art of Loving*, London: Unwin.

Funari, V. (1997) 'Naked, naughty, nasty: peep show reflections', in J. Nagle (ed.), *Whores and Other Feminists*, New York and London: Routledge.

Galbraith, J. K. (1992) *The Culture of Contentment*, Harmondsworth: Penguin.

Garfield, S. (1990) 'Damaged goods', *The Independent on Sunday*, 16 September.

Garnett, L. (1992) *Leaving Care and After Care*, London: National Children's Bureau.

Geertz, C. (1973) *The Interpretation of Culture*, New York: Basic Books.

Geraghty, C. (1991) *Women and Soap Opera: A Study of Prime Time Soaps*, Cambridge: Polity Press.

Gibson, B. (1995) *Male Order Life Stories from Boys Who Sell Sex*, London: Cassell.

Giddens, A. (1984) *The Constitution of Society*, Cambridge: Polity Press.

——(1991a) *The Consequences of Modernity*, Cambridge: Polity Press.

——(1991b) *Modernity and Self Identity: Self and Society in Late Modern Age*, Cambridge: Polity Press.

——(1992) *The Transformation of Intimacy: Sexuality, Love and Eroticism in Modern Societies*, Cambridge: Polity Press.

——(1993) 'Living in a post traditional order', Presentation/paper given to 'De-Traditionalization: Authority and Self in an Age of Cultural Uncertainty', Lancaster University, 8–10 July.

Gilgamesh and Enkidu (1995) Penguin 60s Classics, Harmondsworth: Penguin.

Glaser, B. and Strauss, A. (1967) *The Discovery of Grounded Theory*, Chicago: Aldine.

Gledhill, C. (1988) 'Pleasurable negotiations', in E. D. Pribham (ed.), *Female Spectators*, London: Verso.

——(1997) 'Genre and gender: the case of soap opera', in S. Hall (ed.), *Representation: Cultural Representation and Signifying Practices*, London: Sage.

Glendenning, C. (1987) 'Impoverishing women', in A. Walker and C. Walker (eds), *The Growing Divide*, London: Child Poverty Action Group.

Goffmann, E. (1964) *Stigma*, Harmondsworth: Penguin.

Golding, R. (1992) 'Policing prostitution', *Police Review*, 8 (Spring), 60–72.

Gramsci, A. (1971) *Selections from the Prison Notebooks*, London: Lawrence and Wishart.

Gray, A. (1997) 'Learning from experience: cultural studies and feminism', in J. McGuigan (ed.), *Cultural Methodologies*, London: Sage.

Gray, D. (1973) '"Turning out": a study of teenage prostitution', *Urban Life and Culture* 4, 401–25.

Green, J. (1992) *It's No Game: Responding to the Needs of Young Women at Risk or Involved in Prostitution*, Leicester: National Youth Agency.

——Mulroy, S. and O'Neill, M. (1997) 'Young people and prostitution from a youth services perspective', in D. Barrett (ed.) *Children and Prostitution: Current Dilemmas, Practical Responses*, London: The Children's Society, 90–105.

Hammer, J. and Maynard, M. (eds) (1987) *Women, Violence and Social Control*, London: Macmillan.

——and Saunders, S. (1984) *Well Founded Fear: A Community Study of Violence to Women*, London: Hutchinson.

——Radford, J. and Stanko, E. (1989) *Women, Policing and Male Violence*, London: Routledge.

Haraway, D. (1991) *Simians, Cyborgs and Women: The Reinvention of Nature*, London: Free Association Books.

Harding, S. (ed.) (1986) *The Science Question in Feminism*, Milton Keynes: Open University Press.

—— (ed.) (1987) *Feminism and Methodology*, Milton Keynes: Open University Press.

—— (1989) 'Feminist justificatory strategies', in A. Garry and M. Pearsall (eds), *Women, Knowledge and Reality*, London: Unwin Hyman, 189–202.

—— (1991) *Whose Science? Whose Knowledge? Thinking From Women's Lives*, Milton Keynes: Open University Press.

Harstock, N. (1983) *Money, Sex and Power: Towards a Feminist Historical Materialism*, London: Longman.

Harvey, D. (1989) *The Conditions of Postmodernity*, London: Basil Blackwell.

Haug, F. (ed.) (1987) *Female Sexualization*, London: Verso.

—— (1992) *Beyond Female Masochism: Memory-Works and Politics*, London: Verso.

—— (1995) *Ages of 'Innocence': A Sign of the Times Discussion Paper*, London: Sign of the Times.

Hearn, J. (1990) 'What future for men?', *Achilles Heel* (Autumn), Sheffield: Changing Men Publishing Collective.

—— (1992) 'Researching men and researching men's violences: methodological, empirical and political issues and difficulties', paper presented at the BSA annual conference 'A new Europe' held at the University of Kent, 6–9 April.

—— (1993) 'Theorizing men and men's theorizing: from absence and avoidance to ambivalence and alterity', paper given to the Political Studies Association annual meeting held at the University of Leicester, 20–22 April.

Henriques, F. (1962) *Prostitution and Society*, 2 vols, London: MacGibbon and Kee.

Hersch, P. (1988) 'Coming of age on city streets', *Psychology Today* (January), 28–37.

Hester, M., Radford, J. and Kelly, L. (eds) (1995) *Women, Violence and Male Power: Feminist Activism, Research and Practice*, London: Routledge.

Hetherington, K. (1996) 'Identity formation, space and social centrality', *Theory, Culture and Society* 13 (4), 33–52.

Hirschman, E. C. and Stern, B. B. (1994) 'Women as commodities: prostitution depicted in *The Blue Angel, Pretty Baby, and Pretty Woman*', *Advances In Consumer Research* 21, 576–81.

Hoigard, C. and Finstad, L. (1992) *Backstreets: Money, Prostitution and Love*, Cambridge: Polity Press.

Holland, J., Ramazanoglu, C., Sharpe, S. and Thompson, R. (1994) 'Power and desire: the embodiment of female sexuality', *Feminist Review* 46 (Spring).

Holliday, R. (1999) 'The comfort of identity', paper given to Research Seminar Series, Faculty of Humanities and Social Sciences, Staffordshire University.

Hopkins, J. (1984) *Sex Crimes: Perspectives on Rape and Assault*, London: Harper and Row.

Hothschild, A. (1983) *The Managed Heart*, Berkeley, CA: University of California Press.

Hubbard, P. (1997) 'Red-light districts and toleration zones: changing geographies of female street prostitution in England and Wales', *Area* 29 (2), 129–40.

—— (1999) *Sex and the City: Geographies of Prostitution in the Urban West*, Aldershot: Ashgate Press.

Irigaray, L. (1985) *The Sex Which Is Not One*, Ithaca, NY: Cornell University Press.

—— (1993) *Je, Tu, Nous: Toward a Culture of Difference*, London: Routledge.

Irigaray, L. (1996) *I Love to You: Sketch of a Possible Felicity in History*, London: Routledge.

Jackson, S. (1993) 'Even sociologists fall in love', *Sociology* 27 (2), 201–20.

Jaget, C. (ed.) (1980) *Prostitutes Our Life*, Bristol: Falling Wall Press.

Jaggar, A. (1989) 'Love and knowledge: emotion in feminist epistemology', in A Garry and M. Pearsall (eds), *Women, Knowledge and Reality: Explorations in Feminist Philosophy*, London: Unwin Hyman.

James, J. (1977) 'Ethnography and social problems', in R. Weppner (ed.), *Street Ethnography: Selected Studies of Crime and Drug Use in Natural Settings*, Beverly Hills, CA: Sage.

Jameson, F. (1990) *Late Marxism: Adorno, or the Persistence of the Dialectic*, London: Verso.

Janus, M. D., Scanton, B. and Price, V. (1984) 'Youth prostitution', in A. W. Burgess and M. L. Clark (eds) *Child Pornography and Sex Rings*, Lexington: Lexington Books.

Jarrett, L. (1997) *Stripping in Time: A History of Erotic Dancing*, London: HarperCollins.

Jarvinen, M. (1993) *Of Vice and Women: Shades of Prostitution*, Scandinavian Studies in Prostitution, Oslo: Scandinavian University Press.

Jay, M. (1993) *Force Fields: Between Intellectual History and Cultural Critique*, New York and London: Routledge.

Jennes, V. (1990) 'From sex to sin to sex as work: COYOTE and the reorganization of prostitution as a social problem', *Social Problems* 37 (3), 403–20.

—— (1993) *Making it Work: The Prostitutes' Rights Movement in Perspective*, New York: Aldinede Gruyter.

Jerrard, R. (1992) 'Prostitution and the law', *Justice of the Peace* (7 March).

Jesson, J. (1993) 'Understanding adolescent female prostitution: a literature review', *British Journal of Social Work* 23, 517–30.

John, N. (ed.) (1994) *Violetta and her Sisters: The Lady of the Camellias – Responses to the Myth*, London: Faber and Faber.

Kaplan, L. J. (1991) *Female Perversions*, Harmondsworth: Penguin.

Kelly, L. (1988) *Surviving Sexual Violence*, Cambridge: Polity Press.

—— Wingfield, R., Burton, S. and Regan, L. (1995) *Splintered Lives: Sexual Exploitation of Children in the Context of Children's Rights and Child Protection*, Ilford: Barnardo's and the Child Abuse and Women's Studies Unit, University of North London.

Kempadoo, K. and Doezema, J. (eds) (1999) *Global Sex Workers*, London: Routledge.

Kennedy, H. (1992) *Eve Was Framed: Women And British Justice*, London: Vintage Books.

Kinnell, H. (1989) *Prostitutes, Their Clients and Risks of HIV Infection in Birmingham*, Occasional Paper, Department of Public Health Medicine, Birmingham.

—— (1991) *Safe: HIV Prevention Project*, collection of unpublished papers, Department of Public Health and Medicine, Birmingham.

Kinsey, A. C., Pomeroy, W. B. and Martin C. E. (1948) *Sexual Behaviour in the Human Male*, London: W. B. Saunders Co.

Kishtainy, K. (1982) *The Prostitute in Progressive Literature*, London: Allison and Busby.

Knapp, G. A. (1999) 'Fragile foundations, strong traditions, situated questioning: critical theory in German-speaking feminism', in M. O'Neill (ed.), *Adorno, Culture and Feminism*, London: Sage, 110–40.

Kronhausen, E. and P. (1967) *Walter 'My Secret Life'* (abridged version), vol. 2, London: Polybooks Ltd.

Kuzmics, H. (1993) 'Weber and Elias on civilization: Protestant ethics and sport in England', *ARENA* 1.

—— (1994) 'Power and work: the development of work as a civilizing process in examples of fictional literature', *Sociological Perspectives* 37 (1), 119–54.

—— (1997) 'State formation, economic development and civilization in north-western and central Europe', *Geschichte und Gegenwart* 16 (2), 80–91.

Lawrinson, S. (1995) *The Ethical (Mine)Field of Researching Women Sex Workers*, monograph in the series *Critical Reflections on the Research Process*, Surrey: University of Surrey.

Lee, M. and O'Brien, R. (1995) *The Game's Up: Redefining Child Prostitution*, London: The Children's Society.

Levine, J. and Madden, L. (1988) *LYN, A Story of Prostitution*, London: The Women's Press.

Lim, L. L. (1998) *The Sex Sector: The Economic and Social Bases of Prostitution in Southeast Asia*, Geneva: International Labour Office.

Lloyd, R. (1977) *Playland: A Study of Boy Prostitution*, New York: Blond and Briggs.

Louise (1997) 'Children unheard: a young person's experience', in D. Barrett (ed.), *Child Prostitution in Britain: Current Dilemmas, Practical Responses*, London: The Children's Society, 12–18.

Lowman, J. (1987) 'Taking young prostitutes seriously', *Canadian Review of Sociology and Anthropology* 24 (1), 99–116.

Lupton, C. (1985) *Moving Out*, Portsmouth: Social Services Research Unit.

—— and Gillespie, T. (eds) (1994) *Working with Violence: Dilemmas for a Feminist Practice*, London: Macmillan.

McIntosh, M. (1978) 'Who needs prostitutes? The ideology of male sexual needs', in C. Smart and B. Smart (eds), *Women, Sexuality and Social Control*, London: Routledge and Kegan Paul.

—— (1992) 'Liberalism and the contradictions of sexual politics', in L. Segal and M. McIntosh (eds), *Sex Exposed: Sexuality and the Pornography Debate*, London: Virago.

McKegany, N. (1992) 'Hooked on the killing game', *Times Higher*, 3 July.

—— and Barnard, M. (1996) *Sex Work on the Streets*, Buckingham: Open University Press.

—— Barnard, M., Bloor, M. and Leyland, A. (1990) 'Injecting drug use and female street-working prostitution in Glasgow', *AIDS* 4 (4), 1153–5.

—— Barnard, M., Bloor, M. and Leyland, A. (1992a) *Aids, Drugs and Sexual Risk: Lives in the Balance*, Buckingham: Open University Press.

—— Barnard, M., Bloor, M. and Leyland, A. (1992b) 'Selling sex: female street prostitution and HIV risk behaviour in Glasgow', *AIDS* 4 (4), 395–407.

—— Barnard, M., Leyland, A., Coote, I. and Follet, E. (1992c) 'Female streetworking prostitution and HIV infection in Glasgow', *British Medical Journal* 305, 801–4.

McLeod, E. (1982) *Women Working: Prostitution Now*, London: Croom Helm.

McLintock, A. (1992) 'Gonad the Barbarian and the Venus fly trap: portraying the female and male orgasm', in L. Segal and M. McIntosh (eds) *Sex Exposed: Sexuality and the Pornography Debate*, London: Virago.

—— (1995) *Imperial Leather: Race, Gender and Sexuality in the Colonial Contest*, London: Routledge.

McMullen, R. J. (1987) 'Youth prostitution: a balance of power', *Journal of Adolescence* 10, 35–43.

McRobbie, A. (1993) 'Feminism, postmodernism and the real me', *Theory, Culture and Society* 10 (4), 127–42.

Maraini, F. (1954) *Secret Tibet*, trans. Eric Mosbacher, London: Readers Union/Hutchinson.

Massey, D. (1991) 'Flexible sexism', *Society and Space* 9, 31–57.

Matthews, R. (1991) Prostitution, drugs and HIV: a survey of outreach work with young people, report for Sefton Youth Service.

—— (1986) 'Beyond Wolfenden? prostitution, politics and the law', in R. Matthews and J. Young (eds) *Confronting Crime*, London: Sage, 188–215.

—— (1996) *Policing Prostitution: A Multi-Agency Approach*, Enfield: Middlesex Polytechnic.

Maupassant, G. (1995) *Boule de suif*, Harmondsworth: Penguin.

Mazo-Karras, R. (1989) 'The regulation of brothls in later Medieval England', *SIGNS: Journal of Women in Culture and Society* 14(3), 399–433.

Meil Hobson, B. (1990) *Uneasy Virtue: The Politics of Prostitution and the American Reform Tradition*, Chicago: University of Chicago Press.

Melrose, M. and Barrett, D. (1999) *One Way Street: Retrospectives on Childhood Prostitution*, London: The Children's Society.

Meštrović, S. G. (1997) *Postemotional Society*, London: Sage.

Mienczakowski, J. (1995) 'The theater of ethnography: the reconstruction of ethnography into theater with emancipatory potential', *Qualitative Enquiry* 1 (3), 360–75.

Mies, M. (1983) 'Towards a methodology for feminist research', in G. Bowles and D. Klein (eds), *Theories of Women's Studies*, London: Routledge and Kegan Paul.

—— (1986 and 1991) *Patriarchy and Accumulation on a World Scale*, London: Zed Books.

—— (1993) 'Towards a methodology for feminist research', in M. Hammersley (ed.), *Social Research: Philosophy, Politics and Practice*, London: Sage, 64–82.

Miller, C. and Miller, R. (1972) *Black Players*, Boston: Little Brown and Company.

Miller, G. (1978) *Odd Jobs: The World of Deviant Work*, New Jersey: Prentice Hall Publications.

Modleski, T. (1982) *Loving with a Vengeance*, New York: Methuen.

Moore, H. (1994) *A Passion For Difference*, Cambridge: Polity Press.

Morgan, D. H. J. (1992) *Discovering Men*, London: Routledge.

Morgan Thomas, R. (1990) 'AIDS risks, alcohol, drugs and the sex industry', in M. Plant (ed.) *AIDS, Drugs and Prostitution*, London: Routledge, 88–108.

—— Plant, M. A. and Sales, D. (1989) 'AIDS risks amongst sex industry workers: some initial results from a Scottish study', *British Medical Journal* 299, 148–9.

—— Plant, M. A. and Sales, D. (1990) 'Risk of HIV infection among clients of the sex industry in Scotland', *British Medical Journal* 301, 525.

Morris, A. (1987) *Women, Crime and Criminal Justice*, Oxford: Basil Blackwell.

Morris, M. (1992) 'The man in the mirror: David Harvey's "condition" of postmodernity', *Theory, Culture and Society* 9 (1), 253–79.

Mulvay, L. (1975) 'Visual pleasure and narrative cinema', *Screen* 16 (3).

Munro, R. (1999) 'In denial of what's paid for it: a review of *Not all the time... but mostly...*', in *Not All The Time... But Mostly...*, leaflet for an exhibition of photographs from a Live Art Performance, Nottingham and Stoke-on-Trent: Nottingham Trent University and Staffordshire University.

Murdock, G. (1997) 'Thin descriptions: questions of method in cultural analysis', in J. McGuigan (ed.), *Cultural Methodologies*, London: Sage.

Murray, A. (1995a) 'Mind your peers and queers: female sex workers in the AIDS discourse in Australia and Southeast Asia', *Gender, Place and Culture* 3 (1), 43–59.

—— (1995b) 'Femme on the streets, butch on the streets (a play on whores)', in D. Bell and G. Valentine (eds), *Mapping Desire*, London: Routledge.

Murray, M. (1995) *The Law of the Father: Patriarchy in the Transition from Feudalism to Capitalism*, London: Routledge.

Nagle, J. (ed.) (1997) *Whores and Other Feminists*, New York and London: Routledge.

New Statesman and Society (1990) *Tis no pity she's a whore*, 9 February.

Nicholsen, A. H. (1981) *Youth in Crisis: A Study of Adolescent and Child Prostitution*, Los Angeles, CA: Gay and Lesbian Community Services Center.

Nicholsen, S. W. (1993) 'Walter Benjamin and the aftermath of the aura: notes on the aesthetics of photography', *Antioch Community Record*, 12 February.

—— (1997) *Exact Imagination, Late Work: On Adorno's Aesthetics*, Cambridge, MA and London: MIT Press.

Nicholson, L. (1994) *Feminism/Postmodernism*, London and New York: Routledge.

O'Connell-Davidson, J. (1994) *Prostitution and the Contours of Control*, paper presented at the BSA annual conference held at University of Central Lancashire, 28–31 March.

—— (1998) *Prostitution, Power and Freedom*, Cambridge, Polity Press.

Offe, C. (1984) *Contradictions of the Welfare State*, London: Hutchinson.

O'Hear, A. (1998) 'Diana, queen of hearts (sentimentality personified and canonised)', in D. Anderson and P. Mullen (eds), *Faking It: The Sentimentalisation of Modern Society*, London: Penguin, 183–90.

O'Mahoney, B. (1988) *A Capital Offence: The Plight of the Young Single Homeless in London*, London and Ilford: Routledge and Barnardo's.

O'Neill, J. (1995) *The Poverty of Postmodernism*, London: Routledge.

O'Neill, M. (1991) 'Current responses to prostitution: a multi-agency response', report for Nottingham Safer Cities, Nottingham: Nottingham Trent University.

—— (1992) 'Academic power and social knowledge: prostitution, critical theory and feminist praxis', paper prepared for the international conference on 'Academic knowledge and political power' held at the University of Maryland, 20–22 November.

—— (1994) 'Prostitution and the state: towards a feminist practice', in C. Lupton and T. Gillespie (eds), *Working with Violence: Dilemmas for a Feminist Practice*, London: Macmillan.

—— (1995) 'Prostitution and violence: towards a feminist practice', in M. Hester, J. Radford and L. Kelly (eds), *Women, Violence and Male Power: Feminist Activism, Research and Practice*, London: Routledge.

—— (1996) 'Prostitution, feminism and critical praxis: profession prostitute?', *The Austrian Journal of Sociology* (special edition on *Work and Society*, ed. Johanna Hofbauer and Jorg Flecker) Winter, 333–50.

—— (1997) 'Prostitute women now', in G. Scambler and A. Scambler (eds), *Rethinking Prostitution: Purchasing Sex in Britain in the 1990s*, London: Routledge, 3–28.

—— (1998) 'Saloon girls: death and desire in the American West', in R. Holliday and J. Hassard (eds), *Film and Organization*, London: Sage, 117–30.

O'Neill, M. (ed.) (1999) *Adorno, Culture and Feminism*, London: Sage.

—— and Barberet, R. (2000) 'Victimization and the social organisation of prostitution in England and Spain', in R. Weitzer (ed.), *Sex for Sale: International Perspectives on Prostitution*, London and New York: Routledge, 123–38.

—— Goode, N. and Hopkins, K. (1995) 'Juvenile prostitution: the experiences of young women in residential care', *Childright* 113, 14–16.

—— Johnson, S., McDonald, M., Webster, T., Wellik, M. and McGregor, H. (1994) 'Prostitution, feminism and the law: feminist ways of seeing, knowing and working with women working as prostitutes', *ROW Bulletin* (Autumn), 12–17.

—— in association with Giddens, S., Breatnach, P., Bagley, C., Bourne, D. and Judge, T. (1999) 'Renewed methodologies for social research: ethnomimesis as performative praxis', unpublished paper.

Pakulski, J. (1977) 'Cultural citizenship', *Citizenship Studies* 1, 73–86.

Pateman, C. (1983) 'Defending prostitution: charges against Ericsson', *Ethics* (April), 561–5.

Pheterson, G. (1986) *The Whore Stigma: Female Dishonor and Male Unworthiness*, sponsored by the Dutch Ministry of Social Affairs and Employment, Emancipation Policy Co-ordination, the Netherlands.

—— (ed.) (1989) *A Vindication of the Rights of Whores*, Seattle: Seal Press.

—— (1990) 'The category "prostitute" in scientific enquiry', *The Journal of Sex Research* 27 (3), 397–407.

Philpot, T. (1990) 'Male prostitution: the boys' own story', *Community Care* 820 (28 June), 19–22.

Phoenix, J. (1999) *Making Sense of Prostitution Today*, London: Macmillan.

Piccone, P. (1993) 'Beyond pseudo-culture? reconstituting fundamental political concepts', *Telos* 95 (Spring), 3–14.

Plant, M. (ed.) (1990) *AIDS, Drugs and Prostitution*, London: Routledge.

Plummer, K. (1995) *Telling Sexual Stories: Power, Change and Social Worlds*, London: Routledge.

Porter, R. (1984) *Teenagers Leaving Care*, Social Work Monographs, Norwich: University of East Anglia.

Postman, N. (1987) *Amusing Ourselves to Death*, London: Methuen.

Potterat, J. (1985) 'On becoming a prostitute: an exploratory case comparison study', *Journal of Sex Research* 21, 329–35.

Power, R. (1990) 'A happier lot for the working girl', *The Guardian* (Guardian Women), 3 August.

Presdee, M. (1997) 'Young people and crime', lecture given at the University of Crete, April.

Price, J. and Shildrick, M. (eds) (1999) *Feminist Theory and the Body: A Reader*, Edinburgh: Edinburgh University Press.

Prus, R. and Irini, S. (1980) *Hookers, Rounders and Desk Clerks: The Social Organisation of the Hotel Community*, Toronto: Gage Publications.

Queen, C. (1997) 'Sex radical politics: sex-positive feminist thought', in J. Nagle (ed.), *Whores and Other Feminists*, New York and London: Routledge, 125–35.

Radford, J. and Russell, D. (eds) (1992) *Femicide: The Politics of Woman Killing*, Milton Keynes: Open University Press.

Ramazanoglu, C. (1987) 'Sex and violence in academic life, or you can keep a good woman down', in J. Hammer and M. Maynard (eds), *Women Violence and Social Control*, London: Macmillan, chapter 5.

—— (1989) *Feminism and the Contradictions of Oppression*, London: Routledge.

—— (1992) 'On feminist methodology: male reason versus female empowerment', *Sociology* 26 (2), 207–13.

Ravenscroft, L. (1997) 'The case for soliciting for prostitution by under 18s being decriminalised', MSc dissertation, Social Policy and Administration Department, London School of Economics.

Reich, W. (1983) *The Mass Psychology of Fascism*, trans. V. R. Carfagno, Harmondsworth: Penguin.

Reisman, D. (1950) *The Lonely Crowd*, New Haven, CT: Yale University Press.

Rendall, J. (1997) 'Industrious females and professional beauties, or fine articles for sale in the Burlington Arcades', in I. Borden, J. Kerr, A. Pivaro and J. Rendall (eds), *Strangely Familiar: Narratives of Architecture in the City*, London and New York: Routledge, 32–6.

Rheinarz, S. (1992) *Feminist Methods in Social Research*, New York: Oxford University Press.

Roberts, N. (1992) *Whores in History: Prostitution in Western Society*, London: HarperCollins.

Robson, B. (1994) 'Urban issues', *Voice of the Urban Forum* 2 (November).

Rojek, C. (1995) *Decentring Leisure: Rethinking Leisure Theory*, London: Sage.

Root, J. (1986) *Sexuality: Pictures of Women*, London: Pandora.

Rose, H. (1983) 'Hand, brain and heart: a feminist epistemology for the natural sciences', *Signs* 9 (1).

Ryan, J. (1994) 'Women, modernity and the city', *Theory, Culture and Society* 11 (4), 35–64.

Salomon, E. (1989) 'The homosexual escort agency: deviance disavowal', *British Journal of Sociology* 40, 1–21.

Samuels, A. (1994) *The Political Psyche*, London: Routledge.

Sanders, T. (1999) 'Street working prostitutes: addiction and abuse', Department of Sociology, University of Oxford.

Sassower, R. (1993) *Knowledge Without Expertise: On the Status of Scientists*, Albany: State University of New York.

—— (1995) *Cultural Collisions: Postmodern Technoscience*, London and New York: Routledge.

Scambler, G. and Scambler, A. (1992) 'Health issues for women prostitutes in London: a preliminary report/discussion paper', University College and Middlesex School of Medicine.

—— and Scambler, A. (eds) (1997) *Rethinking Prostitution: Purchasing Sex in Britain in the 1990s*, London: Routledge.

—— Peswani, R., Renton, A. and Scambler, A. (1990) 'Women prostitutes in the AIDS era', *Sociology of Health and Illness* 12 (3), 260–73.

Seabrook, J. (1991) 'Sex for sale: cheap thrills', *New Statesman and Society*, 31 May, 12–13.

Seale, C. (1999) *Researching Society and Culture*, London: Sage.

Segal, L. and McIntosh, M. (eds) (1992) *Sex Exposed: Sexuality and the Pornography Debate*, London: Virago Press.

Seidler, V. J. (1991) *Recreating Sexual Politics: Men, Feminism and Politics*, London: Routledge.

Seidman, S. (ed.) (1994a) *The Postmodern Turn*, New York: Cambridge University Press.

—— (1994b) *Contested Knowledge*, Oxford: Blackwell.

Sellers, S. (1994) *The Hélène Cixous Reader*, London: Routledge.

Sennett, R. (1992) *The Fall Of Public Man*, New York: Norton and Co.

Sereny, G. (1984) *The Invisible Children: Child Prostitution in America, Germany and Britain*, London: André Deutsch Ltd.

Sex Workers and the Law (1997), London: Release.

Seymour-Smith, M. (1969) *Fallen Women*, London: Thomas Nelson and Sons Ltd.

Shrage, L. (1989) 'Should feminists oppose prostitution?', *Ethics* 99, 347–61.

—— (1994) *Moral Dilemmas of Feminism: Prostitution, Adultery, and Abortion*, London: Routledge.

Silbert, D. and Pines, T. (1981) 'Sexual abuse as an antecedent to prostitution', *Child Abuse and Neglect* 5, 407–11.

Smart, B. (1992) *Modern Conditions, Postmodern Controversies*, London: Routledge.

Smart, C. (1978) *Women, Crime and Criminology*, London: Macmillan.

—— (1989) *Feminism and the Power of Law*, London: Routledge.

—— (1992) *Regulating Womanhood: Historical Essays on Marriage, Motherhood and Sexuality*, London: Routledge.

—— and Smart, B. (1978) *Women, Sexuality and Social Control*, London: Routledge.

—— and Smart, B. (1992) 'Unquestionably a moral issue: rhetorical devices and regulatory imperitives', in L. Segal and M. McIntosh, *Sex Exposed: Sexuality and the Pornography Debate*, London: Virago.

Smith, D. (1993) *Texts, Facts, and Feminity: Exploring the Relations of Ruling*, London: Routledge.

Sobey, M. (1994) 'Young people involved in prostitution: a study of literature and a research project examining incidence and agency responses in Nottinghamshire', University of Derby.

Stallybrass, P. and White, A. (1986) *The Politics and Poetics of Transgression*, London: Methuen and Co. Ltd.

Stanko, E. (1985) *Intimate Intrusions? Women's Experiences of Male Violence*, London: Routledge and Kegan Paul.

Stanley, L. (ed.) (1990) *Feminist Praxis*, London: Routledge.

—— and Wise, S. (1993) *Breaking Out Again*, London: Routledge.

Steedman, C. (1997) 'Writing the self: the end of the scholarship girl', in J. McGuigan (ed.), *Cultural Methodologies*, London: Sage.

Stein, M. (1990) *Living out of Care*, Ilford: Barnardo's.

—— (1991) *Leaving Care and the 1989 Children Act*, London: First Key.

Sturdevant, S. and Stoltzfus, B. (1992) *Let the Good Times Roll: Prostitution and the US Military in Asia*, New York: New York Press.

Sunday Correspondent (1990) *Students on the Game*, 25 November.

Taussig, M. (1993) *Mimesis and Alterity: A Particular History of the Senses*, London and New York: Routledge.

Tester, K. (1993) *The Life and Times of Post-Modernity*, London: Routledge.

—— (1994) *Media, Culture and Morality*, London: Routledge.

—— (1995) *The Inhuman Condition*, London: Routledge.

The Children's Society (1990), *Young People Under Pressure*, an information pack, February.

The Economist (1998) 'The sex industry: giving the customer what he wants', 14 February.

The Network of Sex Work projects (1997) *Making Sex Work Safe*, London: Appropriate Health Resources and Technologies Action Group (AHRTAG).

Theweleit, K. (1987) *Male Fantasies, vol. 1: Women, Floods, Bodies, History* Cambridge: Polity Press.

—— (1989) *Male Fantasies, vol. 2: Male Bodies – Psychoanalyzing the White Terror*, Minneapolis: University of Minnesota Press.

—— (1994) *Object–Choice (All You Need is Love)*, London: Verso.

Time International (1993) 'Sex for sale: the skin trade', 21 June.

Trinh, T. Minh-Ha (1989) *Woman, Native, Other: Writing Postcoloniality and Feminism*, Bloomington and Indianapolis: Indiana University Press.

—— (1991) *When the Moon Waxes Red*, London: Routledge.

—— (1992) *Framer Framed*, New York: Routledge.

Truong, T. (1990) *Sex, Money and Morality: Prostitution and Tourism in South-East Asia*, London: Zed Books.

Tseëlon, E. (1995) *The Masque of Feminity*, London: Sage.

Ugwu, C. (1995) 'Keep on running: the politics of black British performance', in *Let's Get It On: The Politics of Black Performance*, London and Seattle: Institute of Contemporary Arts and Bay Press, 54–83.

Van Loon, J. (1999) 'Immateriality', paper presented to Lancaster University Workshop on Materiality, Centre for Science Studies, 13 October.

—— (2000) 'Cultural studies', in P. Atkinson, A. Coffey, S. Delamont, L. Lofland and J. Lofland, *Handbook of Ethnography*, London: Sage Press.

Van Zoonan, L. (1994) *Feminist Media Studies*, London: Sage.

Vance, C. (1992) 'Negotiating sex and gender in the Attorney General's Commission on Pornography', in L. Segal and M. McIntosh (eds), *Sex Exposed: Sexuality and the Pornography Debate*, London: Virago.

Verlade, A. (1975) 'Becoming prostituted: the decline of the massage parlour profession and the masseuse', *British Journal of Criminology*, 15, 251–63.

—— and Warlick, M. (1973) 'Massage parlours: the sensuality business', *Society* 11, 63–74.

Vitaliano, P. D. (1981) 'Perceptions of juvenile experiences: females involved in prostitution versus property offences', *Criminal Justice and Behaviour* 8, 325–42.

Waldorf, D. and Murphy, S. (1990) 'Intravenous drug use and syringe-sharing practices of call men and hustlers', in M. Plant (ed.), *AIDS, Drugs and Prostitution*, London: Routledge, 109–31.

Walklate, S. (1991) *Teenage Prostitution in Sefton*, Sefton: Youth Service.

Walkowitz, J. (1980) *Prostitution and Victorian Society*, Cambridge: Cambridge University Press.

Walter (1994) *My Secret Life*, vols 5–8, London: Arrow Books.

Weeks, J. (1977) *Coming Out: Homosexual Politics in Britain from the Nineteenth Century to the Present*, London: Quartet Books.

—— (1986) *Sexuality*, London: Tavistock.

Welzer-Lang, D. (1993) 'The evolution of prostitution from tradition to modernity', interim report of work in progress, Lyon: University of Lyon.

West, C. (1994) 'The new cultural politics of difference', in S. Seidman (ed.) *The Postmodern Turn: New Perspectives on Social Theory*, New York: Cambridge University Press, 65–81.

West, D. and de Villiers, B. (1992) *Male Prostitution*, London: Gerald Duckworth and Co.

West, J. (2000) 'Prostitution: collectives and the politics of regulation', *Gender, Work and Organization* 7 (2).

White, V. and Harris, J. (1999) 'Professional boundaries re-defined: three discourses on the users of welfare', in M. Dent, M. O'Neill and C. Bagley, *Professions: New Public Management and the European Welfare State*, Stoke-on-Trent: Staffordshire University Press.

Whitehead, P. and Dominelli, L. (1994) 'Masculinity and crime', unpublished paper, Sheffield University.

Whitford, M. (1991) *Luce Irigaray: Philosophy in the Feminine*, London: Routledge.

Whittaker, D. (1995) 'Ethics and feelings: exploring issues raised in health services research with women sex workers', MSc thesis, Department of Genito-Urinary Medicine, University College, London.

Whyte, W. F. (1989) 'Advancing scientific knowledge through participatory action research', *Sociological Forum* 4(3), 367–85.

Wilson, E. (1994) 'Bohemians, grisettes and demi-mondaines', in N. John (ed.), *Violetta and her Sisters*, London: Faber and Faber.

Winch, P. (1990) *The Idea of a Social Science and its Relation to Philosophy*, London: Routledge.

Winnick, C. (1962) 'Prostitutes' clients' perceptions of the prostitutes and of themselves', *International Journal of Social Psychiatry* 42, 289–97.

Witkin, R. (1974) *The Intelligence of Feeling*, London: Heinemann.

—— (1995) *Art and Social Structure*, Cambridge: Polity Press.

Wolfenden (1957) *Report of the Committee on Homosexual Offences and Prostitution*, London: HMSO.

Wolff, J. (1981) *The Social Production of Art*, London: Macmillan.

—— (1983) *Aesthetics and the Sociology of Art*, London: George Allen and Unwin.

—— (1995) *Resident Alien: Feminist Cultural Criticism*, Cambridge: Polity Press.

Wouters, C. (1986) 'Formalization and informalization: changing tension balances in civilizing processes', *Theory, Culture and Society* 3(2).

Wright, M. (1989) 'Personal narratives, dynasties and women's campaigns: two examples from Africa', in *Interpreting Women's Lives: Feminist Theory and Personal Narratives*, ed. The Personal Narratives Group, Bloomington: Indiana University Press.

Young, L. (1996) *Fear of the Dark: 'Race', Gender and Sexuality in the Cinema*, London: Routledge.

Index

Note: Contributors to multi-authored works, all of whom may not be mentioned in the text, are listed with the name of the first author in brackets.